W9-CVA-700

Building the Ultimate Adventure Motorcycle

First published in July 2010

A catalogue record for this book is available from the British Library

ISBN 978 1 84425 836 9

Library of Congress catalog card no 2010924917

Published by Haynes Publishing,
Sparkford, Yeovil, Somerset BA22 7JJ, UK
Tel: +44 1963 442030 Fax: +44 1963 440001
E-mail: sales@haynes.co.uk
Website: www.haynes.co.uk

Haynes North America Inc.,
861 Lawrence Drive, Newbury Park,
California 91320, USA

Printed and bound in the USA

James Mann

Dedication

This book is dedicated to Afghan Heroes, a specialist charity set up to support soldiers and their families affected by the war in Afghanistan. In a remarkable show of support more than 15,000 bikers participated in a motorcycle ride through Wootton Bassett in England on 14 March 2010. Everything that the spirit of motorcycling embodies was on display, including camaraderie, freedom, pride and passion. I was just one of a large number of adventure motorcyclists who took part in the day and it was a truly memorable and moving experience for everyone concerned. As someone who came close to pursuing his own career in the military back in 1987 I would urge you to support Afghan Heroes. For more information please go to: www.afghanheroes.org.uk

Acknowledgements

The author would like to thank the following people for their support and expertise:

Special thanks to Laury Charet, Graham 'Ernie' Clark, Craig Carey-Clinch, Walter Colebatch, Gareth Edmunds, Tzur Gannot, Scott Grimsdall, Tony Jakeman, Grant Johnson, Dom Longman, Sam Manicom, James Mann, Ian Norman, (Motorcycle Sales Promotion & Planning Group, Global Marketing Planning Department, Suzuki Motor Corporation), Joe Pichler, Nick Plumb, Lois Pryce, Benka Pulko, Charlie Rauseo, Kevin Sanders, Nick Sanders, Herbert Schwarz, Chris Smith, Mike Stevens, Ida Tin and Austin Vince

With special thanks to:

Greg Baker – My sincere thanks to Greg Baker for his contribution to the book in his capacity as Technical Editor. Greg brings a great appreciation for and insight to adventure motorcycling and it has been a pleasure to work with him on another book in the series.

Mark Hughes – Editorial Director at Haynes Publishing, for his belief in the project from the start and support throughout the editorial process.

Lee Parsons – Senior Designer at Haynes Publishing, for the outstanding design and interpretation of the subject matter.

Building the Ultimate Adventure Motorcycle

The essential guide to preparing a bike for the journey of a lifetime

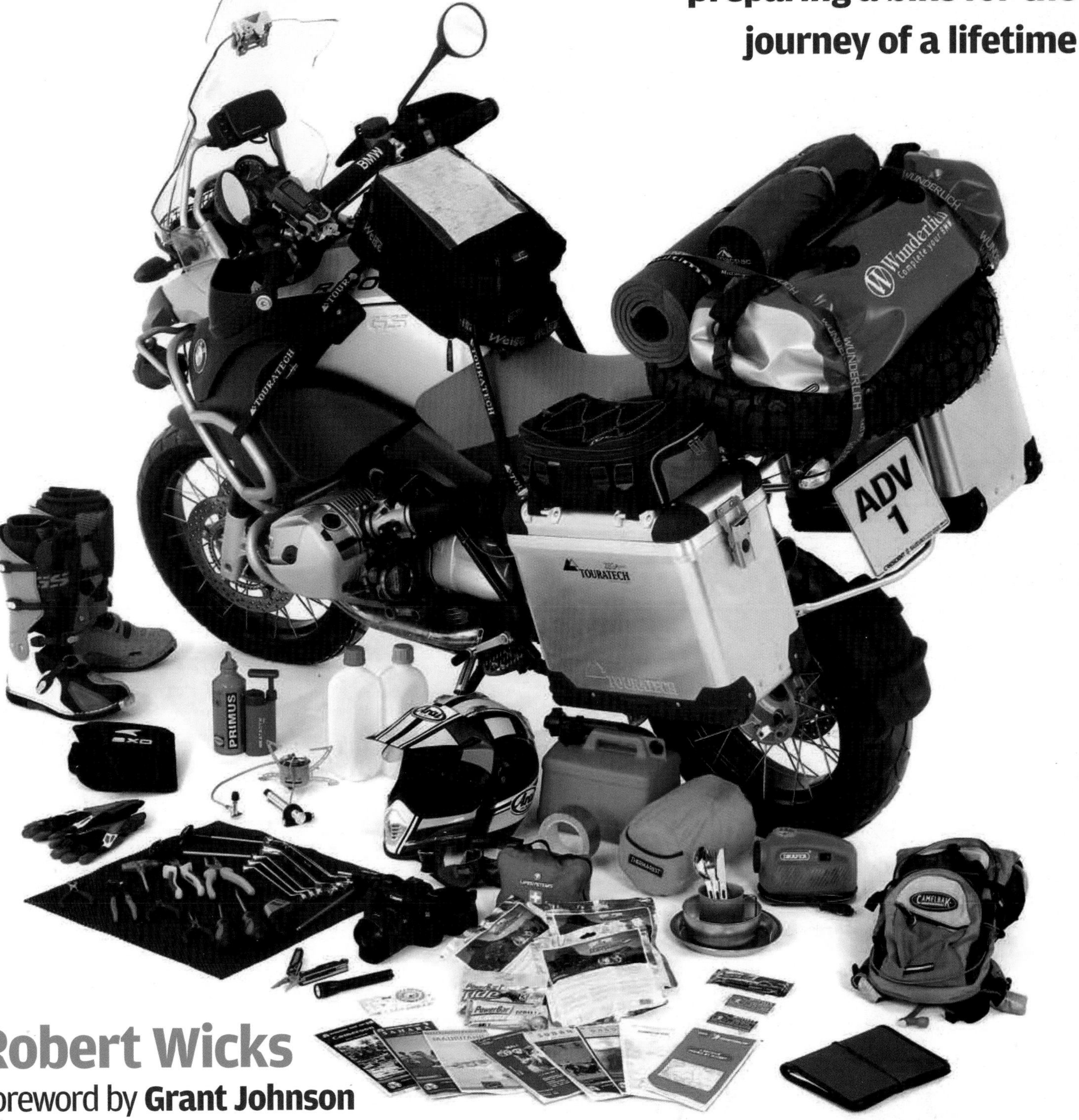

Robert Wicks

Foreword by **Grant Johnson**

Contents

Sibirsky Extreme

Foreword by Grant Johnson

Not so long ago, overland travel by motorcycle through Africa, South America, or India was only contemplated by hardcore adventurers. When my wife Susan and I started off from Vancouver on our own round-the-world (RTW) trip back in 1987, there may have been other travellers out there, but we wouldn't have known about them. Email was unknown, mobile phones were in their infancy and certainly didn't work where *we* were going.

We finally arrived in Prudhoe Bay, Alaska, 11 years later in 1998, having ridden two-up around the world from north to south, through 39 countries and across six continents. The World Wide Web was in its early stages, so we started a website (www.HorizonsUnlimited.com) with stories and pictures from our trip, just as countless others have done since personal websites became an option.

With the launch of a bulletin board (the HUBB) in 1999 and an e-zine in 2000, the site grew phenomenally, to become a home for thousands of motorcyclists around the world. With the addition of other people's travel stories, and the invaluable information contributed by our very active HUBB regulars, the site has grown to over 40,000 pages. It is a tremendous resource for the adventure motorcycle traveller, and a full-time job for us to keep up with! We are sometimes asked, in all seriousness: 'How did you do a RTW trip before there was Horizons Unlimited?'

We hosted the first HU Travellers Meeting in 2001, and the concept has spread worldwide, so that we're now holding more than a dozen meetings a year in the UK, Europe, the USA, Canada, South America, Asia, Australia, and New Zealand. Thousands of adventure travellers and would-be travellers have discovered the joy of meeting people who don't think they're crazy for wanting to ride a bike to South America or Africa or across Asia, or even around the world, and in fact will encourage them, share their experiences, and advise them on how to do it.

There is now a true global community of motorcycle travellers, with over 600 Horizons Unlimited Motorcycle Travellers Communities established in at least 100

countries around the world, to enable motorcycle travellers, both those on the road and those at home, to meet up with like-minded people.

During the past few years tens of thousands of individuals have been inspired by stories of travel to exotic places, and the popular media has discovered adventure motorcycle travel as a result of the *Long Way* series. Today more people than ever are thinking of an odyssey to distant climes – the markets of Marrakech, the Karakoram Highway in Pakistan, the salt flats of Bolivia, the Bungle Bungles of Australia. Not on a package tour, but on their own motorcycle.

We've been helping people to achieve their dreams of travelling to faraway places on their bikes for over ten years now. Some things we can say with certainty. The world is an amazingly friendly and welcoming place, and you don't have to be a movie star or have loads of money to enjoy adventure motorcycling. Whether you go to the next country, the next continent, or around the world, the important thing is to get out there.

Virtually any bike can, and probably has, travelled around the world, but 'which bike' and how to go about preparing it is always a lively topic for discussion among motorcycle travellers. The debate will never end, as everyone has different needs, and different likes and dislikes, so always remember that it's all about what's best for *you*.

Once you've chosen that 'best' bike for your trip, you'll soon find that it's not quite right, and needs 'a little work'. A big part of motorcycle travel for many is getting the bike 'perfect' ... for *them* – for no one else maybe, but certainly it's all theirs and works for them. I'm one of them. A long-time gear-head, I started by taking a clock apart at three, hand-painting my new bicycle at age five, building my own race bikes at 19, and then building my own version of the ultimate around the world bike in 1986, starting with a new BMW R 80 GS. It was an easy choice at the time: it was the first – and at the time, only – real two-up adventure travel bike. Is it perfect? No, and it never will be, but it worked fine for us on our 11-year round the world trip, and in fact it's still working fine today. It's still fun trying to make it better, and I always look at all the new catalogues full of cool bits and pieces with lust.

When I'm asked about the ultimate adventure bike, and what it needs, I always say 'The KISS principle is number one – Keep It Super Simple,' and 'Light is good, heavy is bad.' Past that, it's all up to you. Robert has made the next step a whole lot easier with this book, so get stuck in and enjoy preparing your perfect adventure travel bike!

See you on the road, someday, somewhere...

Grant Johnson

AUTHOR'S NOTE: ABOUT GRANT JOHNSON

As a former winner of the Canadian National Championships in road racing and motocross, and of gold medals in cross-country motorcycle racing, Grant Johnson hatched the crackpot scheme of travelling around the world on a motorcycle. In early 1987, to the dismay of his parents and most of his friends, he and Susan sold everything, quit their jobs and headed for Panama.

At various times Grant has earned his living as a motorcycle mechanic and dealer, as a manager of several sports equipment stores, and as a freelance photographer and writer. In the adventure motorcycling community he is probably best known as the founder of www.HorizonsUnlimited.com – one of the biggest online motorcycle adventuring communities in the world.

'When we travel, we have no schedules to keep,' says Grant. 'We don't make reservations in advance, we stay as long as we want and leave when we decide to go. The travelling just whets our appetite for more, so it will probably be another ten years – or more – before we finish.'

Introduction

Welcome to the third title in the Haynes adventure motorcycling series. What started out as a single book has rapidly developed into a series on what is a truly fascinating subject. *Adventure Motorcycling* was an introduction to the pastime and was followed soon after by *Adventure Riding Techniques* – the definitive guide to off-road adventure riding.

This latest title offers advice on the best possible motorcycle for your trip, and goes into considerable detail on how best to modify and customise the machine still further so that you get the best out of it. Much pleasure can be derived from customising your bike, and the process forms an important part of the preparation for your trip.

Simply put, I don't believe there is a perfect adventure bike – it simply doesn't exist. Such is the extent of the debate about which motorcycle is best for adventure riding that in an ideal world I think we would all own at least five! There may be a few manufacturers disputing this claim, but when one considers that people have navigated their way around much of the world on everything from a 50cc Japanese postal bike or a Yamaha R1 to a Vespa scooter or a Honda Goldwing, one begins to realise that there is a wealth of choice and that it ultimately comes down to personal preferences, your budget, and a healthy dose of common sense.

The principal considerations are *size* (you need to be able to get on it and off it easily enough), *comfort* (long distances over rough terrain will take their toll), *reliability* (for obvious reasons, but especially if you're not too technically minded), *weight* (you want to be able to pick it up if it falls over), and *flexibility* (you want a bike that can eat up the tarmac en route to your adventure but is equally capable of handling potholes and gravel tracks once you're there). There will always need to be an element of compromise too, so factor this into your thinking early on and choose wisely – you're going to be depending on your bike for a significant period of time, and you certainly don't want to find yourself regretting your choice early on. Also be certain about the modifications you make – it's easy to spend the value of the bike again when it comes to accessories, and you may find that many of them are superfluous to requirements.

As a general rule, the tougher the terrain you're likely to encounter, the lighter and more agile the bike needs to be. There is a school of thought which argues that a smaller, lighter bike is the only way to go, irrespective of the terrain. Contrast this with the opposing viewpoint of 'the bigger the better' and you have a truly fascinating debate. I try to address this throughout, including an interesting contribution from adventure motorcycling's ardent DIY advocate, Austin Vince.

It's difficult to cover every motorcycle, modification, and accessory on the market but what follows is a relatively comprehensive guide to the key elements that go into building an adventure bike, and specifications for the vast majority of possible bike choices. On a number of occasions within the book the BMW R 1200 GS Adventure has been used as a base model. This is for no other reason than the fact that I happen to own one and have long been a fan of its near bullet-proof reliability and go-anywhere ability on several adventure rides, including my honeymoon! Also, since I'm six foot four tall it happens to be the ideal size for me. That said, I have tried to make the commentary as universal as possible.

On a final note, as you plan your adventure and prepare your bike it's wonderful to look back in time at how early adventure riders prepared their machines (see Chapter 1). They certainly didn't have the amount of choice we do today, either in machines or accessories, and these pioneers should truly be admired for the adventures they undertook, their tenacity, and their commitment to adventure motorcycling.

I hope you enjoy the read.

Robert Wicks
July 2010

Chapter 1

The modern adventure

motorcycle

James Mann

Before one can appreciate the modern adventure motorcycle it is important to look at how it has evolved over time. Almost one hundred years have passed since the first aspiring adventurers took to the saddle and started to explore the world on two wheels. By today's standards, these machines were very primitive and there was a distinct lack of expertise when it came to preparing a motorcycle for long-distance overland travel. Aftermarket suppliers barely existed and the early solution to carrying spares, provisions and fuel was simply to add a sidecar. These impracticalities failed to deter the early overlanders but it was only by the late 1950s and early 1960s that aftermarket suppliers started to emerge and with an increased range of new products to address the needs of adventure motorcyclists, including integrated luggage systems, touring fairings and bigger fuel tanks. More recently, as adventure motorcycling has gained significant interest the world over, riders find themselves spoilt for choice when it comes both to the range of motorcycles available and all that can be done to prepare them for the journey ahead.

Max Reisch's 1933 250cc two-stroke Puch used in his record-breaking journey across the Middle East in 1933 now recorded as a book – *India The Shimmering Dream* by Max Reisch (published by Panther Publishing 2010, www.panther-publishing.com)
Rollo Turner

Development of the adventure motorcycle

The start of adventure motorcycling can be traced back to the early 1900s, when a small number of intrepid adventurers conceived the notion of using a motorcycle to explore the world. At that time there was certainly no big aftermarket supplier of equipment and accessories for the likes of New Yorker Carl Stevens Clancy to place an order with before he set off on his grand adventure. This journey, which stated in 1913, is widely believed to be the first motorcycle circumnavigation of the globe, and his primary modification was simply to add a sidecar to his four-cylinder Henderson to carry his spares and provisions.

Fifteen years later and the motorcycle and sidecar idea was still popular. In 1928 Stanley Glanfield embarked on a world tour on his Coventry-built Rudge Whitworth motorcycle combination – a tiny 3.5hp single-cylinder motorcycle and a bespoke sidecar. There was no GPS and there were certainly no heated grips to help Glanfield cover some 18,000 miles (28,000km) in just eight months.

The following year two young men from Sydney chose to ride around Australia on a motorcycle for the first time. They bought a Harley Davidson, fitted a stout wooden box on the sidecar chassis to carry their gear, and set out with just £60 and neither a watch nor a compass between them. They returned seven weeks later having achieved their goal.

American Robert Edison Fulton Jr set out four years later in 1932 on a customised Douglas T6 twin for his own 40,000-mile (64,000km) odyssey. His machine also included a sidecar for carrying his camping and cooking equipment, guidebooks, and formal dress clothes. He went a step further than some of his predecessors and customised the bike to add an extra four-gallon fuel tank to the rear of the machine, two small metal panniers for carrying tools, and a secret hiding place for his revolver built into a steel skid plate underneath the engine. He also made sure he had enough room in his luggage for a motion-picture camera and 40,000ft (12,200m) of film. Following a crash he discarded the sidecar and relied on a small suitcase fixed to the handlebars for essential items.

In the 1950s, with road networks improving, there were some further daring attempts. Iranian brothers Issa and Abdullah Omidvar spent ten years completing a round-the-world trip on German-built 50cc Kreidler scooters, with little or no carrying capacity or enhancements to speak of. Other trips were successfully carried out around the same time on

← A 1934 expedition from London to Cape Town – sidecars were widely used for adventures at this time

📷 Pictures from *The Rugged Road* by Theresa Wallach courtesy of Panther Publishing

everything from a Czech-built Jawa CZ350 to Vespa and Lambretta scooters.

By the following decade the Triumph TR6, models from Yamaha's YDS range, and BMW's R75 were quite commonly used for long-distance touring. The last was an extremely capable machine and had been developed in response to a request from the German Army to make a machine more capable in off-road conditions. BMW developed it in such a way that a third (sidecar) wheel could be driven from an axle connected to the rear wheel of the motorcycle, effectively making it a three-wheeled vehicle. Fitted with a locking differential and selectable road and off-road gear ratios, the R75 was highly manoeuvrable and capable of negotiating most surfaces. It was even fitted with a reverse gear. A well-restored R75 can still be used reliably on- or off-road today.

BMW motorcycles of the 1960s were noted as long-distance touring motorcycles and perhaps the best-known BMW rider of the decade was Danny Liska, who rode an R60 from Alaska to Tierra del Fuego in one trip. But none of the BMWs came with fairings or luggage as standard, and these items had to be sourced independently from aftermarket vendors, who were slowly emerging in the industry. The most common fairing options back then were a full kit from Avon in the United Kingdom and an American handlebar-mounted fairing known as the 'Wixom Ranger'.

There were numerous manufacturers of saddlebags and top cases for BMW twins in the 1960s. Wixom's were very popular, as were a set of Craven panniers. Even back then the traditional means of carrying equipment was a set of canvas bags that were strapped to a framework over the then unsprung rear wheel. The result was invariably that the contents were churned and chafed and the frames were prone to breakage over rough roads. Writing about his panniers in the 1977 book *Ride it! The Complete Book of Motorcycle Touring*, Ken Craven said: 'My original design consisted of quickly detachable cases, the dimensions of which were determined by what I considered to be right for the motorcycle, rather than the needs of the rider and passenger, and carrying capacity was restricted accordingly. They were well reviewed in the journals and were a commercial success.'

Aftermarket supplier Butler and Smith offered several styles of luggage carriers for mounting behind the passenger saddle on BMW bikes in the 1960s. With the popularity of the marque growing rapidly, they also offered several styles of windshields, safety bars, a spotlight, and metric toolkits. One expensive and highly sought-after accessory was a

↓ Between 1966 and 1979 Paul Pratt (1926–2010) rode around the world through 48 countries on five continents on his Triumph Thunderbird

📷 Paul Pratt

↑ **Paul Pratt's 102,000 mile (164,000km) journey formed the basis for his book *World Understanding on Two Wheels***
📷 Paul Pratt

mechanical tachometer. All motorcycles came with BMW's famously complete toolkit.

At that time the option even existed for larger fuel tanks – the standard tank held 3.75 gallons (17 litres), though a commonly purchased option were more bulbous 5.5 gallon (25-litre) and 6.6 gallon (30-litre) tanks.

Adventure motorcycling in the 1970s is best epitomised by the exploits of Ted Simon, who between 1973 and 1977 rode 63,000 miles (101,000km) through 54 countries on a 500cc Triumph Tiger in one of the greatest adventure rides of all time, culminating in his bestseller *Jupiter's Travels*. Ted installed low-compression pistons that allowed him to run on low-grade fuel and helped to flatten out the Triumph's notorious vibrations. 'I had high, wide handlebars so that I could sit up and take notice as I went, and good ground clearance to take me over the rough stuff,' he recalls. A number of other modifications were planned but a union dispute at Triumph meant his bike was a rush job and one of the last off the line at the factory for a very long time. In the end, Ted set off with little more than a set of fairly elementary panniers and two saddlebags slung across the top of the fuel tank.

Honda's XL250 also proved popular at the time – it was the first modern four-stroke enduro motorcycle and the first mass-produced four-valve machine. The XL250 and the later XL350 laid the groundwork for the revolutionary Yamaha XT500, which emerged in 1975 and initiated a wave of modern four-stroke enduro machines.

The decision by Yamaha to build a big single was largely inspired by a request from the product planners at Yamaha USA, who believed there was strong demand for a bike with the design and power to cover the great open spaces of the American off-road countryside. The machine would need to be rugged and simple, so it was agreed that a big single was the way ahead.

The project got under way with the clear design aims of building a big single-cylinder motorcycle that was lightweight, compact, highly durable, and beautiful to look at. The bike would need an all new chassis capable of withstanding the vibration of the big single cylinder engine, and strong enough to handle the tough, all-terrain riding it would be subjected to.

The development team tried every means possible to keep the new XT500's weight as low as they could, and this was achieved by making the TT500 Enduro

↓ **Produced from 1976 to 1988, Yamaha's XT 500 became the pioneer of the big single off-road genre. It won the motorcycle division of the first Paris–Dakar Rally in 1979**
📷 Yamaha

machine's crankcase cover out of magnesium, and using aluminium for the fuel tank.

When the bike was launched in 1975 it was an instant success in the American market and soon became the bike of choice for a young generation of touring riders. The big surprise, however, was how these models eventually caught the imagination of riders in the European market. After winning the first two places in the inaugural Paris–Dakar Rally in 1979, and then the top four places in the 1980 event, a new generation of fans with a passion for adventure motorcycling was born in countries like France and Germany. The Yamaha Ténéré brand that grew out of the XT500 would become synonymous with the word 'adventure' among European motorcycle fans in the years to come, and Yamaha would become market leader in the Dakar-style adventure sport market sector.

Norwegian Helge Pedersen set the tone for the 1980s with his carefully crafted BMW R 80 GS. He reinforced the rear sub-frame to carry his heavy load and also went about manufacturing his own aluminium panniers. He added a special 11 US gallon (40-litre) tank. He recalls: 'My BMW had been so profoundly converted for world travel that she seemed to need a more personal name. I chose "Olga", which conjured in my mind the image of a solid, hard-working Norwegian farm woman.' The bike would see him through 77 countries and more than 240,000 miles (402,000km) in ten years.

By the 1990s adventure motorcycling was growing increasingly popular and people were exploring the globe on all manner of machines. Canadian Tom Smith completed 155,000 miles (250,000km) on a stock 1985 Honda Elite scooter without a single modification. He used two soft saddlebags that had side supports and two wide Velcro straps running between them across the passenger seat. The remainder of his gear was tied to a wooden platform that he made before the journey began.

It was this low-budget, DIY approach to adventure motorcycling that lay at the heart of the infamous *Mondo Enduro* journey – the longest land route around the world (some 44,000 miles/71,000km) in the shortest possible time – which commenced in 1995. It was the first recorded motorcycle crossing of the Caucasus, Central Asia, Russia, and Siberia, making the team the first Europeans to reach Magadan following the collapse of the Soviet Union. The trip pre-dated mobile phones and the Internet, making for a quaint, almost 1970s level of technical support. It also featured the rather unprecedented use of small (350cc) dirt bikes with no sponsorship or outside support.

BMW's development continued apace with the

↑ Produced between 1990 and 2003, Honda led the way with the legendary Africa Twin – a bike designed in every respect with adventure in mind
📷 Honda

↑**BMW has been at the forefront of adventure biking, led in many respects to the outstanding R1150 GS model seen here**
BMW Motorrad

→**The aftermarket for accessories has expanded dramatically in recent years leaving riders spoilt for choice**
Touratech

launch of the R 1150 GS at the end of the decade. Other manufacturers saw the gap in the market and began introducing 'adventure' bikes to their own line-ups, but the R 80 GS had laid the foundations for arguably the most successful range of adventure motorcycles ever produced, and today the GS remains a hugely popular choice with adventure motorcyclists. Its proven success and reliability on expeditions such as that of Pedersen years before had generated huge interest in the brand, and led to the establishment of numerous owners' clubs dedicated to the bike, as well as a strong aftermarket of motorcycle accessories for the GS range, including aluminium luggage, padded seats, shock absorbers, bigger screens, lights, and GPS mountings.

The R 1150 GS was rapidly followed by the R 1200 GS and R 1200 GS Adventure, which have together become the best-selling motorcycle built by BMW, the German manufacturer having produced its 100,000th model in August 2007. These two models held the top spot in UK sales for two years running.

At the same time a veritable industry was being built up around the concept of adventure motorcycling, with bike manufacturers providing consumers with increased choice, an explosion of tour operators offering trips to every corner of the globe, and, perhaps most importantly, a burgeoning number of aftermarket suppliers.

BMW's flagship model gained even further exposure when it was used by Ewan McGregor and Charley Boorman for their *Long Way Round* and *Long Way Down* expeditions. These trips saw adventure motorcycling broadcast into more homes than ever before, but there are those that argue it was too 'commercial', too heavily supported, and not in keeping with the ethos of adventure motorcycling. For many purists this may well be true, but on the flip side the trips inspired many more people to at least think about a two-wheel adventure – be that on a continent-conquering GS Adventure, a smaller capacity machine with home-made panniers, or simply from the comfort of one's armchair.

Today's modern adventure motorcycle comes in many forms – from large singles up to twins and even triples, but all have three things in common: their size, their ability to cover long distances on tarmac, and their potential to carry on when the going gets tough or the tarmac runs out. These factors are perhaps best epitomised by BMW's long-running GS and GS Adventure success story.

No matter what your approach is – the choice of motorcycle, the route, or whether you elect to use a GPS or not – the most important thing is that you get out there and enjoy the adventure.

The modern accessories market

As adventurers were pushing the boundaries and travelling further afield, the demand for more specialised products was increasing rapidly. Although much of the market remains a cottage industry, with only a handful of major players, today's adventurers also have an extensive range of OEM (original equipment manufacturer) products and kit parts to choose from, from all the leading motorcycle manufacturers. They also have access to a range of specialist adventure equipment and accessories, and a number of highly skilled overland fabricators to help in the preparation of an adventure bike.

While the market is dominated by a couple of major players like Touratech, who lead the field in adventure-related accessories, and Wunderlich, with an extensive range of enhancements to make touring and adventure-riding safer and more comfortable, its growth has also seen smaller operations like Metal Mule – a favourite with many overlanders – expand their range from panniers to a broad range of bike protection products, custom seats, and exhausts. As mentioned, adventurers also have an extensive range of OEM products and kit parts to choose from.

The market is further supported by a number of specialist fabricators capable of carrying out bespoke work on everything from panniers, frames, racks, engine protectors, reinforced sub-frames, headlight protectors, side/main stands, bash plates, fuel/water carriers, toolboxes, brake/disc protectors, extended footrests, fuel tanks, and custom cockpits. One such operation is UK-based Overland Solutions, run by the one and only Graham 'Ernie' Clark, who has prepared custom solutions for almost every kind of bike, from a full Dakar race machine to panniers on a Harley Davidson.

As panniers are some of the most popular items it is not surprising that there are several luggage manufacturers in the market, such as Hepco and Becker and Stahlkoffer, while Kriega and Ortlieb are renowned for producing some of the best soft luggage in the market.

'Today the accessories aftermarket caters for virtually everything an adventurer needs – from panniers to GPS brackets and windshields to extra headlights,' says Touratech's UK managing director, Nick Plumb. He adds: 'There are some very good stock bikes out there today but people enjoy personalising their machines to meet specific needs and the growth in the market has given people the chance to make a bike their own.'

The Touratech catalogue now stands at over 1,000 pages and 3,500 items. Plumb also believes the accessories market plays a vital role in bike development with the manufacturers. 'We created a range of aftermarket products for the standard GS when it launched, including better protection, luggage and a long-range tank. This

highlighted the bike's potential and not long thereafter BMW launched the GS Adventure model.'

Aftermarket suppliers regularly support trips to test how their equipment functions under harsh conditions. This information is then used to make the products more durable, refined, and efficient.

Touratech

When Herbert Schwarz developed the first 'Tripmaster' for his own use, he had no idea that just a few years later he and Jochen Schanz would be running a company that today employs more than 200 staff in Niedereschach, on the edge of the Black Forest in Germany, and has made a name for itself with its innovative ideas and field-tested accessories for motorcycles.

Touratech products trace their origin to the first illuminated bicycle speedometer and home-made aluminium cases for touring in Africa, the Middle East, the US, and Northern Europe. 1990 saw the development of the first IMO – a waterproof, feature-rich motorbike computer, which helped the newly founded Touratech company get a foothold in the expanding market.

Born of experience garnered through miles of travel, further products are constantly being developed and optimised. Touratech started offering special accessories for all of the new BMW enduros as soon as they hit the market, hired new employees, acquired a large production facility, and in 1999 was transformed into a publicly traded company.

Today the spectrum of Touratech products ranges from navigation (with software developed in-house and electronic navigation aids, including rally-proven mounting brackets), accessories, and special parts for all of the current BMW and other adventure motorcycles, to an extensive outdoor department. Complete rebuilds, such as the R 1100 GS/R 1150 GS based ReVamp, are also part of the product range.

Production has been expanded at dizzying speed in recent years; high-tech manufacturing methods are employed. Following a 2007 expansion of the company's German premises, a shop of 800m² features a variety of ready-to-travel motorbikes, plus accessories and a display of outdoor equipment.

The enthusiasm for motorbike riding and travelling to distant countries is still alive. Touratech only offer products that have proven themselves in practice from Tibet to Mexico and across Africa. Testing also takes place under the toughest conditions in rallies and enduro competitions, such as the Dakar. In 2002, Touratech was the first team in the history of the legendary race to get two motorbikes with fuel injection systems to the finish. The knowledge gained from racing is directly incorporated into the company's work.

For more information go to www.touratech.co.uk and www.touratech.de

↓Touratech's travel days are a great place to meet fellow travellers
Touratech

→Research and development is key to Touratech's success
Touratech

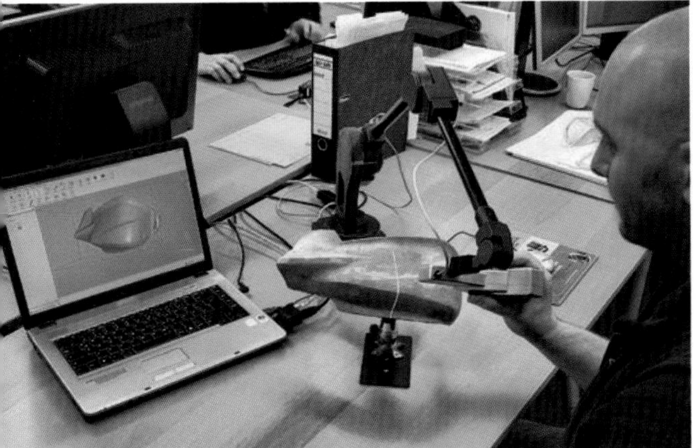

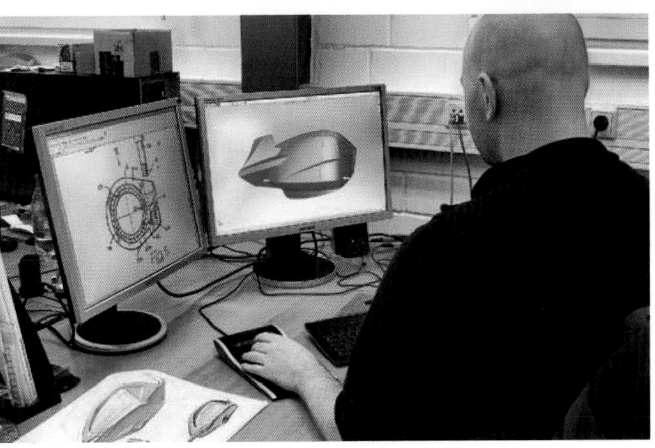

←**Wunderlich have taken precision engineering to a new level and created a broad range of quality products for BMW riders the world over**
Wunderlich

Wunderlich

One of the other leaders in the adventure aftermarket is undoubtedly Wunderlich GmbH, which has produced many high-quality accessories, in particular for BMW machines. Today, a dedicated development department creates tailor-made solutions related to the whole BMW range.

Back in 1985 Erich Wunderlich was still mending his Yamaha single-cylinder XT and SR in his parents' garage. His first modifications aroused a lot of interest very early on. The first eight-page catalogue, still written by typewriter, included a direct lubrication system of the upper camshaft. Just two years later the garage was bursting at the seams and he moved into a bigger workshop. This was followed by an expo at the motorcycle show in Cologne in 1991.

One year later a 67-page catalogue appeared, with more than 200 accessories for different BMWs, and four years later more than 20,000 BMW accessory catalogues were shipped from the company annually. The team, which by then had increased to 12, supported hundreds of customers and began expanding the product range even further.

With business steadily improving the firm opened a development facility using state-of-the-art technology to create 3D functional models. Using a combination of sophisticated CAD/CAM technologies and a 3D laser scanner, test batches of products can be created from a hand-made prototype.

Small batches of new products are produced for testing, as well as a complete first series and moulds for the manufacturing operations. The business doesn't rely solely on the theory of its development engineers: before any product finds its way into the Wunderlich catalogue and ultimately to the customer, its quality and durability are scrutinised in detail and evaluated in real-life test environments, including the legendary Erzberg rodeo in Austria and the company's own adventure tours. These provide important conclusions relating to the strength of the materials used and offer invaluable experience for developing future products. Most of the company's staff are themselves keen bikers and test many of the accessories in everyday life.

For more information go to www.wunderlich.de

➔➔ **No matter the bike or the requirements, Overland Solutions can help you prepare for your trip**
📷 Overland Solutions

Overland Solutions

Overland Solutions specialise in preparing motorcycles that need to cope with extreme conditions or loads. The majority of parts and fabrications are hand-made to ensure top quality and a bespoke fit. This ranges from fabricating a basic side stand to a fully prepared overland motorcycle for extreme riding conditions.

One of Overland Solutions' most successful projects was the work carried out on a bike that crossed the Sahara Desert and endured some of the world's harshest conditions.

'We are in a unique position of having travelled extensively ourselves and prepared many motorcycles for extreme journeys,' says 'Ernie' Clark. 'This has given us a full understanding of what alterations and fabrications are needed on most motorcycles, and we use innovative techniques that we have personally developed. This allows us to offer a personal service that cannot be rivalled. The company sales line is: 'If you want to walk the walk rather than talk the talk, then give us a ring'.

For more information go to www.overland-solutions.com

Vince advocates the use of small, light bikes – 350cc machines were used for the 40,000 mile (65,000km) Mondo Enduro trip

Austin Vince

The DIY approach to adventure motorcycling

Austin Vince
An open letter to those who read this book:

My name is Austin Vince and I am DIY through and through. I ride a bike and live on a boat and don't own a car. Already I'm on the periphery of society. I wish I wasn't, I hate being an outsider.

I have been teaching for 17 years and naturally that means that many of my former pupils are now adults and well over 30 years old. As, over the years, I watch these people develop I relish the thought that I might have influenced them. I remember the hours I spent making entire year groups (not just one class) watch *On Any Sunday*, and the PR efforts required getting the head to agree to holding a dirt bike workshop in the school grounds (using all of *Mondo Enduro* as the instructors!). I want my pupils to get involved. I want people to create, not spectate. That's why I hate professional sport; our society would be richer and stronger if, instead of paying people to play our games for us and then watch them doing it, we played the games ourselves.

Mondo Enduro and *Terra Circa* and, of course, *MotoSyberia* are all about ordinary chaps having a punt. That's not just the *easy* bit of riding along all day, it's the challenge of chronicling your trip too. The damage that some commercially driven adventures have done is incalculable since the message promulgated is one of danger, high risk, possible kidnap, huge expense and huge bikes (that are hugely expensive). Add to that the often cynical refusal by those who take part on trips such as this to neither make their own films, take their

Austin Vince – maths teacher and adventure motorcycling's Mr DIY

Austin Vince

↑Not a long way round, not a long way down, just a long way. Period
Austin Vince

own pictures, update their own websites, nor write their books, and I put it to you that they may be famous, yes, but are they good role models? No. Everything achieved by Horizons Unlimited, Guarav Jani, Chris Scott and Maciek Swinarski's *MotoAfryka* and *MotoSyberia* films show what can be achieved with imagination and effort replacing laziness and bags full of money.

My ethos at school with my pupils and in life is to 'have a go'. Don't listen to anyone who tries to temper your enthusiasm; they're invariably jealous losers craving your ability to dream and then live the dream. Don't listen to the 'expert' in the pub. He will doubtless have an opinion on your plans to do a big bike trip, but will he have ever done it himself? You know the answer.

→No room service here...
Austin Vince

Long-distance overland travel is very easy, it's also very safe (whilst my wife Lois was in the Congo a woman on our road in Uxbridge got stabbed to death in her own living room). DIY adventure is cheap (*Mondo Enduro* was £10,000 for 14 months) and requires no specialist skill or knowledge. It certainly doesn't require determination or mettle. If it did, then our teams on *Mondo* and *Terra* wouldn't have been able to pull it off! All you need is a boyish sense of fun and a desire to step into the unknown. Anybody who tells harrowing stories and describes their trip as being 'against all the odds' is invariably a liar, a show-off, or both.

I have spent many years chatting to all sorts of people about expedition biking. However, only recently have I come to realise that its essential core appeal is how easy it is to execute and enjoy. DIY bike travel should never be compared to true adventures like climbing the Matterhorn, trekking to the North Pole, or canoeing solo down the mighty Limpopo. Such challenges are way beyond the skill and fitness level of your average Joe. They will invariably be truly risky and by definition will need tons of 'practice' before one attempts 'the big one'. No, riding across Russia, or Africa, or the length of the Americas is well within the grasp of any able-bodied adult, male or female. The only skill required is an ability to ride a bike, and many – such as Tiffany Coates and Matt Hill – have shown that even *that* can be mastered 'in country'!

This is the message we need to promulgate: DIY adventure motorcycling offers world-class thrills to all of us in the high street. That's it, extraordinary adventures for ordinary people like us. I'm getting excited just thinking about it.

I want everyone to give up work for three months, borrow £5,000, buy a trail bike (maximum of 400cc), get two old rucksacks, a Poncho, a Thermarest, and a three-season sleeping bag. Hook up with some mates and ride in the same direction for 10,000 miles (16,000km). No GPS, no guided tours, no worries. And go it alone. I don't mean solo, I mean without anyone holding your hand except your chums. The kernel of the experience is coping when it goes wrong. You'll barely remember the easy days! The trip is all about overcoming obstacles through your own mettle, not turning to the tour organiser and saying 'What are we going to do now?' I'm sorry, but in my opinion signing up for an organised, pre-booked 'adventure tour' is completely dishonest and pointless in equal measure.

Hitting the road will be as thrilling a thing as any normal person will experience. However, if you're a stunt man or involved in the sex industry this may not be so. There's no need to spend two years 'finding yourself', but everyone should *eventually* drink from the goblet of DIY adventure motorcycling. Why? Because it's easy, fun, and good for you. How often do we get to say that?

AUTHOR'S NOTE: WHO *IS* AUSTIN VINCE?

He's the man behind the cult movies *Mondo Enduro* and *Terra Circa*. They're well established as the first two adventure motorcycle films ever made. It all started back in 1995, when Austin and company set out to ride around the world by the longest route possible on their second-hand Suzuki DR 350s. En route they became embroiled in a 400-mile (645km) road-less section of Siberia that they nicknamed 'The Zilov Gap'. After this dispiriting section they clattered another 2,000 miles (3,200km), becoming the first Europeans ever to get to Magadan via the so-called 'Road of Bones'. This was immediately followed by the 18,000 miles (29,000km) from Alaska to Chile, then another 10,000 miles (16,000km) from South Africa back to London – all this in an age before mobile phones or the Internet, and, obviously, totally unsupported and unsponsored (Suzuki famously wouldn't even give them a free spark plug!).

2001 saw them filming themselves crossing Russia once more (on the same bikes) and conquering the Zilov Gap. This made them the first team to get across Siberia without using the train. By riding on to New York the *Terra Circa* team firmly established the template that the *Long Way Round* adventure would eventually copy. On his return, Vince couldn't get a single TV channel interested in his footage. How the tapes came to be edited and broadcast is a very long story indeed…

MONDO ENDURO

TERRA CIRCA

Austin Vince

Chapter 2

Choosing a motorcycle

KTM

As you'll see from the rider and bike profiles which follow later in this chapter, it's possible to take almost any kind of bike on an adventure ride. Nick Sanders has ridden around the world on a Yamaha R1, various people have completed significant long-distance rides on scooters, and several Honda Goldwings have covered vast parts of the globe.

I'm sure there are very few people, other than Nick of course, who would even begin to contemplate riding around the world on a bike more suited to Brands Hatch than the back roads of Bolivia – it's certainly possible, but not at all practical or comfortable.

The adventure segment of the bike market has grown significantly in recent years, with almost every major manufacturer launching a new machine, some for the very first time. Even some of the smaller manufacturers who have traditionally not ventured into this market – such as Moto Morini, Moto Guzzi, and even Ducati – have been getting in on the act, leaving aspiring adventurers spoilt for choice.

When it comes to choosing an adventure bike, debate is twofold. Firstly, whether to take a large adventure bike such as a BMW R 1200 GS or KTM 990 Adventure, or a smaller, lighter trail bike, such as a Suzuki DR 650, Kawasaki KLR 650, or one with even less engine capacity – think about Lois Pryce riding the length of Africa on a 250cc Yamaha a few years ago. With varying degrees of modification, smaller machines can be extremely capable and worth considering, particularly if you're looking to keep weight to a minimum and a low seat height.

A smaller, lighter and more nimble off-road trail bike (300cc–600cc) is best suited to smaller riders needing to cover difficult terrain. The downside is that on-road ability may be reduced and load-carrying capacity is generally lower, as is the bike's range unless kitted out with a long-range fuel tank.

There are pros and cons to both categories and much depends on your own ability as a rider, as well as your physical characteristics such as height, weight, and strength to manoeuvre the bike over tough terrain or to pick it up when it falls over. At 195cm tall (6ft 4in) and with reasonable off-road riding skills, I'm comfortable handling my own BMW R 1200 GS Adventure and happen to be a big fan of the bike's 'go-anywhere' ability, so it tends to be my first choice for any adventure ride. For a smaller rider, the biggest downside of a big

trail bike is certainly the weight, and many people make the mistake thinking that it can be loaded up excessively. In fact the complete opposite applies – they're big bikes to start with, and as a result need as little additional weight as possible.

Recently some manufacturers have started to fill a gap in the market with bikes in the 600cc–800cc range. These are proving to be a popular choice with adventure riders, as they offer good engine capacity, load-carrying capacity, and on- and off-road ability but don't weigh the same as traditional big trail bikes. BMW's recent F800 GS and Yamaha's XT660 are great examples of this trend.

The second important choice is the amount of modification work that's going to be required to get the bike to meet the needs of your journey. You can go for the 'all-singing, all-dancing' adventure bike with every accessory imaginable, or a lightweight, machine with minimal accessories and lighter, soft luggage. It's not quite as clear-cut as that and there's always a balance to be had, so Chapter 3 provides details of almost every conceivable accessory and modification.

Aside from your own physical abilities, as a general rule of thumb the tougher the route is, the more likely it is that a smaller, nimble single-cylinder machine with soft luggage is going to be the most appropriate choice. For longer stretches on open gravel roads a bigger bike with big metal boxes is fine. With this in mind it pays to research your route first, then the bike, and finally the modifications. Remember to choose wisely, as you're going to need to be on good terms with your bike for some time to come.

Essential factors

Before making that all-important decision about the choice of motorcycle, you should be clear about a few key points – like knowing about the type of terrain you're likely to encounter, the typical load you'll be carrying, and the average distances between fuel stops on the intended route. These are key points to consider, and the more you know, the more likely you are to make the right choice.

That said, there is no 'perfect' overland bike. What's good off-road isn't necessarily good on-road, and what's right for one person isn't necessarily right for another, so choose the bike that's the best compromise for you and the trip.

Be sure to research and test-ride a range of alternatives before making your final decision. Key factors to look for include:

Budget – remember that a brand new, high-end, all-conquering adventure bike may look like the best choice from the images of remote locations in the sales literature, but this is likely to come at a significant cost, and will have a serious knock-on effect on the price of your carnet, which in turn can put a large dent in your overall budget. Explore second-hand options thoroughly, but be sure you're getting value for money and a machine that's in good condition and capable of the trip.
Range and consumption – consider the distances you'll need to travel between points and be sure that the bike's range is suitable. Fuel consumption is also important – a big 1,000cc engine, for example, can be a thirsty beast, particularly when working hard in the desert.
Load carrying ability – assess how much you need to carry and how the bike will cope with the load.
Terrain – research and understand the terrain you're going to be covering. Some bikes are far better suited to certain types of terrain than others.
Spares and reliability – ideally you want to choose a machine with a good track record, and also one which is likely to have readily available spares that you can either buy on the road or source with relative ease from home.
Mechanical knowledge – appreciate that you'll need a level of mechanical competence to deal with the technical issues that will arise from time to time. At the very least you should know how to carry out a basic service on the machine.
Handling and weight – if possible before purchasing, try to ride a fully laden machine to appreciate what you're in for. A big 1,000cc off-road bike with fully loaded panniers and some additional gear can easily weigh in excess of 300kg (660lb).
Seat height – ensure that the seat height allows you to reach the ground comfortably with at least one foot flat on the road surface. This doesn't sound that important, but it's when riding at slow speeds, in traffic, on uneven road surfaces, or in confined places that you'll appreciate its relevance. Most bikes can be lowered a little so speak to your dealer. The more comfortable you can make yourself on the bike through further modifications the better.

Once you've decided on the bike model, don't delay in getting your hands on it – you'll need as much time with your new best friend as possible, especially if you're planning on some off-road training, which is best done on your own machine, though not essential. The other reason to get going sooner rather than later is that orders for some special parts and accessories may take time to be fulfilled by aftermarket suppliers. Another motivating factor is that it's difficult to complete essential paperwork such as carnet forms without the bike's registration number. So, clear some space in the garage, get your tools out and get cracking.

As you begin to transform your machine, read through trip reports on the Internet to understand the shortcomings of your bike and identify the right places to purchase your aftermarket supplies. Always keep in mind that your goal is to strengthen and prepare your bike for long-distance adventure travel, not to add unnecessary parts that add weight and eat away at your budget.

A comprehensive list of aftermarket suppliers and online resources is available in the reference section at the back of the book.

Aprilia
Pegaso 650 Trail

An excellent long range touring bike with a history dating back more than 12 years, thanks to superior comfort, an advanced new engine and a large number of innovations aimed at improving versatility. It boasts a modern, four-valve, dry sump engine with electronic fuel injection and a 44mm throttle body, a strong diamond shaped steel frame and spoked wheels with medium-knobbly tyres for great handling on and off the road. The 70° steering angle provides agility while the comfortable seat and riding position add to its long distance credentials. At 820mm the seat height makes it easy to get on and off for riders of all statures.

Specifications

Displacement:	660cc	Rear tyre:	130/80–17
Power:	50bhp @ 6,250rpm	Length:	2,160mm
Torque:	61Nm @ 5,200rpm	Width:	810mm
Transmission:	Five-speed / Chain	Height:	1,310mm
Front travel:	170mm	Seat height:	820mm
Front tyre:	100/90–19	Dry weight:	161kg
Rear travel:	170mm	Fuel capacity:	16 litres

Aprilia
ETV 1000 Caponord

This bike has built up considerable following since its introduction in 2005 and is a very capable all-purpose machine with advanced technology, a pace-setting aluminium frame and a highly acclaimed, powerful V-twin engine offering all-round touring versatility. The engine has been derived directly from that of the RSV, but has been thoroughly modified to make it perfect for touring, with overall bike design emphasis on ergonomics, rider and passenger comfort, and total wind protection. Its load-carrying capacity makes it highly versatile.

Specifications

Displacement:	998cc	Rear tyre:	150/70–17
Power:	98bhp @ 8,500rpm	Length:	2,290mm
Torque:	90Nm @ 6,250rpm	Width:	876mm
Transmission:	Six-speed / Chain	Height:	1,436mm
Front travel:	175mm	Seat height:	820mm
Front tyre:	110/80–19	Dry weight:	215kg
Rear travel:	185mm	Fuel capacity:	25 litres

Benelli
Tre-K Amazonas

As Benelli's first foray into the adventure market, the Amazonas is something of an unknown quantity. The engine comes from Benelli's other 1,130cc motorcycles which has been packaged into the frame of an upright adventure tourer. On the plus side are the long travel suspension, comfortable riding position and slim styling and good looks. On the downside, it's not designed to take a hard knock and the engine is prone to vibrate. It also lacks some real world adventure credibility so right now it's unlikely to rival the more established contenders in the market such as BMW and KTM.

Specifications

Displacement:	1,130cc	Rear tyre:	180/55–17
Power:	123bhp @ 9,000rpm	Length:	2,208mm
Torque:	112Nm @ 5,000rpm	Width:	870mm
Transmission:	Six-speed / Chain	Height:	1,375mm
Front travel:	180mm	Seat height:	850mm
Front tyre:	120/70–17	Dry weight:	205kg
Rear travel:	180mm	Fuel capacity:	22 litres

BMW
R 1150 GS

This is undoubtedly one of BMW's most successful models and traces its history back to the original R 80 GS of 1980. Introduced in 1999, the bike emerged with a larger capacity engine, a six-speed gearbox and more radical styling, including a pair of asymmetric projector beam headlights and removable screen. The GS's unlikely combination of a large, heavy touring-bike engine and an off-road chassis offers a much more dynamic package than might be expected. BMW's trademark Telelever and Paralever suspension systems manage to combine soft, long-travel suspension with a degree of firm control not associated with trail bikes.

Specifications

Displacement:	1,130cc	Rear tyre:	150/70–17
Power:	85bhp @ 6,750rpm	Length:	2,189mm
Torque:	98Nm @ 5,250rpm	Width:	903mm
Transmission:	Six-speed / Shaft drive	Height:	1,366mm
Front travel:	190mm	Seat height:	840mm/860mm
Front tyre:	110/80–19	Dry weight:	228kg
Rear travel:	200mm	Fuel capacity:	22 litres

BMW
R 1150 GS Adventure

This is essentially a BMW R 1150 GS with longer travel suspension, a large 30-litre tank, taller screen and decent off-road tyres. Built by BMW between 2001 and 2005, the bike has won countless industry awards and was used by Ewan McGregor and Charley Boorman in their 'Long Way Round' adventure. Whether on gravel paths, sand tracks, rough terrain or over long distances, the chassis ensures optimum comfort and control – even when fully loaded. You'll need to get used to the weight and height but once you do, it's an imposing, durable and highly reliable ride.

Specifications

Displacement:	1,130cc	Rear tyre:	150/70–17
Power:	85bhp @ 6,750rpm	Length:	2,189mm
Torque:	98Nm @ 5,250rpm	Width:	903mm
Transmission:	Six-speed / Shaft drive	Height:	1,366mm
Front travel:	210mm	Seat height:	860mm/900mm
Front tyre:	110/80–19	Dry weight:	232kg
Rear travel:	220mm	Fuel capacity:	30 litres

BMW
R 1200 GS

The latest BMW features a revised boxer engine that sports dual overhead cams. It's allowed for an extra 500rpm, 5hp more and a better spread of torque throughout the rev range making the bike more rideable in off-road conditions. The real benefit comes with the optimised power at low and medium engine speeds. Other new additions include an improved dash with bigger push buttons as well as adjustable handlebars that can be set for more comfortable road use or more aggressive off-road use when you're in the standing position.

Specifications

Displacement:	1,170cc	Rear tyre:	150/70–17
Power:	105bhp @ 7,500rpm	Length:	2,210mm
Torque:	115Nm @ 5,750rpm	Width:	935mm
Transmission:	Six-speed / Shaft drive	Height:	1,450mm
Front travel:	190mm	Seat height:	850mm/870mm
Front tyre:	110/80–19	Dry weight:	203kg
Rear travel:	200mm	Fuel capacity:	20 litres

BMW
R 1200 GS Adventure

The GS Adventure has set the standard for the ultimate long-distance adventure motorcycle ever since its launch in 2005. It's the perfect synthesis of agility, touring ability and off-road capability delivered in the standard package. It is hugely forgiving and stable, infinitely reliable and comfortable and copes with any terrain – a real icon of modern-day adventure motorcycling. BMW continues to enhance and upgrade its top model given competition in the sector from the likes of Ducati's Multistrada and Yamaha's brand new shaft-driven 1,200cc Super Ténéré.

Specifications

Displacement:	1,170cc	Rear tyre:	150/70–17
Power:	105bhp @ 7,500rpm	Length:	2,240mm
Torque:	115Nm @ 5,750rpm	Width:	990mm
Transmission:	Six-speed / Shaft drive	Height:	1,525mm
Front travel:	210mm	Seat height:	910mm/890mm
Front tyre:	110/80–19	Dry weight:	223kg
Rear travel:	220mm	Fuel capacity:	33 litres

BMW
HP2 Enduro

Unfortunately no longer in production, this model was based, in technical terms, on the R 1200 GS, but tailored to the needs of the enduro rider by providing supreme agility and easy control over tough terrain. This is not a bike for the meek – 'HP' stands for 'high performance' and the engine delivers 105bhp combined with lightweight construction, a low centre of gravity and innovative rear suspension making for a formidable machine. Rated by Touratech's Herbert Schwarz as 'the best adventure bike BMW has ever built', the entire drive-train is laid out specifically for off-road use.

Specifications

Displacement:	1,130cc	Rear tyre:	140/80–17
Power:	105bhp @ 7,000rpm	Length:	2,350mm
Torque:	115Nm @ 5,500rpm	Width:	880mm
Transmission:	Six-speed / Shaft drive	Height:	1,266mm
Front travel:	270mm	Seat height:	920mm
Front tyre:	90/90–21	Dry weight:	175kg
Rear travel:	250mm	Fuel capacity:	13 litres

BMW
F 650 GS (Single)

Over an eight year period (1995–2003), BMW sold more than 110,000 F 650 machines, with a large proportion going to female buyers and new riders. Based on the 'enduro' concept, the bike features a relaxed, upright riding position that is the ideal compromise between on-road comfort and off-road control. To accommodate riders of different heights, several seat options are available including a high seat is available that provides taller riders with extra legroom. With a slender engine and under-seat fuel tank the bike's overall centre of gravity is reduced, making it feel both small and light.

Specifications

Displacement:	652cc	Rear tyre:	130/80–17
Power:	50bhp @ 6,500rpm	Length:	2,175mm
Torque:	60Nm @ 5,200rpm	Width:	910mm
Transmission:	Five-speed / Chain	Height:	1,265mm
Front travel:	170mm	Seat height:	780mm
Front tyre:	100/90–19	Dry weight:	176kg
Rear travel:	165mm	Fuel capacity:	17.3 litres

BMW
F 650 GS Dakar

This is the competition version of the BMW F 650 GS, whose forerunners won the Dakar rally on many occasions. It's a very capable machine and has been successfully tried and tested on many adventure rides the world over. Riders benefit from the longer suspension travel, large front wheel and enduro tyres. From the figures, weight (192kg) looks like a concern, but once in motion it carries the weight well and doesn't feel heavy at all – it's a balanced, simple and well constructed package, with emphasis on reliability and durability.

Specifications

Displacement:	652cc	Rear tyre:	130/80–17
Power:	50bhp @ 6,500rpm	Length:	2,189mm
Torque:	60Nm @ 4,800rpm	Width:	910mm
Transmission:	Five-speed / Chain	Height:	1,265mm
Front travel:	210mm	Seat height:	870mm
Front tyre:	90/90–21	Dry weight:	177kg
Rear travel:	210mm	Fuel capacity:	17.3 litres

BMW
F 650 GS (Twin)

Compact and lightweight, practical and well balanced, this bike was used extensively in the making of sister publication *'Adventure Riding Techniques'* and proved to be an agile and capable machine over testing and varied terrain in Iceland. It's built around a punchy twin-cylinder engine, with a rigid steel tube trellis frame, double-sided swing arm, low seat height and narrow design. Cast aluminium wheels and telescopic forks make for a smooth ride. It needs a level of additional protection for any serious off-roading.

Specifications

Displacement:	798cc	Rear tyre:	140/80–17
Power:	71bhp @ 7,000rpm	Length:	2,280mm
Torque:	75Nm @ 4,500rpm	Width:	890mm
Transmission:	Six-speed / Chain	Height:	1,240mm
Front travel:	180mm	Seat height:	820mm / 765mm
Front tyre:	100/80–19	Dry weight:	179kg
Rear travel:	170mm	Fuel capacity:	16 litres

BMW
F 800 GS

Unlike most large-capacity adventure bikes which can sometimes reach their limits because of excessive weight and design issues, the new F 800 GS delivers excellent off-road riding and excellent long-distance performance with a low dry weight of just 178kg. The overall package combines balance, power and weight, excellent ground clearance, long spring travel, precise wheel guidance and sophisticated ergonomics. The inline twin-cylinder engine comes from BMW's well-known F 800 model series. The accessories market expect this to be a popular model with a wide range of modifications and extra kit parts widely available.

Specifications

Displacement:	798cc	Rear tyre:	150/70–17
Power:	85bhp @ 7,500rpm	Length:	2,320mm
Torque:	83Nm @ 5,750rpm	Width:	945mm
Transmission:	Six-speed / Chain	Height:	1,155mm
Front travel:	230mm	Seat height:	880mm/850mm
Front tyre:	90/90–21	Dry weight:	178kg
Rear travel:	215mm	Fuel capacity:	16 litres

BMW
G 650 X-Challenge

Described as 'the hard enduro for the off-road enthusiast', the BMW G 650 is a new departure for BMW and has a lot to offer, including long spring travel and no excess weight. The bike can be transformed into an extremely capable overland machine as shown by Walter Colebatch in his Sibirsky Extreme adventure featured in this book. Fairing components are both light and robust, while the 270mm suspension travel both front and rear means the X-Challenge copes very well off the beaten track. A long-range tank is a must if you're planning on covering big distances.

Specifications

Displacement:	652cc	Rear tyre:	140/80–18
Power:	53bhp @ 7,000rpm	Length:	2,205mm
Torque:	60Nm @ 5,250rpm	Width:	907mm
Transmission:	Five-speed / Chain	Height:	1,255mm
Front travel:	270mm	Seat height:	950mm
Front tyre:	90/90–21	Dry weight:	144kg
Rear travel:	270mm	Fuel capacity:	9.5 litres

Cagiva
Elefant 900

This is a production version of the bike which triumphed in the Paris–Dakar Rally and uses an air and oil-cooled 90-degree V-twin motor (as used on countless Ducati road and race bikes) with a usable spread of torque. Suspension is excellent, with front Marzocchi forks and an Öhlins multi-adjustable rear shock. Its rally heritage is also evident in a large-capacity fuel tank, twin-headlamp fairing and high seat. Low gearing and the flexibility of the V-twin engine make it a very capable machine off-road but beware of overall build quality and high servicing costs.

Specifications

Displacement:	904cc	Dry weight:	204kg
Power:	68bhp @ 8,000rpm	Fuel capacity:	24 litres
Torque:	70.6Nm @ 5,250rpm		
Transmission:	Six-speed / Chain		
Front tyre:	100/90–19		
Rear tyre:	140/80–17		
Seat height:	835mm		

Cagiva
Navigator

This bike is based on Cagiva's Gran Canyon trail bike, but utilises a detuned Suzuki TL1000 engine with modified cam profiles reconfigured for maximum torque. The engine configuration allows for a narrow chassis, complemented by 10-litre plastic tanks on either side of the frame. The tanks are joined by a pipe across the frame so that fuel is evenly drawn from both sides. The soft suspension and strong brakes just about keep up with the engine. A good bike if you can find one; spare parts are also hard to find.

Specifications

Displacement:	996cc	Rear tyre:	150/70–17
Power:	99bhp @ 8,500rpm	Length:	2,104mm
Torque:	95Nm @ 7,000rpm	Width:	820mm
Transmission:	Six-speed / Chain	Height:	1,070mm
Front travel:	150mm	Seat height:	850mm
Front tyre:	110/80–18	Dry weight:	210kg
Rear travel:	150mm	Fuel capacity:	20 litres

Ducati
Multistrada 1200 S

In this new machine, Ducati claim to have produced a bike 'to tackle any kind of journey and road surface', using technology from their race bikes. A single button changes the fundamental characteristics of the bike – power, torque delivery, suspension settings and traction control can all be set on the move, enabling the bike to adapt to the needs of the rider and the terrain. Spares aren't exactly going to be in abundance in remote parts of the world and Ducati does not have much in the way of an off-road pedigree just yet, but the thinking behind this new model might just change that.

Specifications

Displacement:	1,198cc	Rear tyre:	190/55–17
Power:	150bhp @ 9,250rpm	Length:	2,150mm
Torque:	118Nm @ 7,500Nm	Height:	1,400mm
Transmission:	Six-speed / Chain	Seat height:	850mm
Front travel:	170mm	Dry weight:	189kg
Front tyre:	120/70–17	Fuel capacity:	20 litres
Rear travel:	170mm		

Honda
NX650 Dominator

The Dominator was first launched in 1988 as a middleweight dual-purpose bike, with an air-cooled single-cylinder engine in a simple, trail bike chassis. Don't expect significant off-road ability – it's less capable off-road than its styling might suggest. It does offer long-travel suspension and trail-type wheels and tyres but as a package, it's better suited to poorly surfaced roads rather than proper off-road riding. The engine is rather dated now – its four-valve design is unchanged since 1988, and while there is torque in abundance, it struggles at speeds in excess of 70mph (115km/h).

Specifications

Displacement:	644cc	Rear tyre:	120/90–17
Power:	44bhp @ 6,000rpm	Length:	2,200mm
Torque:	53Nm @ 5,000rpm	Width:	903mm
Transmission:	Five-speed / Chain	Seat height:	880mm
Front travel:	220mm	Dry weight:	167kg
Front tyre:	90/90–21	Fuel capacity:	16 litres
Rear travel:	195mm		

Honda
XL1000V Varadero

This is a bike for riders who want long-term comfort twinned with power, ability, and good handling. The Varadero first came into production in Europe in 1999 and was an instant hit. The chassis is comprised of a steel tube cantilever frame, aluminium swingarm and conventional front forks. Bear in mind that the adventure bike styling belies the more road-orientated engineering underneath and the long travel suspension is the only real 'off-road' characteristic of the Varadero. More recent models have a sturdy aluminium sump guard to protect lower engine components.

Specifications

Displacement:	996cc	Rear tyre:	150/70–17
Power:	93bhp @ 8,000rpm	Length:	2,295mm
Torque:	98Nm @ 6,000rpm	Width:	925mm
Transmission:	Six-speed / Chain	Height:	1,500mm
Front travel:	155mm	Seat height:	838mm
Front tyre:	110/80–19	Dry weight:	241.5kg
Rear travel:	145mm	Fuel capacity:	25 litres

Honda
XL 650V Transalp

This has been a stalwart in Honda's line-up for 20 years and was given a major makeover in 2001 when the 583cc engine was bored out to a larger 647cc version, and the bodywork heavily restyled. This is a good bike for riders seeking off-road confidence as the chassis tends to offer safe, predictable handling while the long-travel suspension gives a plush ride. The engine copes well and it's only when you hit motorway speeds it begins to feel the strain. The brakes are not a strong point and suspension offers limited adjustment.

Specifications

Displacement:	647cc	Rear tyre:	120/90–17
Power:	55bhp @ 7,500rpm	Length:	2,260mm
Torque:	56.2Nm @ 5,500rpm	Width:	920mm
Transmission:	Five-speed / Chain	Seat height:	843mm
Front travel:	200mm	Dry weight:	191kg
Front tyre:	90/90–21	Fuel capacity:	19 litres
Rear travel:	170mm		

Honda
XL 700V Transalp

Upgraded from the former XL 650, this remains a versatile machine that handles well-travelled highways and off-road tracks with equal ease and enjoyment. The low-profile seat version lets smaller riders take full advantage of a lighter and more responsive machine. The new model's fuel tank is smaller (down from 19 to 17.5 litres), but the improved fuel consumption of the new fuel-injected engine actually extends the overall range. The bike is equipped with the Honda Ignition Security System (HISS) – a fail-safe electronic interlock to prevent the engine from being started by anything other than the machine's two original keys.

Specifications

Displacement:	680cc	Rear tyre:	130/80–17
Power:	59bhp @ 7,500rpm	Length:	2,250mm
Torque:	60Nm @ 5,500rpm	Width:	905mm
Transmission:	Five-speed / Chain	Height:	1,305mm
Front travel:	177mm	Seat height:	841mm
Front tyre:	100/90–19	Dry weight:	191kg
Rear travel:	173mm	Fuel capacity:	17.5 litres

Honda
XRV750 Africa Twin

With more than ten years of production history, the Africa Twin has become something of a favourite in the off-road community. It's certainly getting on a little now, but still a hugely capable machine offering reliability and range. Supple suspension, a commanding riding position and good ground clearance make you appreciate that this bike was designed to travel a long, long way. This is further supported by the large fuel tank, heavy-duty sump guard, wide handlebars and good fuel economy. Concerns to be aware of are its overall weight and uncomfortable seat.

Specifications

Displacement:	742cc	Rear tyre:	140/80–17
Power:	60bhp @ 7,500rpm	Length:	2,315mm
Torque:	62Nm @ 6,500rpm	Width:	905mm
Transmission:	Five-speed / Chain	Height:	1,430mm
Front travel:	220mm	Seat height:	860mm
Front tyre:	90/90–18	Dry weight:	207kg
Rear travel:	214mm	Fuel capacity:	23 litres

Kawasaki
KLE 500

First introduced in 1991, the KLE is a great dual-purpose bike. Its strongest point is price, offering excellent value for money. You also get smooth power delivery from the reliable parallel-twin engine, while the chassis ensures good all-round handling, performance and versatility for the compromise needed between road and trail. It's a good bike to start out on but beware of the soft suspension and lack of delivery on the throttle. The oversize sump guard almost seems at odds with the rest of the design and may lead you into thinking it's more off-road capable than it is.

Specifications

Displacement:	498cc	Rear tyre:	130/80–17
Power:	44bhp @ 8,300rpm	Length:	2,215mm
Torque:	41Nm @ 7,500rpm	Width:	880mm
Transmission:	Six-speed / Chain	Height:	1,270mm
Front travel:	220mm	Seat height:	850mm
Front tyre:	90/90–21	Dry weight:	181kg
Rear travel:	200mm	Fuel capacity:	15 litres

Kawasaki
KLR 650

First introduced in 1987, this big-bore dual-purpose bike is suitable for all skill levels and provides riders with amazing versatility. Light, durable, immensely off-road capable, its huge fuel tank and thick seat let you keep going longer than you'd ever have thought possible. A big plus is the low-end grunt but also the bike's composure at motorway speeds, making long distance travel a pleasure. It's been ridden to the Arctic, across North and South America, and throughout Europe, Africa, and Asia, as well as on full global circumnavigation rides.

Specifications

Displacement:	651cc	Rear tyre:	130/80–17
Power:	44bhp @ 6,000rpm	Length:	2,204mm
Torque:	46Nm @ 5,000rpm	Width:	940mm
Transmission:	Five-speed / Chain	Height:	1,346mm
Front travel:	231mm	Seat height:	889mm
Front tyre:	90/90–21	Dry weight:	153kg
Rear travel:	231mm	Fuel capacity:	27 litres

KTM
950 Adventure

With heritage closely linked to KTM's success in the Dakar Rally, this bike comes with a strong pedigree. Plus points are a solid chassis and the fully adjustable suspension components. The LC8 engine is a 942cc, liquid cooled, 75° V-twin four-stroke. Clutch pull is easy and smooth, the brakes require only a light touch, steering is easy and shifting between gears is slick. KTM used a dry sump design to enable placing the engine as low as possible in the chassis. Load carrying ability is excellent and there is an extensive array of aftermarket products to enhance the bike still further.

Specifications

Displacement:	942cc	Rear tyre:	150/70–18
Power:	98bhp @ 8,000rpm	Length:	2,260mm
Torque:	95Nm @ 6,000rpm	Width:	950mm
Transmission:	Six-speed / Chain	Height:	1,450mm
Front travel:	265mm	Seat height:	880mm
Front tyre:	90/90–21	Dry weight:	198kg
Rear travel:	235mm	Fuel capacity:	22 litres

KTM 990 Adventure

The popular 990 Adventure is a revised version of the successful 950 Adventure featuring greater displacement, electronic fuel injection and a regulated catalytic converter. It is a touch lower than the companion S model and features improved safety factors with its ABS with the quality WP suspension offering a plush ride. Strong torque is perfect for off-road riding and load/pillion carrying alike. The twin fuel tanks require filling individually, which is a minor inconvenience but helps keep the bike slim-line by tucking fuel storage into nooks and crannies.

Specifications

Displacement:	999cc	Rear tyre:	150/70–18
Power:	104bhp @ 8,500rpm	Length:	2,260mm
Torque:	100Nm @ 6,750rpm	Width:	990mm
Transmission:	Six-speed / Chain	Height:	1,450mm
Front travel:	210mm	Seat height:	860mm
Front tyre:	90/90–21	Dry weight:	209kg
Rear travel:	210mm	Fuel capacity:	19.5 litres

KTM 990 Adventure R

This impressive machine spearheads KTM's adventure family. The reworked engine delivers a 20% increase in power for top class performance. Apart from being more powerful (some novice riders may find the power intimidating), the R model is also 2kg lighter than the standard version and features a higher seat for taller and more experienced riders. The suspension has 55mm extra travel to give it extra off-road capability. ABS is not available on the R model but overall it's a very capable machine with a new cockpit and modified front storage compartment.

Specifications

Displacement:	999cc	Rear tyre:	150/70–18
Power:	113bhp @ 8,500rpm	Length:	2,260mm
Torque:	100Nm @ 6,750rpm	Width:	990mm
Transmission:	Six-speed / Chain	Height:	1,505mm
Front travel:	265mm	Seat height:	915mm
Front tyre:	90/90–21	Dry weight:	209kg
Rear travel:	265mm	Fuel capacity:	19.5 litres

KTM 640 Adventure

Directly descended from successful rally racing bikes, the 640 Adventure is characterised by its low weight, tough exterior, agile chassis with long suspension travel and a robust LC4 engine. Some pre-2004 machines suffered from main bearing failure so make sure the official fix has been completed if you're buying second-hand. Get used to the vibrations – they're evident from the moment you set off and know that the electrics can be fickle. On the plus side you get tremendous handling, good braking and sophisticated WP suspension. Aftermarket suppliers stock a vast array of goodies, including lighting, panniers, protection and cockpit conversions.

Specifications

Displacement:	625cc	Rear tyre:	140/80–18
Power:	53bhp @ 7,500rpm	Length:	2,200mm
Torque:	55Nm @ 5,500rpm	Width:	640mm
Transmission:	Five-speed / Chain	Height:	640mm
Front travel:	275mm	Seat height:	945mm
Front tyre:	90/90–21	Dry weight:	158kg
Rear travel:	300mm	Fuel capacity:	25.5 litres

Moto Guzzi
Stelvio NTX

The iconic Italian manufacturer has taken some of the key ingredients from their other machines – a big, air-cooled twin-cylinder engine, shaft drive and a single-sided swingarm and mixed them into an off-road styled chassis to create the Stelvio to take on BMW's class domination. The seat height is a fair bit lower than the 1200 GS and the Stelvio is marginally lighter too (by 5kg), but at this stage of its development it's not an accomplished off-roader. Perhaps worth a look if you're after something a little different.

Specifications

Displacement:	1,151cc	Rear tyre:	180/55–17
Power:	104bhp @ 7,500rpm	Length:	2,250mm
Torque:	108Nm @ 6,400rpm	Width:	1,025mm
Transmission:	Six-speed / Shaft drive	Height:	1,475mm
Front travel:	170mm	Seat height:	840mm
Front tyre:	110/90–19	Dry weight:	214kg
Rear travel:	155mm	Fuel capacity:	18 litres

Moto Morini
Granpasso

Performance and versatility are the main attributes of this new machine. An extra-large fuel tank, twin headlights and aluminium sump guard give it an adventurous demeanour, enhanced by a wire-spoked 19-inch front wheel. The seat height will prove challenging for shorter riders who may also struggle with a machine that is wide. Some comfort will come from the fact that it's over 10bhp more powerful than rivals such as BMW's R 1200 GS and Moto Guzzi's Stelvio. Öhlins rear suspension and front Marzocchi forks complement the package.

Specifications

Displacement:	1,187cc	Rear tyre:	150/70–17
Power:	118hp @ 8,500rpm	Length:	2,170mm
Torque:	103Nm @ 6,750rpm	Width:	850mm
Transmission:	Six-speed / Chain	Seat height:	830mm
Front travel:	190mm	Dry weight:	198kg
Front tyre:	110/80–19	Fuel capacity:	25 litres
Rear travel:	200mm		

Suzuki
V-Strom DL 650X

This new model offers a step-up in off-road credentials from the earlier dual-purpose DL 650 V-Strom. The new DL 650X is based on the non-ABS version of the V-Strom 650 and comes with an alloy bash plate, hand guards, steel engine protection bars and a decent screen. It's aimed at riders who intend to use the bike's off-road ability which has received mixed reviews and many Suzuki fans would like to see the Japanese manufacturer go one step further to lift the model's off-road credentials to a more acceptable level.

Specifications

Displacement:	645cc	Rear tyre:	150/70–17
Power:	87bhp @ 8,800rpm	Length:	2,290mm
Torque:	60Nm @ 6,400rpm	Width:	840mm
Transmission:	Six-speed / Chain	Height:	1,450mm
Front travel:	150mm	Seat height:	820mm
Front tyre:	110/80–19	Dry weight:	199kg
Rear travel:	150mm	Fuel capacity:	22 litres

Suzuki
V-Strom DL 1000

Surprisingly no longer part of the Suzuki range given EU emissions ratings, this bike delivers comfort, convenience and a good range from the tank. It's not as off-road capable as the market leading heavyweights and needs a fair bit of modification for even moderate off-road use but a smooth throttle response of the fuel injection's Dual Throttle Valve system ensures easy riding. Although the rear shock offers preload and rebound adjustability, this is not a bike for heavy off-road work but certainly capable enough on wide trails where the surface is smooth.

Specifications

Displacement:	996cc	Rear tyre:	150/70–17
Power:	96bhp @ 7,600rpm	Length:	2,295mm
Torque:	101Nm @ 6,400rpm	Width:	910mm
Transmission:	Six-speed / Chain	Height:	1,395mm
Front travel:	150mm	Seat height:	840mm
Front tyre:	110/80–19	Dry weight:	208kg
Rear travel:	160mm	Fuel capacity:	22 litres

Suzuki
DR 350

This is a small and affordable trail bike with a single cylinder four-stroke engine. It's rugged, easy to ride and simple to maintain. Negatives to consider are a poor finish and modest power output (some may see this as a plus), but generally speaking it's an endearing machine. If you're buying a Suzuki DR 350, make sure you get a post-1995 electric start version and pay attention to the suspension – by now most Suzuki DR 350s will have thinned fork oil and a tired shock – replacing or refreshing these will make a huge difference to the handling.

Specifications

Displacement:	349cc	Rear tyre:	110/90–18
Power:	30bhp @ 7,600rpm	Length:	2,335mm
Torque:	29Nm @ 6,200rpm	Width:	885mm
Transmission:	Six-speed / Chain	Height:	1,245mm
Front travel:	280mm	Seat height:	890mm
Front tyre:	80/100–21	Dry weight:	130kg
Rear travel:	255mm	Fuel capacity:	9 litres

Suzuki
DR 650

A long-standing model in Suzuki's range, the DR 650 was first introduced in 1990 as a replacement for the DR 600 model. This is a lightweight single cylinder and a very popular model for adventure riders. It is easy to handle and highly reliable, with a good power to weight ratio. A major plus is the compact and lightweight four-stroke engine which has been tuned for strong low- and mid-range power and fuel efficiency. The seat height can be lowered 40mm and the tyres come with an on/off road tread pattern fitted to 21 inch front and 17 inch rear wheels.

Specifications

Displacement:	644cc	Rear tyre:	120/90–17
Power:	43bhp @ 6,400rpm	Length:	2,255mm
Torque:	54Nm @ 4,600rpm	Width:	865mm
Transmission:	Five-speed / Chain	Height:	1,195mm
Front travel:	260mm	Seat height:	885mm
Front tyre:	90/90–21	Dry weight:	147kg
Rear travel:	260mm	Fuel capacity:	17 litres

Suzuki
DR-Z400S

The Suzuki DR-Z400S was launched in 2000 both as a commuter and as a veritable off-roader and the bike performs both functions well. Models from 2002 onwards have an electric starter. Power and torque of the water-cooled 398cc single-cylinder, DOHC, four-valve engine were gradually improved in later models. It's reliable and has very few known issues. Biggest concerns are the small tank and narrow motocross-style seat. Plus points are strong low-rpm power, a fully adjustable rear shock absorber and multiple function digital display.

Specifications

Displacement:	398cc	Rear tyre:	120/90–18
Power:	40bhp @ 8,500rpm	Length:	2,310mm
Torque:	39Nm @ 6,600rpm	Width:	875mm
Transmission:	Five-speed / Chain	Height:	1,230mm
Front travel:	295mm	Seat height:	935mm
Front tyre:	80/100–21	Dry weight:	132kg
Rear travel:	295mm	Fuel capacity:	10 litres

Triumph
Tiger

This bike's heritage dates back to 1994, having built up a reputation as a dependable, multi-purpose machine with some off-road ability. At the heart of the latest model is an excellent 1,050cc, fuel-injected, three-cylinder engine. That said, unfortunately Triumph seemed to have moved away from the off-road character almost completely – gone are the knobbly tyres, hand guards and sump protector and in their place is a slim new look with firmly road-focused capabilities. Older Tiger models are therefore probably better suited to adventure biking if you're planning on using a Triumph.

Specifications

Displacement:	1,050cc	Rear tyre:	180/55–17
Power:	112bhp @ 9,400rpm	Length:	2,110mm
Torque:	100Nm @ 6,250rpm	Width:	840mm
Transmission:	Six-speed / Chain	Height:	1,320mm
Front travel:	150mm	Seat height:	835mm
Front tyre:	120/70–17	Dry weight:	198kg
Rear travel:	150mm	Fuel capacity:	20 litres

Yamaha
1200 Super Ténéré

This model signifies Yamaha is serious about regaining the high ground of the adventure market it enjoyed in the late 1980s with its XTZ 750 Super Ténéré which went on to win six Dakar Rallies. Key features include a good size 23-litre tank for reasonable range, seat adjustment from 845–870mm to suit different rider heights, a sleek shaft drive requiring no running maintenance, a powerful electronics package for different engine settings, tubeless rims and a sturdy aluminium sump guard. The limited first production run will also come with panniers as standard. Expect to see many of these on your travels.

Specifications

Displacement:	1,199cc	Rear tyre:	150/70–17
Power:	108.4bhp @ 7,250rpm	Length:	2,250mm
Torque:	114Nm @ 6,000rpm	Width:	980mm
Transmission:	Six-speed / Shaft drive	Height:	1,410mm
Front travel:	190mm	Seat height:	845mm / 870mm
Front tyre:	110/80–19	Dry weight:	233kg
Rear travel:	190mm	Fuel capacity:	23 litres

Yamaha
XT 660 R

This is an all-rounder that is light and slim, with a fuel-injected 660cc single-cylinder water-cooled engine. A new electronic fuel injection system together with twin catalytic converters offer strong green credentials. The bike is tall with reasonable suspension but the low-slung exhaust pipes are vulnerable and need protection. The bodywork seems to favour style over functionality. These touches together with the engine's claimed 48hp match it up against Suzuki's V-Strom 650 or BMW's F 650, though the XT probably edges out both of these competitors as somewhat more capable off-road.

Specifications

Displacement:	660cc	Rear tyre:	130/80–17
Power:	47.3bhp @ 6,000rpm	Length:	2,240mm
Torque:	60Nm @ 5,250rpm	Width:	845mm
Transmission:	Five-speed / Chain	Height:	1,230mm
Front travel:	225mm	Seat height:	865mm
Front tyre:	90/90–21	Dry weight:	165kg
Rear travel:	200mm	Fuel capacity:	15 litres

Yamaha
XT 660 Z Ténéré

This is the bike which resurrected Yamaha's legendary XT model. Powering the new XT 660 Z Ténéré is a 660cc liquid-cooled 4-stroke single cylinder SOHC engine which delivers strong low to mid-range power. It's equipped with an all-new chassis whose rugged, go-anywhere character perfectly complements the big-single engine. It's off-road credentials are enhanced by the long-travel forks which give 210mm of front wheel movement, complemented by a lightweight aluminium swinging arm with 200mm of rear wheel movement. A large-capacity 22-litre fuel tank underlines the machine's serious long-distance potential.

Specifications

Displacement:	660cc	Rear tyre:	130/80–17
Power:	48bhp @ 6,000rpm	Length:	2,246mm
Torque:	58Nm @ 5,250rpm	Width:	865mm
Transmission:	Five-speed / Chain	Height:	1,477mm
Front travel:	210mm	Seat height:	895mm
Front tyre:	90/90–21	Dry weight:	183kg
Rear travel:	200mm	Fuel capacity:	22 litres

Yamaha
TTR250

This bike once won the national enduro championship so it's certainly a capable machine. An air-cooled, four-stroke, four-valve, DOHC single engine with electric start, six-speed gearbox and disc brakes front and rear, the TTR also features plush long-travel suspension and nimble handling. Other plus points include a comfortable seat, excellent reliability and light weight. The low seat height and forgiving ride make this an ideal bike for those starting out on trail riding. This is the bike used by Lois Pryce on her trans-Africa trip.

Specifications

Displacement:	249cc	Rear tyre:	100/100–18
Power:	19bhp @ 8,500rpm	Length:	2,195mm
Torque:	20Nm @ 7,000rpm	Width:	835mm
Transmission:	Six-speed / Chain	Height:	1,255mm
Front travel:	280mm	Seat height:	914mm
Front tyre:	80/100–21	Dry weight:	113kg
Rear travel:	280mm	Fuel capacity:	12 litres

One of the best things when it comes to adventure motorcycles is that as riders, we are spoilt for choice both in terms of the range of models available but also by way of the extensive range of modifications which can be made and the accessories that can be added to personalise the machine to our specific journey and needs. These choices are brought to life through the following bike and rider profile pages featuring some of the well-known faces in the international adventure motorcycling community. These people have completed significant miles in the saddle and you will see that bike choice is more often than not determined by one or a combination of the following factors – type of route, allegiance to a particular brand, price, weight, fuel capacity, seat height and load carrying capacity. Each profile details the reasons why specific bikes were chosen, reasons for the various modifications made, as well as the strong and weak points of each bike.

BIKE AND RIDER PROFILES

Sibirsky Extreme

TOURATECH
BMW

Benka Pulco

Bike:	**BMW**
Model:	**1996 F 650**
Route:	**All seven continents**
Distance:	**111,856 miles (180,016km)**
Date:	**19 June 1997–10 December 2002**

Main reason for choosing this bike/ model: As I didn't know much about bikes, and never consider learning from the experience of others as a bad thing, BMW was the only serious candidate. With my whole life packed onboard, and me weighing only 57kg, I couldn't imagine using anything but their smallest bike.

Preparation time: 6 weeks.

Principal modifications: Scottoiler, GIVI windscreen, Metzler Enduro 4 tyres, Garmin GPS on Touratech mount, Hyper Lites, Acerbis lever protectors, and 27-litre fuel tank.

Luggage: Homemade 5mm aluminium cases, Aerostich tank panniers, GIVI 45-litre top case, Road Gear tank bag.

Anything you wish you had done? Put less trust in the guys who knew so little about bikes, but much more about showing off.

The best thing about the bike? Reliable, still stable even though heavily loaded, strong and fast enough for most of the roads this planet has to offer, and excellent unmodified performance at high elevations.

The weak point about the bike? Not equipped with a serious skid plate or lever protectors. No clock, and for me personally a calendar would be handy. If I was to hit the road again, I would surely take another BMW F 650 for the adventure.

Tip: Don't overlook the little things which help keep you on the road – it isn't only the bike that requires attention. I maintained my sanity with a small bottle of my beloved perfume.

Sam Manicom

Bike:	**BMW**
Model:	**1991 R 80 GS**
Route:	**Africa, Australia and New Zealand, South-East Asia, Asia, Middle East, Africa, South America, Central America, USA, Canada, Alaska**
Distance:	**200,000 miles (322,000km)**
Date:	**1992–2000**

Main reason for choosing this bike/ model? Two guys in the pub. One told me the GS was bulletproof, and his mate said they were idiot proof. So I thought I'd better have one. They were right too.

Preparation time: 3 months.

Principal modifications: WP shock and progressive fork springs, Acerbis 43-litre petrol tank, additional ten litres of spare fuel (only used once and dumped as soon as I realised it wasn't needed) and ten-litre water tank, additional fuel filters, an engine bash plate, fitted trail-type tyres, and some hand guards.

Luggage: Originally BMW standard plastic panniers. They were rubbish for overlanding, so an 80-year-old Australian millionaire made me some excellent 2.5 mil aluminium panniers – still happily in use today. If I had to buy some now, I'd get Metal Mule.

Anything you wish you had done? Should have fitted an oil cooler. The bike pinked like mad in places like the Sahara.

The best thing about the bike? Tough, simple to work on, reliable, low centre of gravity.

The weak point about the bike? Weight in the most extreme conditions (approximately 5% of the trip only, though a good 40% of the trip was in bush/off-road conditions) and fuel consumption – she drinks like an old lush!

Tip: Did I use a GPS? No. I like maps, a compass, and asking the way. It's a great way to meet people and the best adventures almost always start with the people you meet. I think that finding suitable maps is part of the adventure and the way you start to learn about a country – not just your route. Too much electronic gear takes away from the money you'd have to put petrol in your tank, and it's more to break or get nicked along the way.

Chris Smith & Liz Peel

Bike: Honda
Model: 1999 XRV 750 Africa Twin
Route: North, Central and South America (north to south)
Distance: 72,000 miles (116,000km)
Date: 2004–2006

Main reason for choosing this bike/ model? We needed a bike that was large enough for a rider and pillion to be comfortable on rough roads, and one that was reliable, suitable for unpaved roads, and could be repaired easily in the middle of nowhere.
Preparation time: Eight months (bike modifications by me and Overland Solutions).
Principal modifications: Pannier racks and aluminium panniers, engine crash bars with tool boxes, front and rear luggage racks, frame strengthening, long-range 37-litre fuel tank, raised front mudguard, ignition switch cover, modified seat (for comfort), side-stand with extra large foot (for soft ground).
Luggage: Modified Touratech ZEGA panniers to fit an Overland Solutions luggage rack.
Anything you wish you had done? Added a better centre stand.
The best thing about the bike? Reliability and the ability to be able to mend it on the side of the road.
The weak point about the bike? The original un-stepped seat was uncomfortable and without a step in the seat the pillion would slide forward under braking
Tip: Let others work on your bike only as a last resort, not the first resort, and when planning a trip, and once you've left there are very few problems that cannot somehow be put right.

Kevin Sanders

Bike: BMW
Model: 2009 R 1200 GS Adventure
Route: London to Beijing
Distance: 13,000 miles (21,000km)
Date: 28 March–24 June 2009

Main reason for choosing this bike/ model? I've always taken the BMW GS on any long-distance adventure trip. Back in 1998 I took the R 80 GS to ride the Americas; now it's the 1200 GS Adventure. I have achieved two Guinness World Records on R 1150 GS bikes, and when you need reliability it's the best available. I first went for the GS because of the shaft drive and the overall strength of the engine.
Preparation time: For this trip, I only got the bike a month before departure, but I've prepped these bikes before, so I knew exactly what I wanted to do.
Principal modifications: Upgraded battery to Hawker Odyssey, bash plate, steering stop, additional xenon lights, fuel injector protector, Kahedo aftermarket seat. Engine bars and cylinder head protection are standard with the Adventure model.
Luggage: Touratech standard panniers, Touratech tail bag, Touratech tank bag.
Anything you wish you had done? No – the bike and the modifications worked well for the journey.
The best thing about the bike? 100% reliability. It never failed, even on the roughest of roads across the Tibetan plateau at over 5,000m altitude. I threw it down the road at 60mph too. The engine bars did their job. The bike was battered, but it started first time and kept on going. I scraped snow off it regularly in the morning, where it had stood outside in below freezing temperatures, and it still started without problems.
The weak point about the bike? You could argue that, for loose dirt roads, deep sand and gravel, it's a bit of a lump. If I was setting off on a journey that I knew to be all those types of road conditions, I'd seriously consider something lighter. Having said that, with off-road training it's amazing what these bikes will do.
Tip: When setting off on any motorcycle trip, pack light. Use kit and equipment that is multi-functional and takes up little space. Most riders on a GlobeBusters expedition find that around a third of the kit they take doesn't get used!

Ida Tin

Bike: Aprilia
Model: 2006 Pegaso Strada 650cc
Route: California, Nevada, New Mexico, Arizona, Utah
Distance: 18,500 miles (30,000km)
Date: August 2007–March 2009

Main reason for choosing this bike/model? I wanted an 'all-round motorcycle', suitable for any kind of road ranging from gravel, dirt, and back roads to windy roads and even the occasional freeway.
Preparation time: Three months.
Principal modifications: Most importantly I constructed a steel crash bar that doubled as a holder for ten litres of fuel on one side of the bike and ten litres of water on the other side. To charge my laptop, satellite terminal, and other electronic devices I installed a transformer to get 220v from the motorcycle battery. To make sure not to end up with a flat battery, a relay was also installed so it would only connect when the engine was on. I also changed the tyres to Bridgestone Battlax to have something more appropriate for gravel riding.
Luggage: On the sides I had Aprilia clip-on side bags. I called them my Italian handbags because they were so small. They weren't waterproof, so I had plastic bags inside them the few times I had heavy rain. At the back was an Aprilia top-box, an additional soft bag on the rear of the seat, and a tank bag.
Anything you wish you had done? Installed heated grips or at least wind/crash guards. I had really cold weather and my gloves had holes melted in them from me desperately trying to heat my frozen fingers on the engine.
The best thing about the bike? That it's light enough to pick it up myself, its turning capabilities, and good brakes. It's the perfect bike for small windy roads and fun to ride. Easy going and with single-cylinder character!
The weak point about the bike? The fuel efficiency is not impressive, and with no real screen I developed strong neck muscles from holding myself up against the wind.
Tip: Don't underestimate how cold the desert gets in the winter! And always go for a lighter bike – it's a lot more fun.

Craig Carey-Clinch

Bike: BMW
Model: R 1200 GS 2007 (standard edition)
Route: North and West Africa, London to Dakar, via Mali and Banjul
Distance: Approximately 3,000 miles (4,800km)
Date: Twice in 2008

Main reason for choosing this bike/model? Its 'go-anywhere' characteristics.
Preparation time: Six months for the first trip! A few weeks nowadays. Includes gathering paperwork, visas, carnet, checking route research, and current situation in countries.
Principal modifications: A range of Touratech essentials fitted: engine bars, full engine bash plates, oil cooler protector, headlamp protector, sidelights, fuel injector and potentiometer protectors, luggage rack plate, GPS.
Luggage: Touratech metal side-boxes, a tank bag, and luggage rack plate. Clothing and other personal items go in an Ortleib bag. This allows an easy 'day end' routine (off the bike and in the bar in seconds!).
Anything you wish you had done? I'm still working on getting the electronics and communications gear right and reducing the size of the infamous 'bag of wires' which gets hauled about on every trip.
The best thing about the bike? Its ability to survive the serious pounding it gets on rough and broken roads is impressive.
The weak point about the bike? Fuel capacity! It may carry 220 miles (355km) in the tank, but in developing countries unreliability of fuel supply means that in reality I'm hunting for fuel after 150 miles (240km), or carrying fuel cans. I love this bike, but BMW did the right thing by launching the Adventure.
Tip: Leave early, make the most of the cool of the day in hot countries, and avoid the urge to rush your day's ride. In developing countries try and avoid the psychological urge to spend all your time on the familiar 'comfort zone' of your bike, by taking time to meet local people and enriching your own life by finding out more about theirs.

Greg Baker

Bike: KTM **Model:** 950 Adventure S
Route: Bournemouth, UK, to Ouarzazate, followed by Talouine, Tazenacht, Foum Zguid, Zagora, Mhamid, the Draa Valley, Nekob, Alnif, Merzouga, Erfoud, Tinerhir, Lake Iseli and Tislit, Msemir, Boumalne Dades, and return to Ouarzazate
Distance: 1,900 miles (3,000km) **Date:** August 2006

Main reason for choosing this bike/model? More appropriate for my skills and needs and had a good pedigree, given KTM's off-road success.
Preparation time: Six to eight weeks.
Principal modifications: Engine bars to protect the lower tanks, an HID (high-intensity discharge) lighting upgrade.
Luggage: Hepco and Becker.
Anything you wish you had done? Fitted a proper comfort saddle rather than trying to modify/improve the OEM version, which led to some daft comments about my sheepskin seat cover!
The best thing about the bike: We experienced every kind of terrain – easy hard-packed piste, narrow boulder-strewn mountain tracks, pebbled river beds, deep soft Sahara sand, and the KTM coped with consummate ease. Its nimble handling and seamless power delivery made short work of most obstacles.
The weak point about the bike? The fuel capacity should have been greater.
Tip: With hindsight it's easy to see that I took too much stuff, tools I didn't need, clothes I didn't wear – valuable lessons learned which will make the next trip a lot easier.

Nick Sanders

Bike: Yamaha **Model:** R1
Route: Parallel World – from London to Cape Town via Sudan and the East Trans African Highway, then up and down India, South-East Asia, up and down Australia, and the length of the Americas from Tierra del Fuego to New York.
Distance: 40–45,000 miles (65–73,000km) **Date:** April–August 2008

Main reason for choosing this bike/model? Bikes are like a nice pair of shoes – if they fit well, why wear wellies? The GS school of thought goes right over my head – it's all in the mind. You could do all I do on a 125cc bike with a basket on the front; but R1s are also so lovely to look at how could you not ride one around the world?
Preparation time: None – well, nearly none. I kind of work out where I want to go, grab a load of visas (in the case of Africa), and go like the clappers until the countries I want to go to start to fall out with each other. Problem with despotic rule is that they're run by men with very fragile egos and if they get offended for whatever reason they go to war with someone.
Principal modifications: Nothing to the bike, but my mindset changes. I begin to adopt an attitude of extreme single-mindedness where nothing matters except the journey. After all, that's what I'm paid to do.
Luggage: Not a lot...except I take a movie camera and a laptop. I make films and write books, so this is all I need apart from the usual paperwork and a toothbrush. Do you really want to trust a dentist in southern Ethiopia?
Anything you wish you had done? No.
The best thing about the bike? Superb and indescribably necessary reliability. Also, girls love sitting on the back, it makes them feel nice. I actually took my girlfriend from Nairobi to Cape Town on it.
The weak point about the bike? It's rubbish in sand. Having said that, I did cross the Nubian Desert on it, and also the Trans African bit across the Didu Gagalu desert (it was a 500km field!), but that was due more to ridiculous and dogged determination than it's off-road capability.
Tip: Just go. Don't over-pack. Ask yourself if you can live without what you're taking and then don't take it. Ten seconds after your kids leave home, go. Take your wife, or get a new one. Don't come back until you are satisfied with what you've done. Be nice to people in uniform. Don't think anyone really cares what you are doing, they don't...you're on holiday, they're not.

Joe Pichler

Bike:	KTM
Model:	990 Adventure S
Route:	Amazon Rainforest
Distance:	15,000km
Date:	June–September 2008

Main reason for choosing this bike/ model? I have used KTMs for most of my adventure trips, but in essence I wanted a bike that was not only capable of tough off-road riding but one which was suitable for a pillion passenger, as my wife Renate joined me for much of the trip.
Preparation time: One year.
Principal modifications: 45-litre tank. Instead of the original rims I mounted the narrower rims of the 950 Super Enduro, which were perfect for the Pirelli MT 21 tyres I used. Luggage had to be kept to a minimum, as I had to take along extensive photo and video equipment.
Luggage: Rack and panniers from Touratech.
Anything you wish you had done? No – I am happy with it as it was.
The best thing about the bike? I had no problems with the bike, whether I was on the muddy slopes of the rainforest or at

the icy altitude of 5,300m in the Andes. The engine and suspension did a perfect job.
The weak point about the bike? Only the fuel consumption, which with an average of 7.5 litres per 100km is a bit high, but with the large tank it was not a real problem.
Tip: Just do it.

Herbert Schwarz

Bike:	BMW
Model:	HP2 Enduro
Route:	Off-road from Canada to Mexico
Distance:	3,400 miles (5,500km)
Date:	November–December 2006

Main reason for choosing this bike/ model? The HP2 is the best choice for off-road adventure travelling if you want to have a boxer-engine. It has good ground clearance and the suspension offers reasonable travel.
Preparation time: Two months (includes the time to develop the parts).
Principal modifications: Large fuel tank to take capacity from 13 litres to 30 litres in total, xenon twin-headlight, aluminium sump guard, fuel line protection, crash bars, oil cooler guard, frame protectors, handlebar risers, a minor modification to the side-stand, and a ceramic clutch.
Luggage: On one of the bikes we used our Touratech pannier system with 35/29-litre aluminium ZEGA cases and a large photo tank bag size. On the second bike we used the ZEGA-Tex soft luggage and another large photo tank bag.
Anything you wish you had done? No – it all worked really well and we learnt a lot about the bike and the parts on this trip.
The best thing about the bike? It is quite simply the best boxer for adventure travelling ever made!
The weak point about the bike? Nothing to say other than it is a pity that BMW didn't continue with the production of this model. I hope they'll return soon with an updated version.
Tip: If you can find one of these in the market, you should buy it!

Lois Pryce

Bike: **Yamaha**
Model: **TTR250**
Route: **London to Cape Town**
Distance: **10,000 miles (16,000km)**
Date: **October 2006–March 2007**

Main reason for choosing this bike/model? I wanted a smallish, lightweight trail bike and had used a 225 Yamaha on my previous trip in the Americas. A mechanic friend of mine recommended the TTR250.
Preparation time: Six months.
Principal modifications: Changed the stock nine-litre tank for a 22-litre tank, had the seat remodelled to make it more comfortable and covered it with sheepskin, fitted a bash plate, fitted a small screen, fitted super-heavy-duty inner tubes, attached a piece of Perspex over the headlight with heavy-duty Velcro, and before I left I replaced the brake pads, cables, wheel bearings, and the chain and sprocket with brand new original Yamaha parts.
Luggage: One metal top box, two soft pannier bags (Andystrapz) and a waterproof dry-bag.
Anything you wish you had done? No!
The best thing about the bike? The bike took an almighty hammering across Africa, particularly crossing the Sahara, the Congo, and through Angola, but I had no mechanical problems whatsoever – it just kept on going no matter what was thrown at it, and is still going strong to this day. But maybe that's just my ladylike riding style!
The weak point about the bike? Simply that it was too tall for me, so I had to lower it, which then slightly affected the suspension.
Tip: There is no need to spend loads of money or buy lots of fancy kit for your adventure bike. The most important thing is to use quality parts and never to scrimp on the preparation – any money you save at home you'll pay for on the road when you break down and have to have parts sent out to you, and waste time and money waiting around for them to arrive.

Walter Colebatch

Bike: **BMW**
Model: **G 650 X-Challenge**
Route: **Central Asia, Road of Bones, BAM Road, Mongolia**
Distance: **31,000 miles (50,000km)**
Date: **March–October 2009**

Main reason for choosing this bike/model? The X-Challenge is one of the lightest possible bikes to base a properly durable adventure touring platform on. Its base weight is just over 140kg.
Preparation time: Five weeks
Principal modifications: X-Tank 12-litre additional tank, giving a total capacity of 22 litres, BMW F 650 steel gear lever, Hyperpro front springs and coil-over-shock, Rayz custom saddle (the standard seat of the X-Challenge is most definitely not made for touring), Touratech front rally fairing to give space for maps, GPS, and power sockets (the fairing also adds wind protection and space for proper headlights), Touratech hand guards, chain guard, risers, and large engine bash plate, Mefo MFE99 Super Explorer Tyres, and HID50 custom twin Hi/Lo Projector 50W HID lights.
Luggage: I rode with a Touratech/Kahedo tank bag, a pair of Ortlieb 'Bike Packer Plus' Panniers and an Ortlieb XL (89-litre) 'RackPack' roll bag. Nothing weighs an adventure touring bike down more than adding 20kg of steel frame and aluminium boxes. We cut over 15kg out by going with soft panniers.
Anything you wish you had done? Wish I had tried to fit a 400W alternator.
The best thing about the bike? Lightweight and superb engine – it ran on straight 76 octane for 250 miles (400km) in Siberia at one point without any problems.
The weak point about the bike? The subframe is made from alloy and is not as strong as a steel version.
Tip: Take weight seriously. Don't necessarily follow the default line of thinking and believe you need a big bike with metal boxes.

See page 124 for more information on Walter Colebatch's impressive BMW G 650 X-Challenge.

Chapter 3
Equipment & accessories

Touratech

Modifications are essentially undertaken for ergonomic reasons to enhance rider comfort, for protection to reduce risk, for improved performance and handling, and ultimately to make for a better all-round riding experience. They form an important part of your pre-trip preparation and should be initiated as soon as possible.

Some modifications may be purely cosmetic (be careful of the additional weight these can add), while others may be considered necessities, so choose wisely to keep the weight down. Some stock parts can also be removed to reduce weight but keep in mind that there's a fine balance to be had between what can be taken off and what starts to have a detrimental effect. It's also useful to research what modifications other people have made to the same model and the reasons these were made or why they didn't work out as planned. The well-documented case studies of Adam Lewis and Walter Colebatch later on in the book are a great place to start.

You should try to get all your preparation and modifications done around three months before you set off on the adventure. This will avoid any early failures that might happen with new parts. And make sure you don't trust new parts until you've trialled them for at least a month, ideally on a short test run over similar terrain to that which you're expecting to cover.

Most modifications will need some degree of 'tweaking' to get them just right, and most importantly you should understand how they're assembled and how they function – particularly if they've been fitted or made by someone else – in case they need disassembling, replacing, or repairing.

Starting early gives you the maximum amount of time to sort things out, and you'll undoubtedly find that time is very limited as your departure date approaches.

Ergonomics and comfort

Adventure riding is often quite physically demanding, especially if the terrain is tough, so it's important that you should be able to ride all day and ideally not feel any aches or pains. Discomfort of some description is likely to mean some kind of problem with the interaction between your body and the bike.

In the second book of the Haynes adventure motorcycling series – *Adventure Riding Techniques* – it was emphasised that you should be able to easily go from the sitting position to the standing position and vice versa. Much of this ability is determined by the set-up of the bike – the position of the handlebars, the size and position of the seat, how well protected you are from the wind, in particular the interaction your feet have with the foot pegs and your hands with the levers, as well as various other key considerations.

You should also be able to move freely on the seat, backwards and forwards. It's essential to experiment and get the bike set up in such a way that you feel comfortable, but be sure to do this over a few days of riding.

Suspension

Given the terrain an adventure bike is likely to encounter it's no surprise that its suspension has to work very hard indeed. Having a well set up and balanced suspension system can make a huge difference to the way your bike will feel and ride. Its job is to keep the wheels in contact with the ground at all times – after all, if a wheel isn't in contact with the ground it can't steer, brake, or drive. By controlling the rate at which the suspension compresses or rebounds over irregularities in the road surface, a full contact area can be maintained, ensuring good control and manoeuvrability.

Standard OEM units will be adequate under 'normal' situations, but may start to struggle after many miles off-road. On uneven terrain the suspension will be working constantly, which will cause the damping oil to heat up, often so much that it becomes thinner, vastly reducing its damping effectiveness. With poor damping, the compression and rebound strokes of the suspension become uncontrolled, leading to erratic and unpredictable handling and very poor rider comfort.

Checking the bike's settings is the first thing to do. Riders often fail to take into account the additional weight of their luggage, so ensure that the bike is loaded before making adjustments. Check your manual for the recommended settings and the method of adjustment, then aim to use about 30% of the available travel with the rider and luggage aboard. Check now to see if the front and rear suspension move equally when you sit on the bike, and adjust accordingly. With the suspension correctly set up, a comfortable and level attitude can be maintained on the road.

If you can't achieve this position of balance, then you'll probably need to consider modification of your existing suspension, or fitting a high-end unit such as from the likes of Öhlins, which can be built to your exact

↓An aftermarket shock absorber is worth considering if the going is likely to be tough
KTM

specification. One of the most frequent failures on long-distance overland rides is the rear shock losing damping, usually caused by the seal failing and allowing oil to escape. Aftermarket shocks tend to do a better job at absorbing shocks than the standard units on most bikes, and most suppliers will be able to build a unit from off-the-shelf components to your specific requirements on the basis of your weight and riding style. Ensure at least that the rear unit is serviced a minimum of three months before you depart, as it's not easy on the roadside as you typically need special tools and pressurised nitrogen.

If your front forks have adjustments for damping and pre-load, be sure to set these in accordance with the manual. If you choose to alter the settings, be sure to only change one thing at a time so that you can change it back if you're not happy with the result. If changing the forks' pre-load cannot give you the range of suspension travel required, or you have non-adjustable forks, then there are a few options open to you. Swapping the OEM fork-springs for some higher-rated springs will restore ride height and suspension travel, and changing the oil in the forks will allow you to alter their damping characteristics. If you have non-adjustable forks, the Italian company BiTubo offer a kit consisting of a 'cartridge' that replaces your existing fork internals, fork springs rated according to rider weight, and fresh fork oil. The new cartridge gives a superior and more linear damping effect that's fully controllable by the rider, and the correctly rated springs restore lost ride height.

↑ Simon Pavey puts the BMW HP2 through its paces in Iceland
Thorvaldur Orn Kristmundsson

← A suspension unit that is fully adjustable offers increased flexibility
KTM

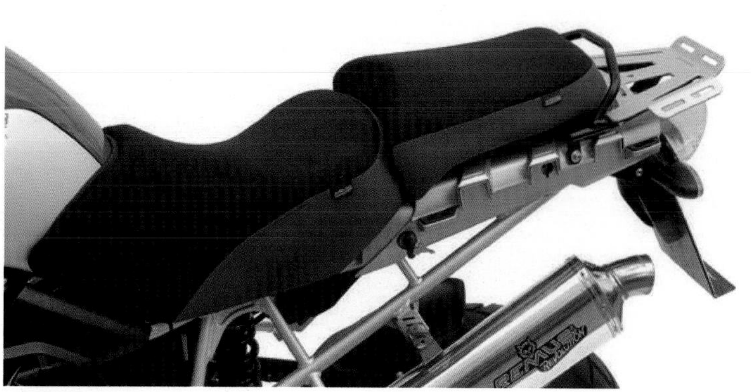

↑ **An aftermarket seat can make the most of BMW's multi-adjustable seat**
Touratech

Seats

True overlanding bikes are capable of travelling vast distances in a single day, but peculiarly, the one component that restricts most bikes' potential will almost always be the saddle. OEM saddles are generally too hard or have a profile that doesn't support the rider's buttocks properly, and can become painful quite quickly. Some models have a well-proportioned and wide seat base which gives great support, while others have a reputation for thin and unyielding seats. Some riders will find that their seats will in time become more comfortable, but others will need to have their seats reworked or modified to relieve pressure points on the buttocks and give them day-long comfort.

An easy and relatively cheap first step would be to try a sheepskin pad on top of your existing saddle. Natural sheepskin has a surprisingly dense and resilient quality that resists compression and is capable of spreading a load evenly over its area. As it's a natural material it allows good air circulation and is inherently water repellent. Another device to try might be an Airhawk pneumatic seat pad. This performs a similar function of spreading the load over a greater area; however, the design of the individual pneumatic cells within the pad can create a feeling of 'squidginess' or separation from the saddle which might not suit all riders.

If neither of these options works for you, then it's worth thinking about replacing the saddle with either a factory 'comfort' item, or reworking your OEM seat from the inside. The factory option will probably be a similarly profiled saddle, with a different combination of padding foams and usually a silicone gel pad inserted at the area of highest

↑ **A sheepskin seat cover adds comfort but needs to be fitted securely**
Robert Wicks

↓ **A good ergonomic design can give day long comfort in the saddle**
Touratech

→ **If you're tall then an aftermarket windshield and/or a spoiler are a necessity**
KTM

pressure. A better option might be to have your own seat reworked by a specialist motorcycle saddle upholsterer, who'll discuss your requirements with you before starting work and, based on a variety of factors such as your build, inseam, and riding style, will reprofile your seat, replacing or reworking the original seat foam with a more forgiving padding combination. This may include a visco-elastic polyurethane (memory) foam or a gel pad and refit of the cover in an appropriate material. Surprisingly, this kind of 'ergonomic tailoring' might not cost much more than an OE 'comfort' equivalent, but you're virtually guaranteed of day-long performance and comfort, as the seat will have been built around you.

Windshields

There's an almost bewildering selection of windscreens and shields that are available for just about every adventure bike on the market today, and making an appropriate choice is not necessarily as simple as it might first appear. Many factors have to be taken into account, including riding style, terrain, rider physique, and apparel. By and large the screens as fitted by the manufacturer will be a compromise between a styling aesthetic and functionality in use – they have to look good whilst still performing some function, but some riders might demand more.

The main function of the screen is clearly to provide protection for the rider, but not all riders will fit the 'average' criteria and may benefit from a different size or style of screen. Decide beforehand what you need the new screen to do – if it's adjustable, has the full range of adjustment been explored? Could the addition of an aftermarket screen-mounted spoiler make a positive difference? Be aware that full wind protection will require quite a large shield, but will probably require you to look through the screen rather than over it, and a screen of this size will be very unwieldy in any off-road situation. A shield that's just a few centimetres too short may cause buffeting around your helmet, and while this might not be a problem for a few miles, hours of high-speed motorway riding might make it intolerable. Will your helmet affect your choice? Some dual-sport helmets have quite a large peak that can be affected by wind-flow putting additional strain on the rider's neck.

You can get a good idea of how well your screen works by exploring the airflow around it while you're riding. Find a quiet stretch of road, preferably straight, and drive at a constant but reasonable speed. First of all, duck down behind the screen to get an idea of what still air feels like. Then stand on the pegs to lift yourself above the screen to see what 'clean' airflow feels and sounds like. When you sit down again, the chances are that you'll find your face is right in the middle of those areas that are the most turbulent and noisy. Now use your left hand to feel how the airflow moves over the screen and find the still air behind the shield. If you can,

↑ Some stock screens offer a level of adjustment but nothing beats a custom product
Wunderlich

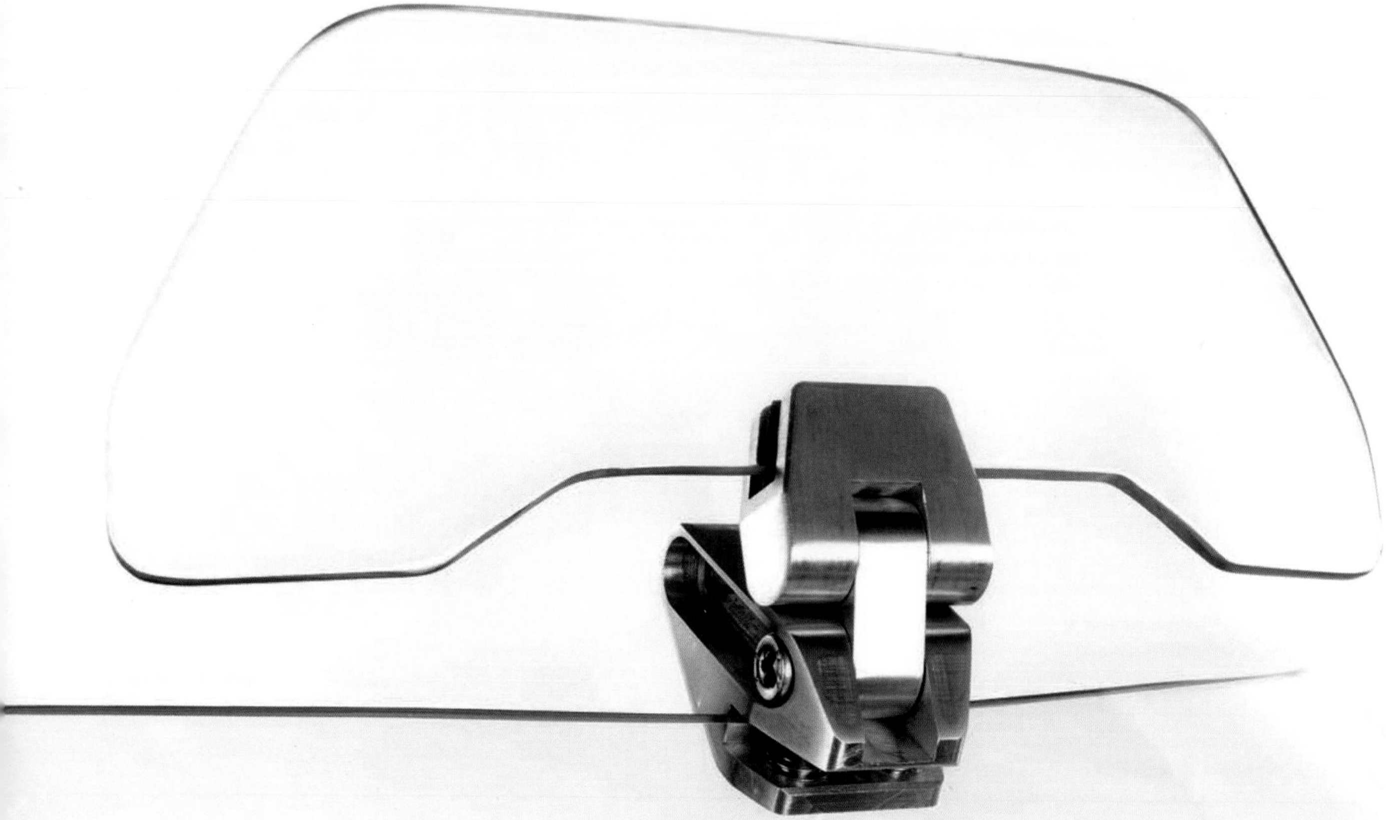

Even a simple clip-on extension can provide a surprising difference in airflow
Wunderlich

This spoiler includes a locking mechanism for added security and flexibility
Touratech

put your hand towards the top of the screen and find the boundary between the still air behind the screen and the faster-moving air going over the top. You can use your hand to deflect or disrupt the airflow to give you an idea of how a taller screen might work. Similarly work your way around the screen to see how the airflow moves round the sides of the screen, which will give you an idea of whether you need a wider shield. You might find that a shorter screen works better for you, keeping the wind pressure off your chest but leaving your helmet in a clean and quiet airflow.

Windshield spoilers

A windscreen spoiler is by no means a compulsory accessory but may be one to consider if you find yourself getting buffeted about when riding. Long periods of exposure to buffeting can become very uncomfortable, and if this is the case then a spoiler is certainly worth a try, especially as it's often cheaper than investing in a completely new screen, with the additional versatility of being removable if needs be.

The spoiler is designed to effectively raise the windscreen height. This higher profile in front of the rider provides better airflow over the screen and greater wind deflection around the rider. The reduction in buffeting also helps to reduce noise levels when riding at higher speeds, which can be very useful when communicating via radio. There are different versions available, but one that can be clamped on and easily removed is usually the best variety. Some spoilers can be mounted at different angles to precisely fit your height and comfort preferences.

An OEM windshield can also be supplemented with smaller side wind-deflectors, often called 'winglets'. These are additional spoilers, usually mounted to the upper edges of the fairing, designed to disrupt the air turbulence round the sides of the screen, smoothing the airflow around the rider's hips and lower torso. They're small but very functional accessories that provide a discernible improvement in rider comfort. As with the screen spoiler, they're manufactured from a clear plastic and are very unobtrusive in use.

Handlebars and risers

At first sight, your motorcycle's handlebars might not appear to be too complicated, but this is far from the truth. As they form a critical link between rider and machine, they must be comfortable and effective in use. Once again the OEM fitment is designed to fit the majority of riders, requiring little in the way of adjustment. Since all of us have a different build, it's recommended that each rider set up their bike to suit themselves and their riding style.

The bend of a handlebar is very important, as it determines the angle of the hand and wrist while riding. If the bar profile is very curved, then this will force the rider's wrists and elbows inwards, restricting the amount of leverage and steering effort that can be applied. If the bars are too straight, the rider is forced into a more forward riding position, and the wrists can be put under a lot of strain at full lock.

Adjusting the handlebars for height is not as simple as loosening the yoke clamps and twisting the bars up. Doing this completely changes the angle of the grips and seriously affects the ergonomic position of the arm from the shoulder through the elbow to the wrist, impacting both rider control and comfort. When adjusting the handlebar position it's equally important to adjust your brake and clutch levers to fit correctly within comfortable reach.

Touratech

Most handlebars are marked with an adjustment range that will align with the clamps. These are good for rotating the handlebars but do nothing to add to their height. If you cannot find an optimum position within this range, then you'll probably need to use a handlebar riser to get

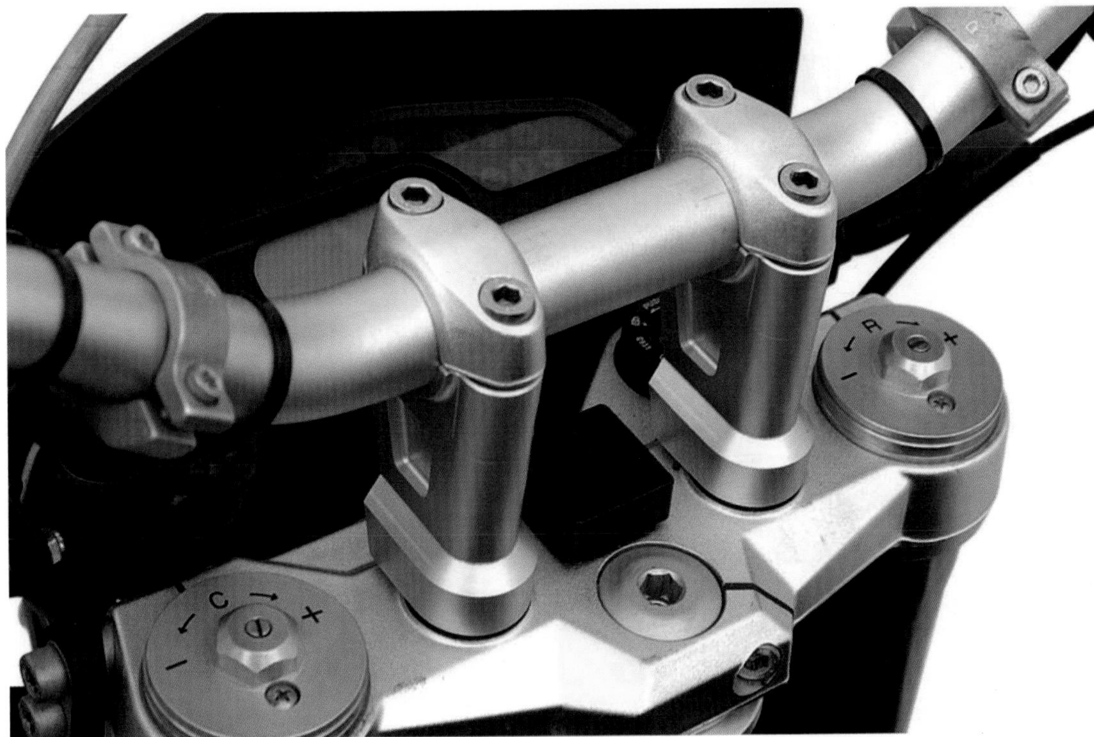

Bar risers are an easy way to customise your riding position
Touratech / Wunderlich

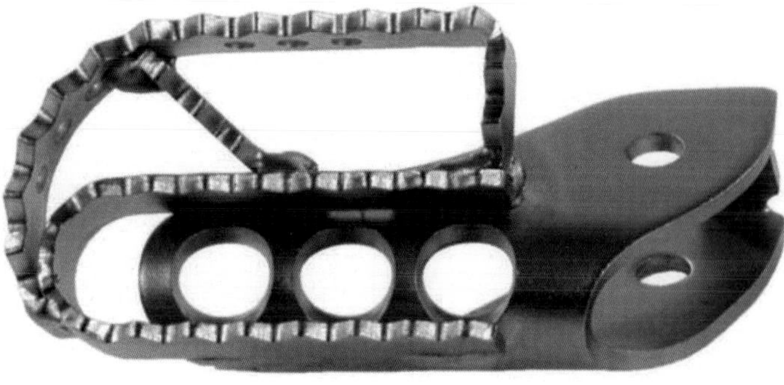

↑Don't underestimate the value that an aftermarket set of foot pegs can add in terms of control
📷 Touratech

the best position. Risers come in various configurations and can be used to alter the position of the bars, either simply upwards or upwards and backwards, which can be beneficial for shorter riders or for riding for long periods standing on the pegs. Be aware, though, that changes of more than about 20mm may require the fitment of longer cables or brake lines.

Once you've found your optimum adjustment, you'll find that your level of control and comfort on the bike will vastly improve.

Foot pegs

Foot pegs are another of those 'invisible' components that largely go unnoticed, despite performing an integral role in the control of your motorcycle. Second only to the handlebars in terms of control importance, they provide a principal point of contact between the rider and his motorcycle, the pivot point around which every movement for balance is made. When you're riding in the 'attack' position all of your weight is bearing on the foot pegs, which are generally no more than 9 x 4cm in size; and at times it can be the rider's full weight on just *one* peg. In these conditions, it makes a lot of sense to make the foot peg size bigger, to spread this load over a greater area, easing the pressure on your feet and effectively increasing the control you have over the motorcycle.

Replacement pegs are available which provide a much enlarged area for the rider's feet, being both wider, which gives greater support to the instep, and longer, which helps prevent the ankle being strained or twisted.

A recent innovation is the foot peg that pivots about its mounting point, which is especially effective in allowing the foot to stay in full contact with the peg if the bike is pitching fore and aft, or on a steep ascent or descent. As the whole surface of the rest is in contact with the sole of the boot rather than

→Heated grips will come in useful if you're travelling in cold climates
📷 Yamaha

just an edge, the rider can achieve much greater levels of grip and security and therefore more confidence on tricky terrain.

If the OEM rests are to be retained, take a close look at them to see if the rubber insert can be removed to reveal the serrated top edges of the peg, as these vastly increase grip on the boot sole.

Heated grips

Once considered a luxury fitment on only the most highly specified bikes, heated grips have become another one of those 'must-have' options. A rider's hands are always in the airflow, and even in moderately cool conditions they can become chilled to the point of losing fine motor control and some degree of feeling. Go beyond that point and you risk numbness and stiffness in your fingers and hands to the point that it can be very difficult to operate the controls properly. Using thicker gloves may not address the problem effectively as they can be very cumbersome, making it difficult to operate switches and control levers. Heated grips provide a source of warmth that's readily absorbed by the hands, keeping your blood flowing and fingers flexible.

Aftermarket fitments come in three types: under-grip 'thin-film' elements, whole grip replacement assemblies, and bar 'wraps' which simply fit over the existing grips.

Looking at the wraps first, their principal advantage is simplicity and speed of fitment – once you have a set of terminals attached to your battery, simply plug them in, wrap them around the handlebar grips, and switch on. As they fit over the existing grips they're insulated from the metal of the bar, so most of the heat they produce gets to the rider. The downside of this design is that they increase the overall diameter of the grip, which may not suit all riders, and in extreme cases might make it harder to fully use the controls.

Under-grip element systems have the advantage of being 'printed' on a thin polyester film. This flexible film is then bonded to the handlebar and the grip reinstalled as normal. Once the wiring has been connected this is a low-profile solution that retains all original components, so it's relatively low-cost and adds negligible additional thickness to the grips.

The remaining option is the whole grip replacement. In this case the heating element is pre-installed between an additional secondary plastic tube and the grip. The whole assembly is then permanently fixed to the handlebar with a cyano-acrylic glue. Extreme care must be taken when fixing this type of system, as once the glue is set there's little or no chance of repositioning the grip! The finished result is fairly robust and is quite close to the original grip thickness.

↑ The low profile printed film option allows you to maintain the original grip thickness
Adam Lewis

↑ **Some aftermarket brake levers feature a folding pedal to protect in the event of a crash**
📷 Touratech

Lever and pedal extensions

It goes without saying that control levers need to be within reach to be able to operate them properly. Some riders might find, for example, that their clutch or brake levers are too far from the bars, or that they miss the brake pedal or gear lever. Various devices and accessories are available that can help with these issues by either extending or reprofiling the levers and even the rear brake pedal.

Original brake and clutch levers can be replaced with shorter-bladed 'stubby' items that can increase clearance from the bar-ends, and dog-leg or span adjustable levers that reduce the reach required to operate the brake or clutch without compromising leverage. Foot controls can also benefit from extensions, making it easier to 'find' the levers and lessening the chances of missing a gear change or your foot slipping off the brake pedal.

📷 KTM

→ **A larger brake pedal area offers more control**
📷 Touratech

Safety and protection

Your bike will need an increased level of protection once you're out on the trail. The idea is to shield vulnerable parts of the bike that could be damaged during a crash or compromised by coming into contact with rocks, mud, and dust.

There's a vast array of items which can be added, and it's easy to go overboard with everything listed in an aftermarket catalogue, so choose wisely, and look at what other people have done with the same bike to protect the key parts and keep the weight down.

←KTM's crash bars sit neatly alongside the fairing
KTM

Crash bars

If you're considering overlanding on your bike, then fitting some type of engine protection system is an absolute must. Engine bars or 'crash' bars have one function – to provide protection to the engine casings and other vulnerable components. To achieve these levels of protection, they'll invariably be manufactured from high-quality steel tube, giving them maximum rigidity when mounted on the bike's chassis. Various styles are available for most bikes. Some will offer simple protection to the lower part of the engine, while other styles extend their safety cage around upper parts of the engine and fuel tank. The horizontally opposed cylinders of BMW Boxer twins present a unique challenge in terms of protection, and despite their bulk they're still quite vulnerable and easily damaged. The primary protection must be the bar-type system, but this would be usefully augmented with a cylinder head cover.

Whilst a cover might initially seem to be a cosmetic accessory, it can offer good protection to the exposed cam-cover area of the boxer twin, reducing the possibility of the cover being punctured or cracked by a large stone.

The systems manufactured from steel bar will give greater structural protection, at the expense of increased weight and bulk, although they can also provide another quite neat opportunity for mounting small items of luggage or auxiliary lighting.

Be aware that compatibility issues can arise when mixing and matching accessories from different suppliers – for

←In this instance the crash bars really did their job
Wunderlich

↑ **This takes engine protection to a whole new level**
Overland Solutions

→ **Exhaust pipe protectors are largely cosmetic but may prevent small stones from doing damage**
Wunderlich

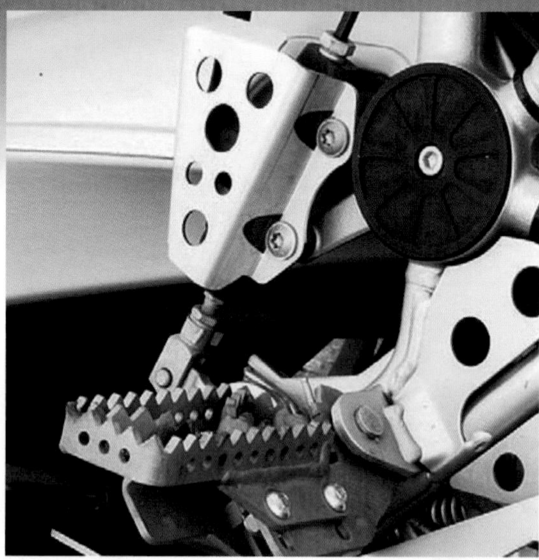

↑ **Protection of the brake master cylinder is essential**
Touratech

example, one manufacturer's engine bars might not fit round another manufacturer's bash plate. It's always best to check with a dealer or supplier first, then offer the component up to the bike and carry out a visual check that all the mounting points it needs are actually free.

Also look to add some form of protection for the rear brake master cylinder, which can often be extended to offer protection to the frame as well, preventing it being scuffed by the rider's boots.

Hand protectors

Hand protectors are designed to offer protection from wild brush and branches. They also provide wind and weather protection, and at the same time act as highly effective protection for clutch and brake levers in the event of a fall.

Unfortunately adventure motorcycles don't always come with hand protectors fitted as standard. Invariably, the manufacturers' own design of guards will be a better, first-time fit, but in some cases aftermarket accessories can be a better choice.

Various styles of protectors are available, from the basic steel or alloy bar type (BMW F 800 GS) to a low-profile, injection-moulded handguard (R 1200 GS), which can be extended with a touring deflector to provide increased wind protection. Brush guards can also be reinforced with an alloy insert (KTM 950/990), providing a great increase in rigidity and protection. Typically, though, they're made of high impact polyethylene plastic, which makes them highly resilient and impact resistant whilst retaining a degree of flexibility.

→ Low profile lever protector
Yamaha

→ Greater protection from a brush guard
Robert Wicks

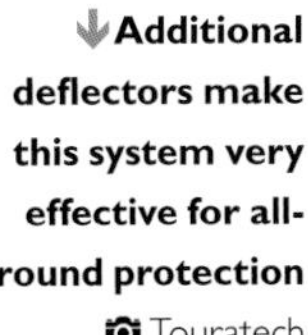

↓ Additional deflectors make this system very effective for all-round protection
Touratech

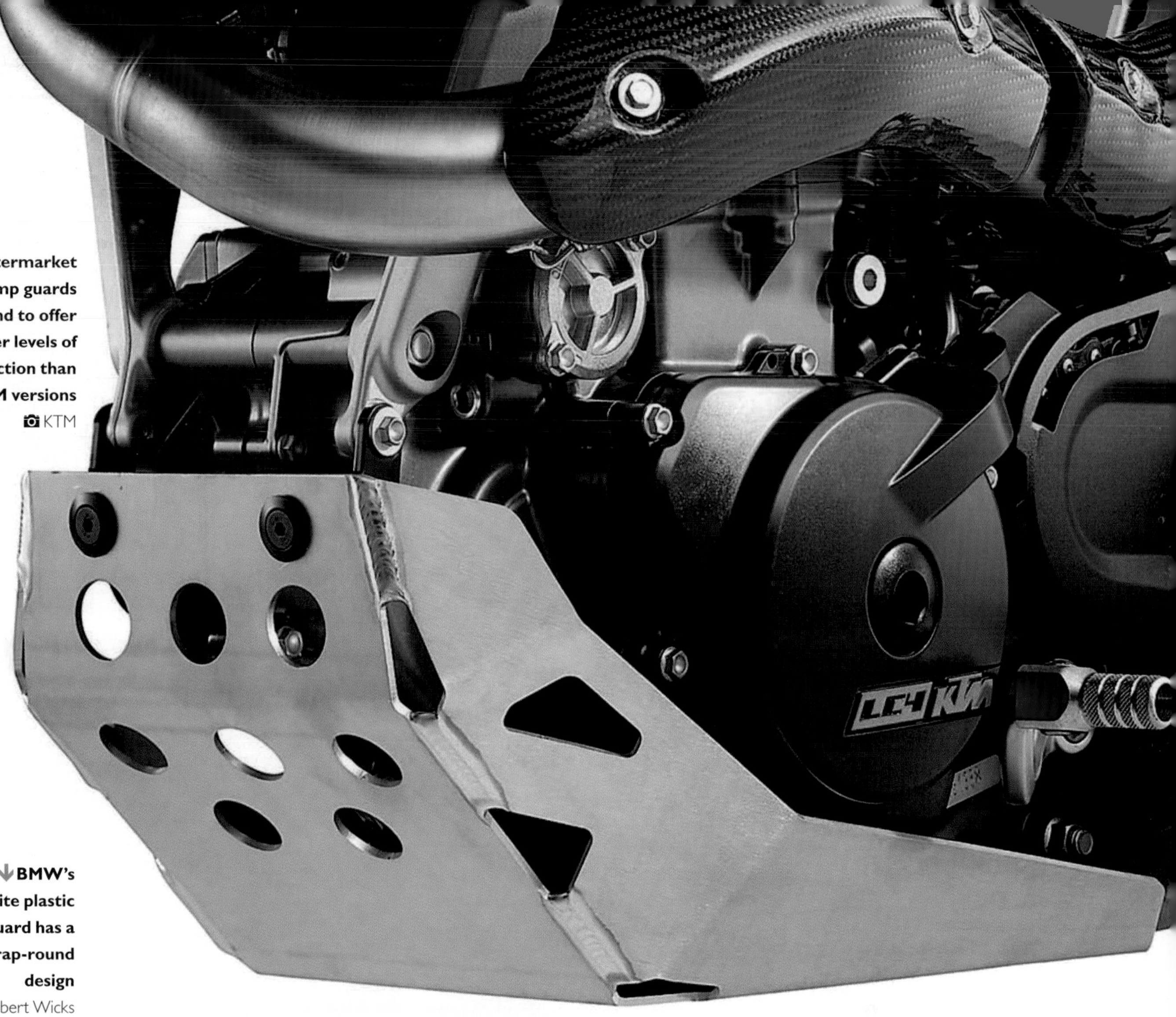

➔ **Aftermarket sump guards tend to offer greater levels of protection than OEM versions**
KTM

↓ **BMW's composite plastic sump guard has a good wrap-round design**
Robert Wicks

Fitting hand protectors is usually quite straightforward, but attention must be given to cable and brake line routeing to ensure that no cables or wiring will be rubbed or chafed. It's imperative to check that the guards you intend to fit don't contact the screen at full lock. If they do, you're severely restricting steering lock, as well as risking damage or breakage of the screen if you have a tumble.

Whether protectors are fitted or not, it's always advisable to slightly loosen the clamp holding the clutch and brake levers to the handlebars. Even with handlebar protectors it's possible to break a lever, but in the event of a spill there's a good chance the clamp will simply turn on the bar, thus saving the lever.

Sump guard

The purpose of a sump guard, sometimes known as a 'bash plate', is to protect the engine casing by distributing the impact of any knock from rocks or when crossing uneven terrain. It's arguably one of the most important additions to any adventure motorcycle. Most adventure bikes will come with a sump guard of some description as a standard fitment, but it will be up to you to decide whether this will provide adequate protection on your trip, given the terrain and conditions you're likely to face.

The term 'bash plate' is very descriptive of its function, providing protection to the motor's sump from stones or rocks kicked up from the front wheel, or if the front wheel drops over a ledge and the bike lands on its sump. A typical OEM fitment will be very basic, manufactured from relatively thin plate or composite plastic, generally with single surface welding and offering minimum protection to the sump pan, while often leaving the exhaust pipes exposed. An aftermarket plate will be a much more sturdy affair, constructed from 3–4mm aluminium plate, folded and formed in such a way as to offer protection to the whole of the underside of the motor and the exhaust pipes, often extending up the sides of the engine casing and back as far as the catalytic converter. It will be double surface welded to maximise its rigidity and strength, and will have holes punched into it to prevent mud or water accumulating behind it.

Premium models can be further adapted to provide a small storage area at the front sufficient to carry a small tool-case or even, on some examples, an auxiliary water carrier.

Again compatibility issues must be considered when mixing and matching accessories from different manufacturers. It will often be found that bash plates won't fit round a different manufacturer's engine bars, or that they'll be drilled to use the same mounting points on the engine. Research well and try before you buy.

↑Even a skid plate can offer a degree of protection for vulnerable parts
Wunderlich

Headlights

Riding in Third World countries can be hazardous at the best of times, particularly in built-up areas, and it's always

←This Yamaha sump guard fits well with the engine protection bar
Yamaha

→ **This combination of fog and driving lamps will give optimal lighting in all conditions**
📷 Touratech

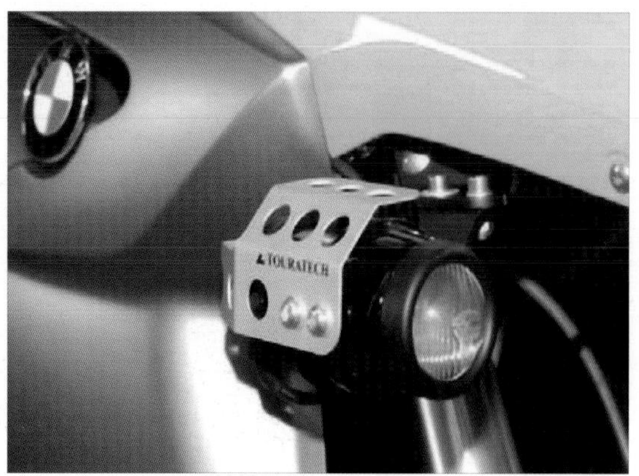

advisable to maintain a high degree of visibility. One of the best ways of doing this is by keeping your headlight(s) on at all times. EU directives now require all European motorcycles to have a permanently switched-on dipped beam, but surprisingly a lot of modern bikes still come with relatively poor headlights, so that in adventure riding – where visibility is key – it's necessary to upgrade or supplement the lighting system. This can be achieved in a variety of ways depending on the flexibility of your budget and personal preferences.

The cheapest and simplest upgrade is to replace the standard OEM halogen filament bulb with a more efficient high output one. High output bulbs use a combination of a different filament material and inert shielding gas (usually xenon) to make the filament glow more brightly whilst drawing the same current as a standard bulb. Various light output levels are available. Some manufacturers claim as much as a 90% increase in output, though this may come at the cost of a reduced operating life for the bulb. It is, however, imperative to ensure that

→ **Factory-fitted auxiliary lights complement the existing lighting arrangement on Yamaha's new Super Ténéré**
📷 Yamaha

Walter Colebatch

the wattage of the bulb remains the same as the OEM fitment, as a higher wattage bulb may well upset the bike's on-board computer and trigger a fault code.

Rally bulbs are available, although designated 'for off-road use only', in much higher wattages than standard, in some cases up to 100W. However, the current required to power these can be close to twice that needed for a standard bulb, and the bulbs themselves generate a terrific amount of heat, which may either burn the reflector or melt the plastic terminal block. Additionally, the bike's wiring harness may not be able to carry more than the OEM levels of current without overheating and causing a catastrophic electrical failure.

Another upgrade possibility that's rapidly gaining popularity is the use of HID (high intensity discharge) lamp systems. The principle behind HID is very similar to that used in fluorescent tubes. A ballast unit supplies a very high voltage to electrodes encased in a sealed glass capsule containing an inert gas, such as xenon. The resulting electrical discharge between the electrodes ionises the gas, creating a superheated ball of plasma that produces a high intensity light.

The way in which HID systems work makes them far more efficient than a regular incandescent filament bulb, which equates to a much greater light output for the same power draw, which is its main advantage. However, they can sometimes take a few seconds to 'warm up' and give full light output, making them less than ideal for use in a high-beam lamp.

All HID systems require quite a high starting current that a standard bike's loom may not be able to supply. If this is the case, then a switching relay must be used. Fitting an HID system can present a challenge, as the ballast box can be quite bulky, and there's the additional problem of routeing its electrical supply. However, once your bike's bodywork is removed you'll generally be able to find the small space required to mount the box and route the cables. Once fitted it's imperative to ensure that your headlamp is correctly adjusted to prevent glare affecting other road users. The quality of the kits available can vary, so it's essential to research the marketplace and ensure that the kit you buy will comply with local motoring and traffic regulations.

Headlight protectors

Stones, branches, and other debris on the road can easily damage your headlights, so fitting a headlight protector of some description is always a good idea. The protector is very useful if you're constantly riding with someone else, as the chances of a stone coming up off the road are that much higher. That said, even if travelling alone, whether on- or off-road, your bike is constantly exposed to unpredictable hazards which can cause damage that's both expensive and unsafe.

There are typically two variants of headlight protector available on the market. One is made from transparent polycarbonate while the other comes in the form of a powder-coated steel wire mesh.

→ This headlight protector has been integrated into the crash bar and carrier frame
Overland Solutions

The wire mesh version tends to stop the bigger stones but not the smaller ones. Importantly, it doesn't distort the light in any way. On the other hand, the Perspex version covers the whole light unit, so in theory it offers better all-round protection. The reflected glare can be distracting, but is also easily controllable by using a glare shield clipped to the top of the headlamp. The build-up of dirt and road grime on the Perspex can also seriously affect the amount of light transmitted through it.

When the protector is fitted it's essential to leave enough space to get in and clean the headlight when necessary – and to allow for cooling, given the heat generated by the headlight; typically about 2.5cm between the two surfaces is sufficient for this. Fitment is generally quite simple, requiring no more than the removal of the two bolts on either side of the headlamp housing.

↑This Aprilia's wire mesh headlight protector could stop a kangaroo
Overland Solutions

←This Perspex protector folds forward for easy access to the headlight
Wunderlich

←←Headlight protectors attach directly to the headlight bracket making for easy fitment
Touratech

↑ **A lightweight radiator protector on a BMW F 800 GS**
Touratech

Radiator protectors

Some bikes have radiator protectors fitted as standard. They're designed to stop damage from sticks and stones and also to prevent mud from clogging up the radiator itself. If a plastic model isn't available, an alternative is a strong mesh guard capable of dealing with any possible intrusion.

Fork protectors

The relatively simple design principle of telescopic forks means they have areas of vulnerability that need to be protected from the rigours of overland travel. The greatest enemies of any suspension system are stones, mud, and dust, which can quickly wreck the delicate surfaces of the fork tubes and seals, which in turn can allow the damping oil to leak, ruining the handling and possibly making the bike difficult if not impossible to ride.

Clearly the protection required will depend on the type of suspension fitted – USD (upside-down) forks can either use a hard plastic slider attached to the lowest part of the fork-leg or cover the exposed plated area of the slider with a neoprene 'sock'. Conventional forks will have to rely upon a gaiter attached to the top of the fork-leg. Protecting the bearing surfaces of the forks in this way will help prevent the ingress of damaging water and dust into the seal. In any event it's important to ensure that your forks and suspension are in good condition before you embark upon your voyage, as any sign of oil seepage is an indicator that a component has failed and needs replacing.

Rear suspension units are equally vulnerable, and as they're generally pressurised they can suffer extremely rapid failure if an oil seal is damaged. A very simple method of protection is a tubular neoprene cover that slips over the unit completely enclosing it, effectively sealing it from external penetration. Hard plastic covers that clip or bolt on to the swingarm are also available, but these tend to be less resilient and can become clogged with mud, which can create a different set of problems.

BMW Telelever systems are significantly different in that they have a wishbone-style suspension system, and have a centrally mounted single spring/damper unit. While this unit is not as exposed as conventional fork systems, it can also be effectively protected by a simple neoprene sock.

→ **Both types of forks need a level of protection**
Wunderlich

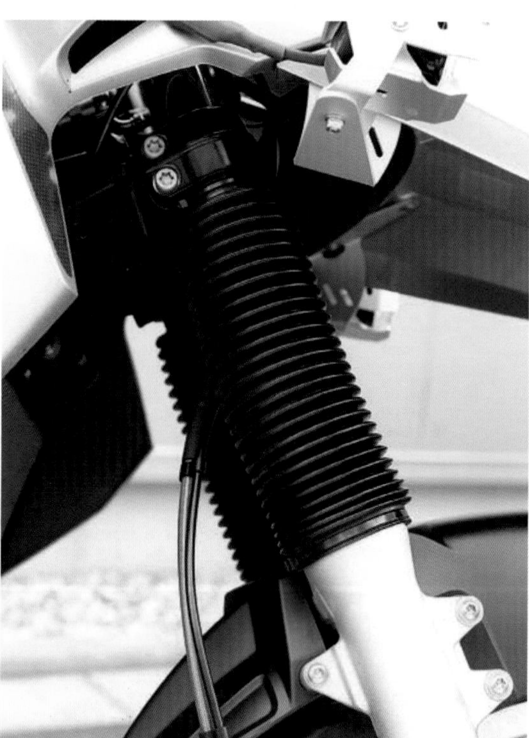

↑ **Long range tanks add weight but remove the need for carrying bulky fuel containers**
Touratech

Performance

Various items can be replaced or enhanced on your motorcycle to improve its performance, whether it's a bigger tank to give you an extended range, better tyres to suit the terrain you're going to be covering, or an aftermarket exhaust that not only boosts performance but also reduces weight. Here are some typical performance enhancements to consider:

Fuel tanks

For long-distance overlanding, one of the most important modifications you can make is the addition of a long-range fuel tank, the single biggest benefit of which is not necessarily the ability to travel huge distances between fuel stops, but relief from the worry of running short of fuel. For example, if you know your maximum fuel range is 310 miles (500km), and that fuel is available before 350km, you have a safety margin of at least 95 miles (150km). This margin is always maintained if you take every advantage to refuel and rest at the same stop.

Some manufacturers can save you the trouble of fitting an aftermarket product. For example, BMW offer the standard R 1200 GS with a 20-litre tank, but they also offer the R 1200 GS Adventure with a massive 33-litre capacity, which is more than adequate. The KTM 990 Adventure, on the other hand, has a tank capacity of just over 19 litres, and would really benefit from a supplementary tank of some kind. Thankfully various options are open to you, ranging from full replacement of the original tank with a 40-litre version, to a system which utilises a 2:1 conversion of the exhaust to provide space for an 8.3-litre auxiliary tank in the vacated space.

Another clear advantage of using larger tanks is removing the hassle of loading and safely stowing jerrycans, and not having to deal with the adverse effect they may have on the bike, or maintaining an optimal weight distribution.

Assuming you decide to make this modification, there is a good selection of custom-designed aftermarket fuel tanks available for most models. However, there are some important points to bear in mind when considering a long range tank:

Choice – make sure you purchase the model required for your specific motorcycle (there may be small differences for each model variant that aren't immediately apparent).
Range – be aware of your fuel consumption (it will vary depending on the terrain you're covering and the speed

→ **Additional fuel supplies can be difficult to stow safely and awkward to carry**
KTM / Overland Solutions

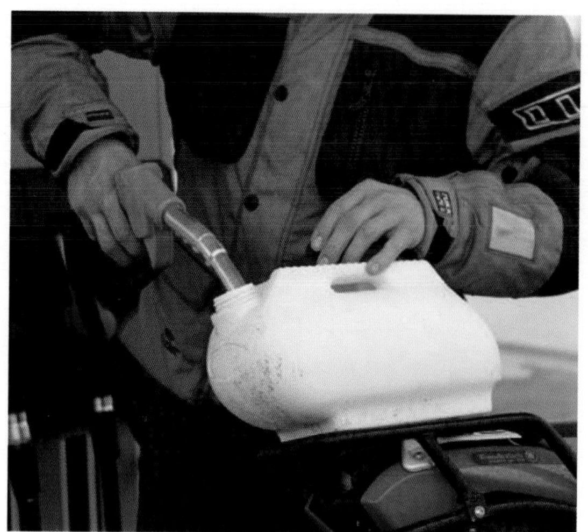

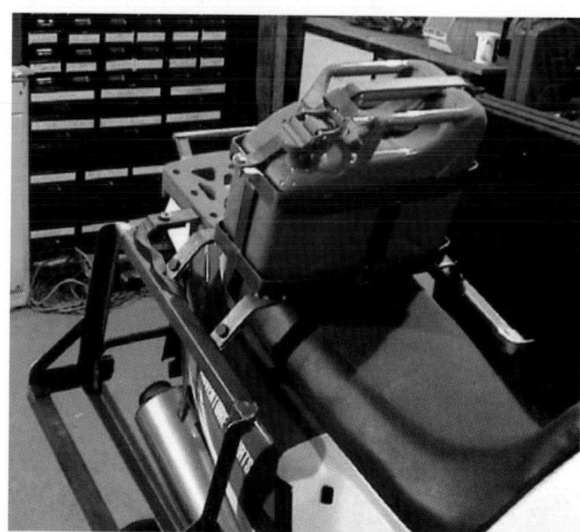

you're riding at) and the maximum distance the fuel you carry will take you. If your bike has good fuel consumption you'll need to carry less fuel to achieve the same distance. For example, a KTM 640 with a 28-litre tank can travel 310 miles (495km), whereas a KTM 990 with a 19.5-litre tank can only travel 160 miles (255km) before needing refuelling, or would need to carry more than 18 extra litres of fuel to travel the same distance.

Parts – it's useful to check if items such as the fuel cap and fuel pump on the long-range tank are interchangeable with the same standard items, which may be easier to source.

Design – ensure that the bigger tanks are properly supported (some require an additional subframe to be attached to the chassis). Airflow through the radiators must be maintained – check that the bigger tank has adequate venting. Check also that the larger tank doesn't interfere with other protection such as crash-bars, or create problems with handlebar controls if a tank-bag is fitted.

Space – risers may need to be fitted to provide adequate clearance for the handlebars above the modified tank. Care must be taken that the raised bars don't foul the screen.

Weight – always take into account the weight of the additional fuel load, which might compromise your overall load capacity and place stress on the chassis.

→ **In this kind of environment KTM's 28-litre rally tank is essential**
Overland Solutions

→→ **This long range tank on Steve Coombs' BMW F 650 Dakar is a thing of beauty**
Robert Wicks

BMW
WP
racing
BMW

↑The right tyre will find grip on almost any surface
📷 Robert Wicks

↓These tyres are certainly past their 'best before' date
📷 Adam Lewis

Tyres

Tyre choice is ultimately always a compromise between the ability to grip the road and the longevity of the tyre. The softer the rubber compound the better it grips, but it won't last as long as a harder tyre. The harder the compound, the less it grips, but the longer it will last. Assuming you have a good idea of what the route is likely to be like, the key points to consider are whether to run with tubed or tubeless tyres and then to consider the tyre tread choice – either a dual-purpose (intermediate) tyre, or a full knobbly more suited for rougher off-road riding. It's not uncommon to start with dual-purpose tyres and carry more serious off-road rubber with you for use over tougher terrain.

If your route takes you over reasonably easy off-road terrain and sealed roads, then an intermediate (dual-purpose) tyre is probably best. Most of the leading manufacturers produce tyres in this category, which tend to feature a chunky tread pattern that delivers impressive traction on dirt roads. This, together with the choice of compound, allows for a combination of both on- and off-road use. Be wary of road-biased tyres masquerading as 'inters' just because they have a deeper tread.

The choice of whether to run with tubed or tubeless tyres is essentially dictated by the construction of the

↑ **The Continental TKC80 provides the *de riguer* finish to the adventure style motorcycle**
📷 Wunderlich

wheel rims in the first instance, the tyre itself in the second, and finally the nature of the riding you plan to do. Rims with wire spokes that go right through the middle of the rim need tubes, while alloy rims that are cast as a single unit can accept tubeless tyres. Rims with spokes that attach to the rim on the side rather than the middle can be used with or without tubes.

Tubed tyres and their associated spoked rims are hardier and offer more flexibility (eg one can deflate the tyre to a greater extent when travelling over thick desert sand). They can also tackle tough off-road conditions with stones, rocks, and potholes, as the spoked wheels can handle this type of abuse better than alloy wheels.

Tubed tyres tend to generate more heat than their tubeless counterparts and in the event of a sudden puncture can be more dangerous, as the tyre can come adrift from the rim (unlike tubeless).

Tubeless tyres and their light alloy rims are not always that well suited to tough conditions, as they could lose their shape following an impact, which would result in the tyre no longer sealing itself against the rim. However, one of the big advantages of tubeless tyres is the ease of repair when one has a puncture, as the tyre can generally always stay on the rim during the repair process (large sidewall punctures are the exception, of course). The tyre also fits more tightly on to the rim, meaning that a sudden puncture is less of a threat, plus they tend to be safer at high speeds.

These benefits come at the expense of it being a far tougher job to remove the tyre from the rim (so called 'breaking the bead') in the first place. It's also worth bearing in

Intermediate tyres

Wear life front:	**6,500 miles (approx)**
Wear life rear:	**3,800–5,000 miles (approx)**
Terrain:	**These offer increased levels of grip and feedback compared to their enduro counterparts but will obviously not perform as well over rough ground. Will last much longer than a full knobbly tyre**
Brands/models:	**Continental Escape, Michelin Anakee, Bridgestone Trail Wing, Metzeler Enduro 3**

Enduro tyres

Wear life front:	**3,000–5,000 miles (approx)**
Wear life rear:	**2,000–3,000 miles (approx)**
Terrain:	**These will work best in tough off-road conditions but can perform well all season, in varying weather conditions, regardless of continent. The Continental TKC80 has become the benchmark tyre for world travel**
Brands/models:	**Continental TKC80, Michelin Desert, Bridgestone Trail Wing, Metzeler Karoo, Pirelli MT21**

↑ **Snow chains should only be used when absolutely necessary**
Wunderlich

↓ **Taking tyres with you can save the headache of trying to find spares later**
Adam Lewis

mind that badly punctured tubeless tyres can accept a tube in an emergency.

When looking at tyre choice, consider the following four specifications:

- The size (refers to the rim diameter, typically 17, 18, 19, 21 inches).
- The tyre width (refers to the cross-section, typically 120, 130, 140mm).
- The speed rating (denoted as a single letter A to Z, with Z being the highest speed).
- The load rating (typically between 20 and 80 – the larger the number the higher the weight the tyre can cope with).

Finally, remember that motorcycle tyres come in pairs – each particular model has a front wheel version and a rear wheel partner, and both tyres have the same characteristic profile. Generally you'll wear out two rear tyres to every front tyre, but this depends to a large extent on your style of riding, the terrain, and the weight being carried.

Popular brand names include the Avon Distanzia, Bridgestone's Battle Wings, the Metzeler Tourance, Pirelli Scorpion, Dunlop Rally Raid, and Michelin Anakee and Desert variants.

Wheels

There has long been debate over the pros and cons of the various types of wheels available, and indeed each type of wheel – spoked and cast – has advantages over the other. Manufacturers will occasionally put aesthetics above function when it comes to designing a bike to look 'good'. Sadly, it's also often seen that costs affect the quality of the component used, and it's for a combination of these reasons that an adventure bike might end up with inappropriate wheels fitted.

It's easy to overlook the amount of work a wheel has to do. It's not just a question of it rotating! It has to transmit the bike's power to the ground in order to drive it forward; it has to transfer the huge forces exerted upon it during heavy braking; it has to resist the lateral forces applied to it when the bike is leaning hard into a corner; and it has to be strong enough to work with the loading it receives when the suspension is working hard. The humble wheel does all of these things whilst having to stay completely undistorted and free rotating. For the most part an OEM wheel will do all these jobs and do them well, but the increased stresses that adventure riding puts on a bike's wheels will soon reveal their shortcomings.

Consider a relatively high-speed impact with a rock. A spoked wheel might deform slightly, perhaps break a spoke or two, but the chances are quite good that the tyre would stay inflated and secure. A cast wheel in a similar situation may not fare as well, as it's far more likely to crack or fracture, leading to an immediate deflation of the tyre and possible catastrophic failure of the wheel. If this were the case, the spoked wheel is probably repairable and will get you home, but a cast wheel won't. A cast wheel does have some advantages over a spoked wheel, though – simple punctures can be repaired with the tyre still on the rim, and they tend to run cooler than a tubed tyre, which can help to ensure longer tyre life.

Rebuilding wheels is not something to be approached lightly and making the correct choice of the replacement components is critical. The OEM rims will generally be budget items and will rarely give the same performance in terms of strength and integrity as a high-end 'performance' rim, such as Excel. Be sure that the rim you select will be appropriate in terms of spoke configuration as well as strength, and that the spokes to be used will be suitably uprated and corrosion resistant. The complexity of the configuration of a spoked wheel puts repairing it outside the scope of the average home mechanic and it's best left to a specialist wheel-builder to assemble the wheel to your specification.

A good example is provided by BMW's R 1200 GS and R 1200 GS Adventure models. The standard model comes with cast wheels while the hard-core Adventure features BMW Motorrad's proven, extra-strong cross-spoke wheels, with superior benefits particularly on extreme tracks, at high off-road speeds, and under high permanent loads. With the spokes on the outside of the rim it goes without saying that

→↓BMW's standard R 1200 GS comes with cast wheels while the Adventure variant features more hard core spoked wheels
BMW Motorrad

→Excel manufacture the toughest off-road rims available
Robert Wicks

'Petal' discs keep the pad surface clean, and maintain braking efficiency
Wunderlich

the machine may be fitted with tubeless tyres and the spokes can be replaced individually one by one.

On a final note, wheel bearings are often overlooked, so rather than wait for them to fail it's always a good idea to replace them before a trip or when the wheel's off for a tyre change. When doing so be sure to select an industrial-quality bearing such as SKF or NSK, specifying the need for 'double sealed bearings'. If possible it's a very good idea to carefully prise the grease seal away from the bearing and repack the balls and races with a liberal quantity of high-quality grease. This will protect the bearings from most adverse conditions and will extend their life considerably.

Brakes

The braking systems on modern adventure bikes are one area that has minimal potential for modification. Almost all large-capacity bikes are fitted with ABS systems which are to all intents and purposes non-adjustable save for the replacement of consumable components. Modifications that can be achieved are:

- **Replacement of hydraulic brake lines** – if the hoses are old or damaged, or the brake feels 'spongy', it's imperative that the brake lines are replaced. Various types of replacement hoses are available, but it will be preferable to fit a set of stainless steel 'braided' lines,

Simon Pavey demonstrates effective rear brake control
Thorvaldur Orn Kristmundsson

← Brake discs and pads can wear quickly when used for extended periods in adverse conditions
📷 Robert Wicks

which will give an immediate improvement in braking performance as well as being more resilient than a plain rubberised line. Custom lines can be manufactured to your specification to accommodate the extra length needed after the fitment of handlebar-risers.

- **Brake discs and pads** – you'll find that brake pads and discs will wear much more quickly in an off-road environment and certainly the pads will need more frequent replacement than normal. Special care must be taken when inspecting them to ensure that both the discs and the pads are well within acceptable wear limits, and will last the duration of any journey. If there's *any* doubt, they should be replaced. If you're considering aftermarket brake discs be sure to check the composition and fit pads to suit – some discs have high iron content and need a softer 'organic' pad to minimise disc wear.
- **On-board switching of ABS function** – the ABS systems on modern ADV bikes will in almost every case be switchable. Great care must be taken to explore the differences in braking characteristics between the various modes, to avoid being taken by surprise if the wheels lock up properly. The switching function can't normally be operated without a deliberate input from the rider so there's no danger of the ABS being inadvertently disabled.

↓ This KTM floating disc will be effective in all conditions
📷 KTM

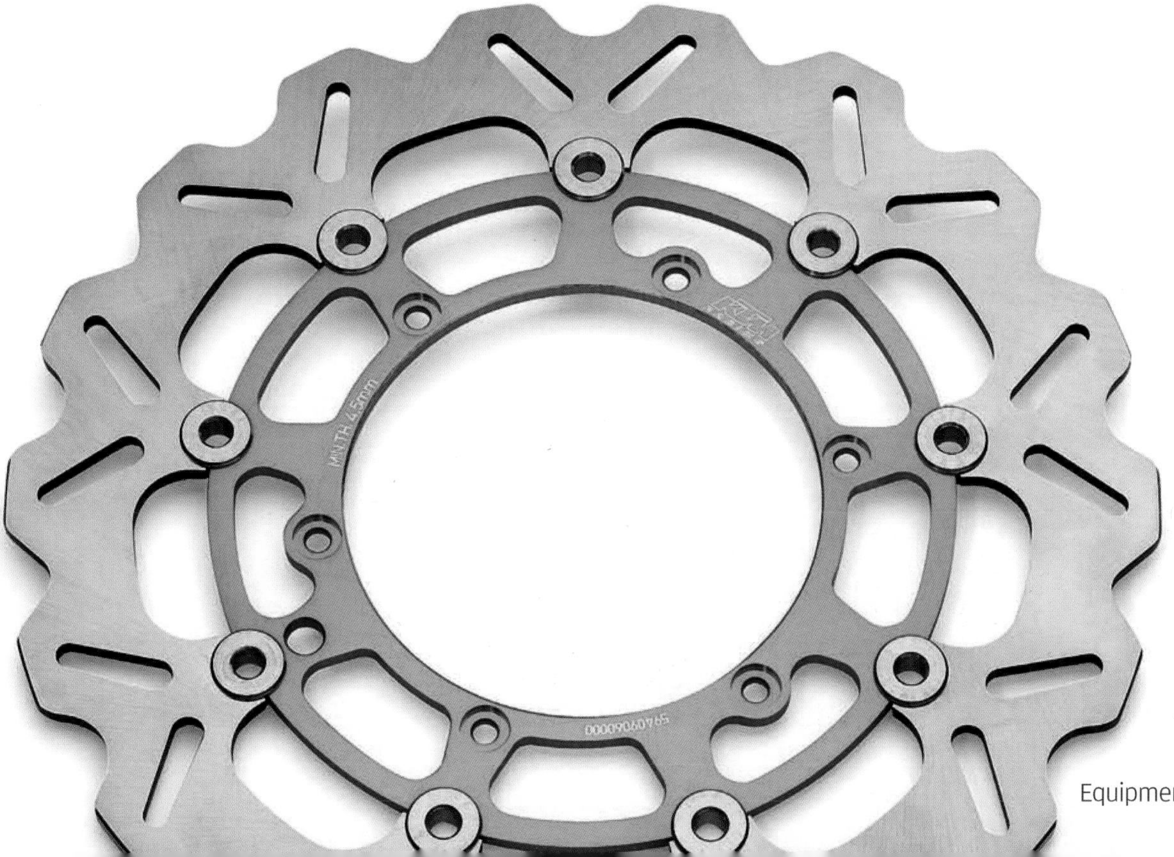

↑ **An aftermarket exhaust kit will reduce weight and can improve performance**
KTM

Exhaust systems

The exhaust system on many motorcycles is one of the first things that can be easily modified. OEM systems tend to be quite heavy and sometimes rather bulky, so there can be some real advantages to be gained from replacing them with a lighter and perhaps slimmer design of silencer. An OEM silencer can weigh 6–7kg, while an aftermarket replacement can weigh as little as 2–3kg depending on the materials used. OEM systems are designed to meet the stringent regulations attached to new motorcycles, while the replacement systems criteria are less restrictive while remaining road legal. It will often be the case that an aftermarket exhaust system can be more free-flowing, which is likely to change the power characteristics of the engine. A well-designed pipe can provide more tractability through the rev range, perhaps increase the power slightly too, although you should also be aware that the converse can apply to a poorly designed pipe.

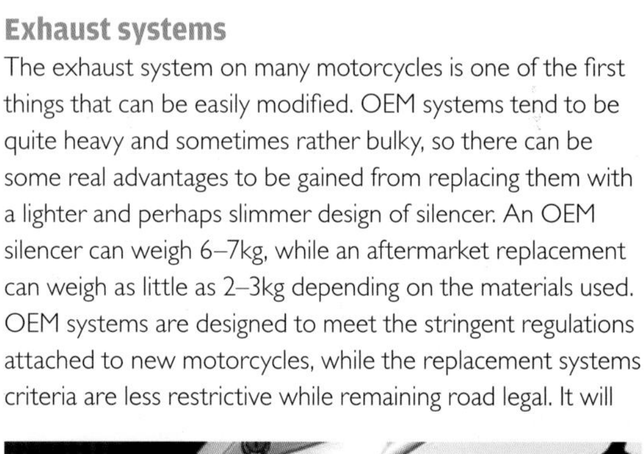

→ **This is an ultra-light version of the Remus exhaust**
Touratech

For the more serious modifier there's the possibility of replacing the whole system, including the exhaust headers. Whilst this might be quite an extreme step to take, the design of the headers will often improve primary exhaust gas flow, which in conjunction with a redesigned exhaust can often result in a noticeable improvement in the engine's power characteristics. Full replacement systems will also often allow the removal of the catalytic converter, which extends the possibilities of fuel choice in Third World countries, although the engine management system may need to be re-mapped for optimum performance.

Using a replacement exhaust silencer can also increase your luggage carrying capacity – for example, Metal Mule's pannier arrangement relies upon the use of an oval-shaped exhaust system to reduce the overall width of their pannier mounting racks, which in turn allows for a more balanced pannier package to be fitted, equalising packing capacity on both sides of the bike.

Chains and sprockets

This is the final part of the transmission, transferring the engine's power to the bike's rear wheel. A lot of power can be sapped by a neglected transmission – indeed, losing a chain can potentially ruin your adventure.

Check your existing chain and sprockets for wear and replace them if there's any doubt about their condition. Use this opportunity to explore the gearing possibilities for your bike – using an engine sprocket with one tooth less than standard lowers the gearing, which is generally better for off-road situations but at the expense of outright top speed. Using an engine sprocket which is one tooth larger raises the gearing and is ideal for extended periods of highway riding, but can make off-road riding harder. The same effect can be achieved in degrees by using larger or smaller rear wheel sprockets: a larger sprocket reduces the gear ratio while a smaller cog increases it. Be sure, though, that there's still scope for effective chain adjustment by increasing or reducing the number of links in your chain accordingly.

Touratech

Engine management issues

Modern engine management systems can cope with a variety of differing conditions, but their main job is to keep the engine running efficiently whilst meeting stringent emissions and noise regulations. But if you're riding in less than optimum conditions, at altitude, and with low octane gasoline, then the bike isn't going to be giving its best. Some bikes have switchable fuel mapping, which allows the use of low-quality fuel, but other bikes will need to have their engine management programmes reset by a dealer.

Modern fuel injection systems can be usefully augmented by 'piggy-back' systems, such as the Power Commander, which are designed to optimise the engine's fuelling, improving torque or pulling power and in a lot of cases greatly improving fuel consumption. These systems can help make a fuel-injected bike much more 'rideable' in an off-road situation by smoothing throttle response, and when correctly set up on a dyno will maximise mid-range torque – exactly where it's needed most.

It's certainly worth investing in good quality sprockets and chains especially given this type of terrain

Thorvaldur Orn Kristmundsson

Globebusters

Cockpit

However long your journey, be sure that you arrange your cockpit in the most effective way possible. It will be your 'office', for want of a better description, and needs to be set out in a way that works best for you at all times. It can be as simple or as sophisticated as you want it to be, and can contain a GPS, a road book or route notes, a trip meter, and paper maps. The navigation equipment needs to be positioned in such a way that it's easy to read, and still allows you to maintain a focus on the road ahead. Additional navigation equipment should also not obscure the bike's main instruments, such as the rev counter, speedometer, and warning lights. Large or heavy accessories are best on a frame-fixed mount, whilst lighter items can safely be carried on a handlebar mounting.

GPS units

Of all the visible technologies that have grown in recent history, the most useful to the adventure rider is undoubtedly the GPS or Global Positioning System. Modern GPS units are compact and have fast processors that can provide metre-accuracy in positional location, and have both route planning and track logging capability. The latest units also act as multi-functional devices, offering in addition a phone and a music player option. The range available is extensive, with significant differences in functionality, but few if any can match Garmin's rugged suitability for overland travel. Whichever unit is appropriate for you, all of the requirements discussed in this section need to be satisfied – secure vibration-proof mounting, an accessible power supply in clear line of sight, and ideally waterproof.

GPS technology can also be used for personal security in the form of a simple tracker unit, either stowed on the bike or carried by the rider. These are 'active' units that both receive and transmit positional data, which can then be securely distributed via a web link. This data can be used to track the unit or, in the worst case, locate a fallen rider. For some the notion of other people knowing their exact location goes against the very notion of adventure motorcycling and 'getting away from it all', but aside from the safety aspect this type of technology is a great way for family and friends to keep in touch with your journey, and potentially a great tool if you're trying to satisfy the needs of a sponsor.

Some argue that using a GPS can take the novelty (and art) of navigation away from map reading, but ultimately the best solution is to use both a map and GPS in tandem. Relying on just one aspect can leave your navigation open to error, and when riding in remote areas in particular this can create unnecessary and sometimes significant problems. In the book entitled *Chasing Dakar*, Jonathan Edwards MD and rally veteran Scot Harden comment that, used correctly, these various elements will 'help to keep you on the correct

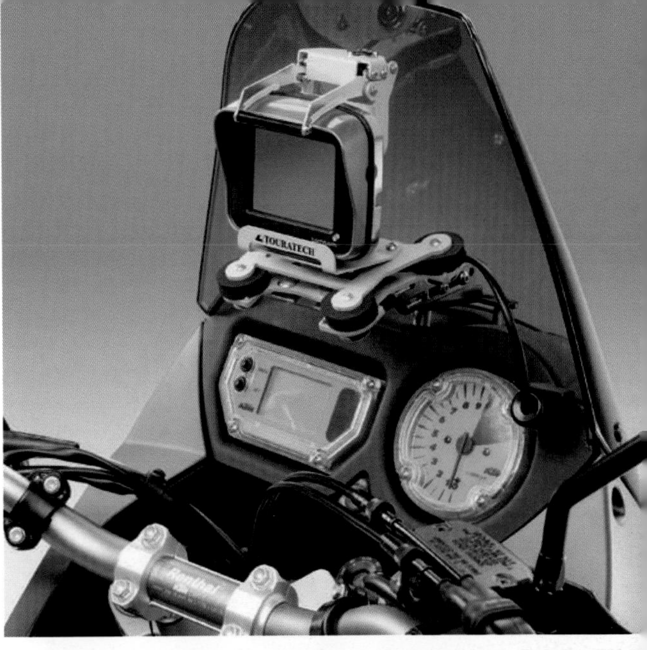

➔ No matter what type of GPS you prefer there is a bracket available. Units fitted here to a KTM 990 are a Tom Tom, Garmin 276C and a Garmin Street Pilot
KTM

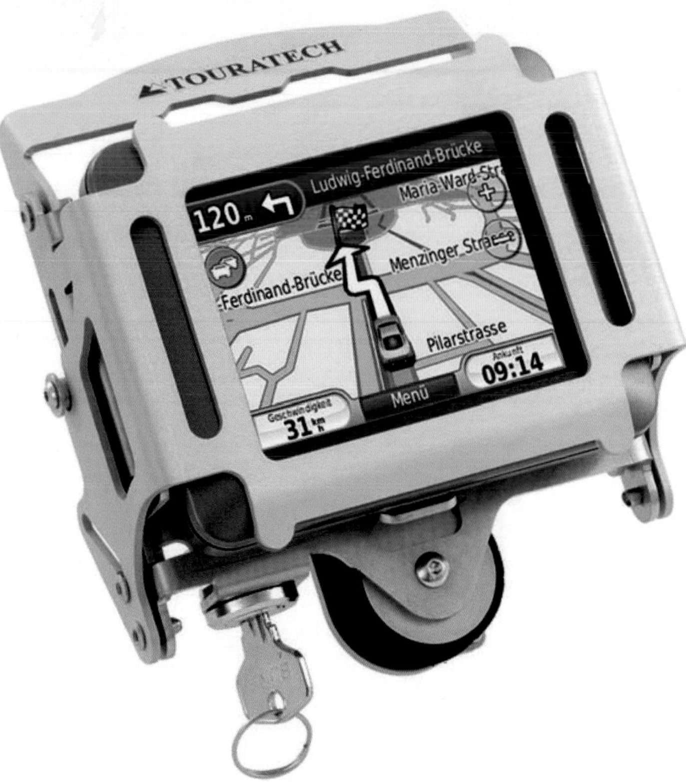

↑ This heavy-duty Touratech bracket will certainly keep your GPS unit secure
Touratech

trail, prevent you from getting lost and may even save your life'. They rightly state that 'riding with and using navigation equipment is multi-tasking in its highest form; one must learn to shift one's attention from the trail to navigation without compromising your safety'.

Mounts

Some bikes have a pre-fitted accessory bar that can be utilised for mounting a variety of instruments. These can be frame-mounted or, more usually, can be an extension of the screen mounting system. These place the accessories in a perfect line of sight, clearly visible without obscuring any other instruments or taking your eyes too far from the driving line. Handlebar mounts are also very popular, but care must be taken to minimise movement and vibration by keeping them as central as possible.

There are a huge variety of accessories available for adventure bikes and each one will have a mounting option, either specific or universal. Making sure that your accessory mount is compatible with your mounting system is critical – the last thing you want is an accessory that you can't fit on your bike. In choosing your mount, look for one which offers a locking mechanism so that you can keep the GPS unit safe if the bike is left unaccompanied, and above all remember that vibration is a killer, so try to minimise it wherever possible by using vibration-proof mounts.

Road books

Road books have their origins in the world of off-road rallies and act as an 'itinerary' in the form of a succession of information on the direction changes (way points), with relative and absolute distance information. It's really just a roll of paper with navigational instructions and information designed to fit in a holder, which can be advanced forward or backwards. It contains route information such as direction, checkpoints, fuel stops, distance headings, GPS waypoints, warnings about road hazards or dangerous areas, and overall distance travelled. The road book is designed to provide the rider with all this

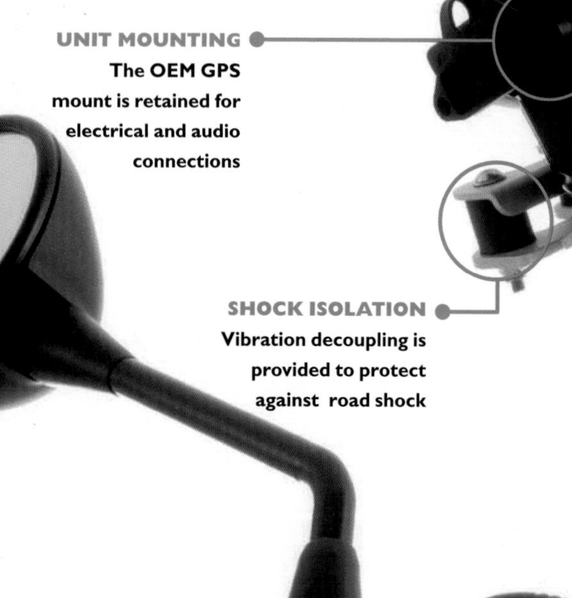

information while they're on the move and it becomes quite an art to keep your concentration on the road and to take in the information at the same time.

More and more adventure riders want to benefit from this type of system, but traditionally rally road book holders have been too big, and on many motorcycles there's simply not enough space to accommodate the device, and the bike's instruments – such as the speedometer – can no longer be read. However, manufacturers are now producing smaller road book units. If you're after one of these, they need to be waterproof and be made with a rugged aluminium housing.

Pre-designed routes for road books aren't widely available just yet and if you have a specific route in mind and want to use the road book format, then this may mean you'll need to knit and stick together your own pages and information to obtain the complete roll of the itinerary you want to ride. In order to be able to follow a paper road book, frequent resets of the odometer are required along the route in order to avoid inaccuracies resulting from the calibration deviations between your own speedometer compared to the one used to make the road book.

Power

An accessible power supply is essential for navigation equipment so determine what accessories you intend to use and make sure you have an appropriate power terminal close to it. Be sure that the cabling doesn't interfere with any other controls, and isn't chafed or trapped anywhere. See the section on electrical issues further on in this chapter.

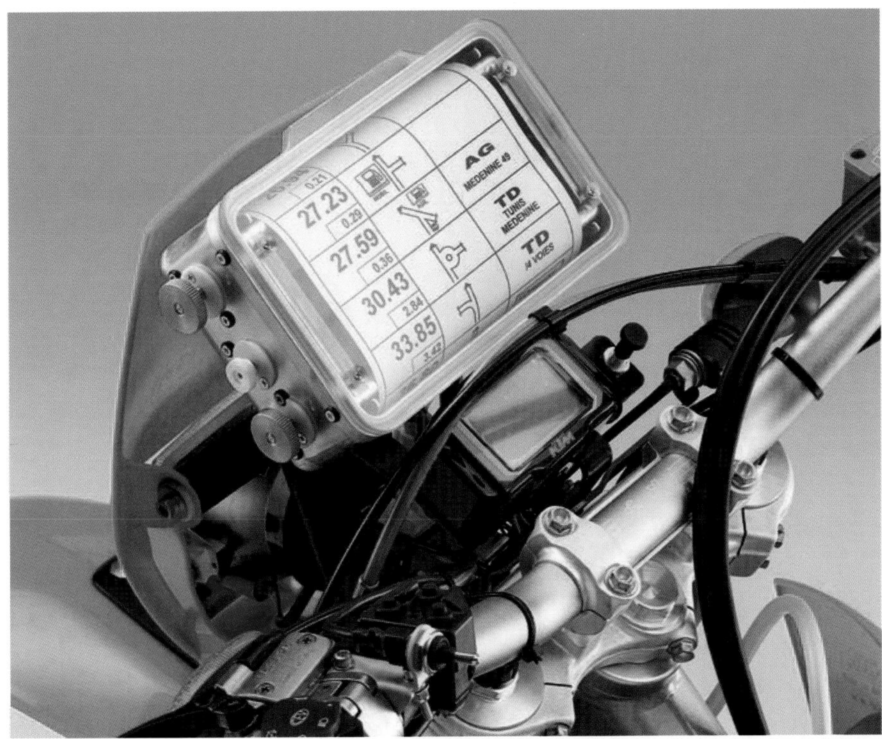

←↑Road books can be a challenge to fit but are essential for safe and effective rally navigation
📷 KTM & Touratech

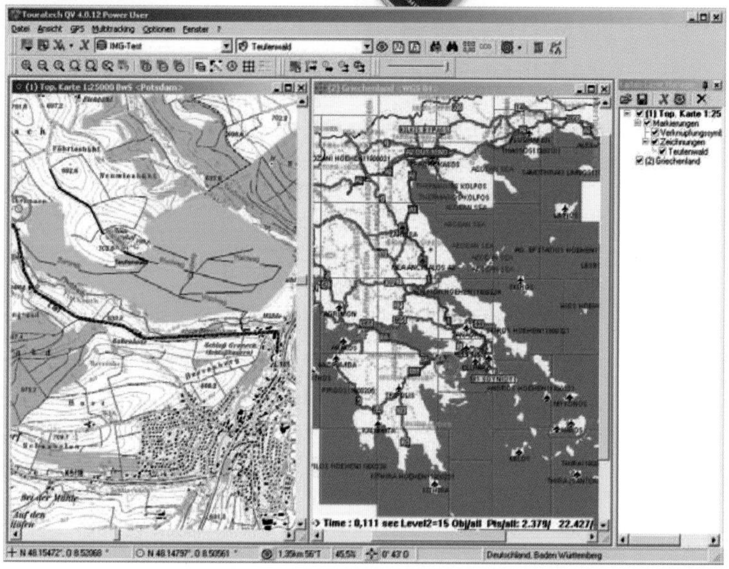

↑ There's nothing like the feel of a real map when it comes to planning your trip
📷 James Mann

↓ A tank bag is the ideal place to store your maps
📷 Touratech

→ Touratech's mapping software makes it easy to transfer routes to your GPS
📷 Touratech

Maps

Maps are a vital ingredient for an adventure ride, but don't take it for granted that what the map says is indeed what you'll find. While the road systems in some areas are being upgraded and this can provide a nice surprise, other roads suffer from serious neglect and may be very different to what you're expecting. Some sealed roads may, in fact, be quite difficult to negotiate, with potholes, sand, broken sections, and rock falls. There will be extreme variations in some roads that are indicated as being the same on a map – a 'gravel road' in say, Botswana or Namibia, is likely to be better quality than one in Tanzania or Ethiopia, though they'll both have been identified as similar in quality by the map's legend.

Before heading off ensure you're comfortable with basic map reading, understand how coordinates are defined, and how map scales, latitude, and longitude work. Maps are best carried in a clear sleeve in the top of your tank bag, where they can easily be seen while riding. An innovative idea is to take Walter Colebatch's lead and make provision for a waterproof, tear-resistant version – these are more expensive but worth the investment if you can afford it.

➔ Radio communication technology for use on bikes has advanced dramatically in recent years
Touratech

Radios

Communication between riders in a group can often be problematic. Thankfully these days it's relatively easy to interface a simple PMR hand-held radio to an intercom unit, which makes communication between bikes readily achievable. PMR-446 is a licence-free communication radio band, using 446MHz. The radios are hand-held, small, and compact, which makes them easy to stow on a bike. On specific installations there'll be an output from the intercom unit that provides the power for the radio, removing the need for batteries.

PMR radios are limited to a relatively small 0.5W transmission output, but in ideal conditions in open terrain this can give a usable range of up to six miles (10km). This range is reduced in built-up areas, but should still be effective at up to 0.6–1.2 miles (1–2km). Under normal circumstances it's not usually necessary to change transmission frequencies, so the radio can be tucked away in a convenient place on the bike, generally close to the intercom unit. Using them is simplicity itself, as the intercom's 'vox' setting gives voice-activated transmission, but a PTT (push-to-transmit) button can be fitted as an option if required. If you're planning on bike-to-bike communications, take the time to carefully install the headset and microphone boom into your helmet and test the system thoroughly to make sure it works before heading off.

↓ Radio communication can be a real asset when riding with friends
Thorvaldur Orn Kristmundsson

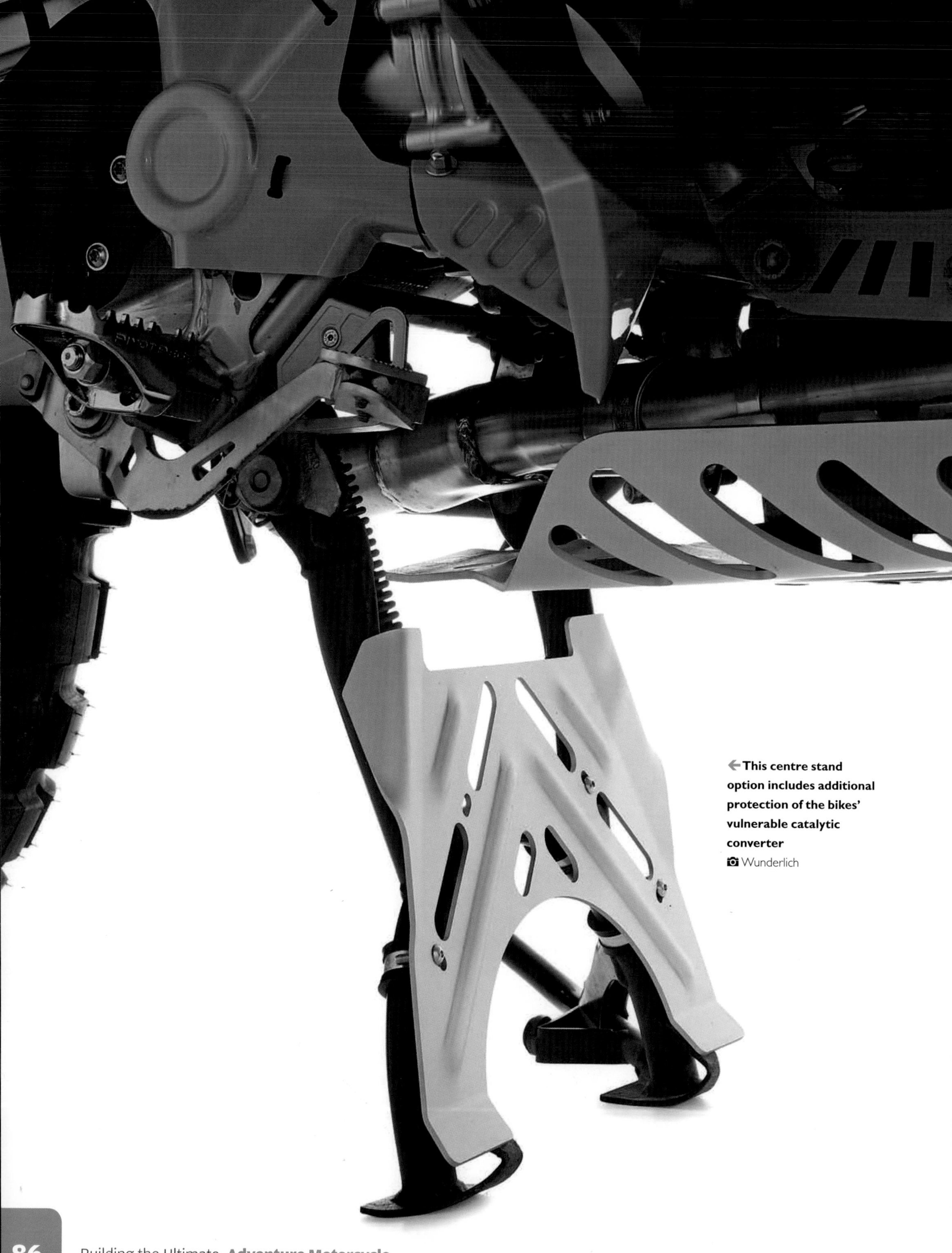

←**This centre stand option includes additional protection of the bikes' vulnerable catalytic converter**
Wunderlich

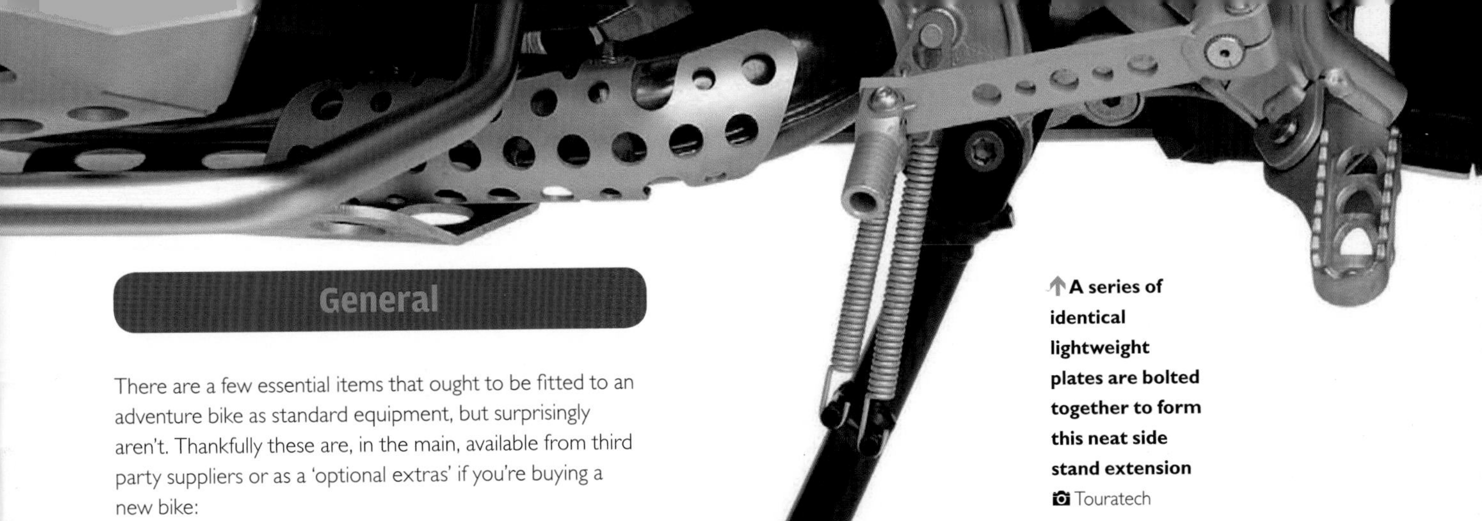

↑A series of identical lightweight plates are bolted together to form this neat side stand extension
📷 Touratech

General

There are a few essential items that ought to be fitted to an adventure bike as standard equipment, but surprisingly aren't. Thankfully these are, in the main, available from third party suppliers or as a 'optional extras' if you're buying a new bike:

Centre stand

Wheel removal for tyre changes or puncture repair can be a veritable challenge without a centre stand, as it can often be difficult to support a heavy bike with either wheel off the ground relying upon the side-stand alone. It typically bolts on to the bottom of the existing stand with a combination of interlocking plates.

Side-stand support extension

A side-stand footprint enlarger is a vital piece of equipment on almost any motorcycle and minimises the risk of the side-stand sinking into soft ground or hot tar, and tipping the bike on to its side.

Mudguard extension

A fender extender (or 'crud-catcher') is a very simple yet extremely effective accessory. On liquid-cooled bikes, it will help maintain airflow through the radiator by preventing it becoming clogged by mud or road-debris thrown up by the front wheel.

←This fender extender prevents mud from reaching the engine casing
📷 Wunderlich

←←A rear mudguard extension is a useful addition on any bike
📷 Wunderlich

↑A sturdy chain guard will protect both the bike and the rider in the event of a chain failure
Touratech

↓Don't assume pedestrians have seen or heard your approach
Globebusters

Chain guard

Whilst the chainguard is a fairly simple component, it is both an essential and a legal requirement for chain driven motorcycles. Its purpose is to prevent damage being caused in the event of the chain breaking, but this means that it is very close to the wheel, so it's important that it is in good condition and sturdy enough not to flex and get tangled in the spokes.

If you are changing a drive sprocket, you would also be wise to check that the case saver is still going to do its job. Its function is to protect the engine casings, and often the clutch slave cylinder from damage that might be caused by a broken chain. Various sizes are available according to the gearing fitted to the bike, check with your dealer which one you'll need.

Horn

In more developed urban areas of Third World countries, the one thing you'll probably hear most is a cacophony of vehicle horns at almost any time of day, and at some time or other you'll be certain to need your horn to attract attention or avert disaster! If your OEM horn is a little feeble, consider replacing it with a louder item, or augmenting it with a second unit to increase volume. If you have a CAN bus electrical interface, you may need to have a dealer reprogramme the control unit to correct any error messages that a second horn might cause.

Electrics

The natural environment of an adventure bike will be a world away from the convenience of a domestic electrical supply, so you must ensure that you have the means to use the accessories you take. The bike's alternator provides the electrical current required for running the bike, ignition, and battery recharging, but it has a maximum output which cannot be exceeded without risking a flat battery.

Consult your bike's manual for details of the alternator's output and make sure you have a good idea of the current requirements of your accessories, prioritising their use if necessary. If you need more power, then some bikes may have an alternator that can be upgraded – check with your dealer if this is possible.

There's a multitude of accessories available for which a 12V supply will be required, for example heated clothing, a phone charger, or a compressor. Remember that you can use your bike to recharge devices, which gets you away from having to take different plugs and transformers and means you won't need to find a household supply that works. Newer adventure bikes will have an auxiliary 12V outlet mounted somewhere, but it may not be conveniently placed, and perhaps not be compatible with your accessories. The control unit on a bike equipped with a single wire CAN-bus system can also be upset by non-compliant accessories, or it may not be able to supply sufficient current to a high wattage device. Installing an auxiliary power supply will resolve all these issues, giving you a lot more flexibility with how you can use your power, especially if you have a good idea of the accessories you'll be using.

Non-CAN-bus systems are relatively straightforward to adapt, with most wiring harnesses having readily available switched outlets – your manual will show you where these are, and what power they'll be able to supply. These are most likely to be wrapped up in the wiring loom, generally at the front of the bike, and will have a simple connector marked 'AUX' or similar, and may be permanently live or switched by the ignition. These can be used for almost any accessory depending on the fused rating of the supply. If you need more flexibility or an additional outlet, then it's best to install an independent supplementary harness. Using a combination of a simple 12V switching relay and fused distribution unit to protect your primary wiring harness gives you the possibility of four or five individually fused supplies. If you're in any doubt about how to achieve this kind of modification consult an automotive electrician or your dealer.

Any accessory should be fused, and ideally that fuse should be as close as possible to the battery's positive terminal. Simply put, after the fuse things are protected, before it things are not.

For auxiliary sockets, visit a boating shop as they offer products with rust-free components. Whatever you decide on, make sure they're hard-wearing and can withstand vibrations. On a final note, remember that the electrical system's regulator/rectifier unit is often placed in an area of high airflow, which is needed to keep it cool. Unfortunately this also means that it's likely to be susceptible to physical damage from either the rider or the terrain. Small plates designed to bolt on to the assembly can cover it effectively, but still allow the airflow required to keep it cool.

← Keep any auxiliary wiring neat and away from heat sources
Touratech

Hard-wiring accessories is relatively straightforward, and can be achieved in a variety of ways, depending on the configuration of your wiring harness. Again, look for the spare wires in your loom marked 'AUX', which will have their own fused protection. In the majority of cases the accessory can be plugged directly into the terminator, but others might require the fitting of a different connector. CAN-bus controlled bikes will have an auxiliary terminator somewhere in the loom, but these require the accessory to have a specific connector fitted. Check the power consumption of the accessory to be fitted and be sure that the fuse and cabling will be appropriately rated, and always ensure that your new cabling is routed and protected in such a way to minimise chafing or trapping.

← Know your way around the fuse box and electrics on your bike
Robert Wicks

When fitted, the pannier will hide this neat tool box arrangement from view
Overland Solutions

Integrated sump guard and tool box combination keep weight low down
Overland Solutions

Tools, spares, and maintenance

There's no way of telling exactly which tools and spares you're going to need on an adventure ride, and it's even less certain what might be available to you en route. As a general rule of thumb, if you know something has a high probability of failing during the trip given its age then you should replace it before you leave, and this should avoid you having to carry it as a spare part.

Given the weight and space constraints it will boil down to a selection of the key items you're most likely to need. Try wherever possible to keep tools low down on the bike and as central as possible. Overland Solutions make some of the most ingenious toolboxes – an integrated version that's either attached to or forms part of the sump guard, as well as a version that sits neatly behind the panniers and out of sight.

A basic technical knowledge and awareness of any weaknesses the bike may have will enable you to carry out at least a degree of routine maintenance and simple repairs. Leaving home with the bike in good condition in the first place and then ensuring that it's looked after on the road will go a long way towards reducing potential technical issues.

←←Careful design allows for two tool boxes to be located around the lower part of the engine
Overland Solutions

←Regular maintenance will improve longevity of key parts
Thorvaldur Orn Kristmundsson

Australian adventure rider Frank Warner says: 'You should be able to perform normal essential servicing on your bike, so learn at home where you can get assistance and do a full service on the bike before you leave. Get to know your bike – understand what things are, what they do and where they are. This is essential if something does go wrong.'

It's also important to have a good contact back at home who can source particular parts from your local dealer and arrange to get them shipped out to you if needed. For long-distance trips make sure you have all the tools needed to strip and rebuild the bike. Garages in remote areas may have some heavy tooling but not necessarily all the basic hand tools you need to work on your specific bike.

On a related note, be sure to fix any small problems quickly. On a long ride these can easily develop into more significant problems, so either eliminate it, fix it, or change it.

When it comes to maintenance, Warner makes a valid point: 'One hint when you're travelling is to try and have all the maintenance happen at one time rather than several small maintenance sessions. Three two-hour sessions on three separate days over a month are much worse than one whole day. Those two-hour sessions tend to take the best travel parts of the day.'

Finally, always ensure you carry a good range of

↓Take care that bush welding doesn't fry your ECU!
Metal Mule

↑ **Easy access to your tool kit is important**
Overland Solutions

consumables, such as duct tape and cable ties – these will invariably be put to use on even the shortest of trips in a variety of different applications.

What follows is a reasonably comprehensive list designed to cater for a long trip, but you should always adjust these recommendations for your own bike, which may have a specific tool requirement of some sort:

- Spare keys
- Motorcycle repair manual
- Actual toolkit supplied with the motorcycle
- Puncture repair kit
- Tyre levers
- Spare rear tyre
- Spare front tyre
- Heavy-duty inner tubes (most people carry a rear, as that's where a flat is more prevalent, but one option is to carry a front, as that will also fit the rear if needed)
- Spoke key
- Air filter (washable/reusable variety)
- Fuel filter
- Brake, throttle, and clutch cables
- Brake and clutch levers
- Length of fuel hose
- Selection of electrical spares – bulbs, fuses, and connectors
- Spanners
- Set of Allen keys
- Extension tube to allow high torque fastening of wheel nuts etc
- Screwdrivers
- Pliers
- Mole grips
- File
- Spark plugs
- ¾in drive ratchet and sockets
- Small hacksaw and spare blades
- Engine oil
- Coolant fluid
- Small 12V compressor
- Surgical gloves
- Small selection of consumables
- Water displacement spray (like WD40)
- Scotch lock
- Electrical connectors
- Fuses
- Duct tape
- Electrical tape
- Selection of cable ties in various sizes
- Collection of nuts and bolts as used on the bike
- Superglue
- Araldite
- Metal putty
- Small tub of grease

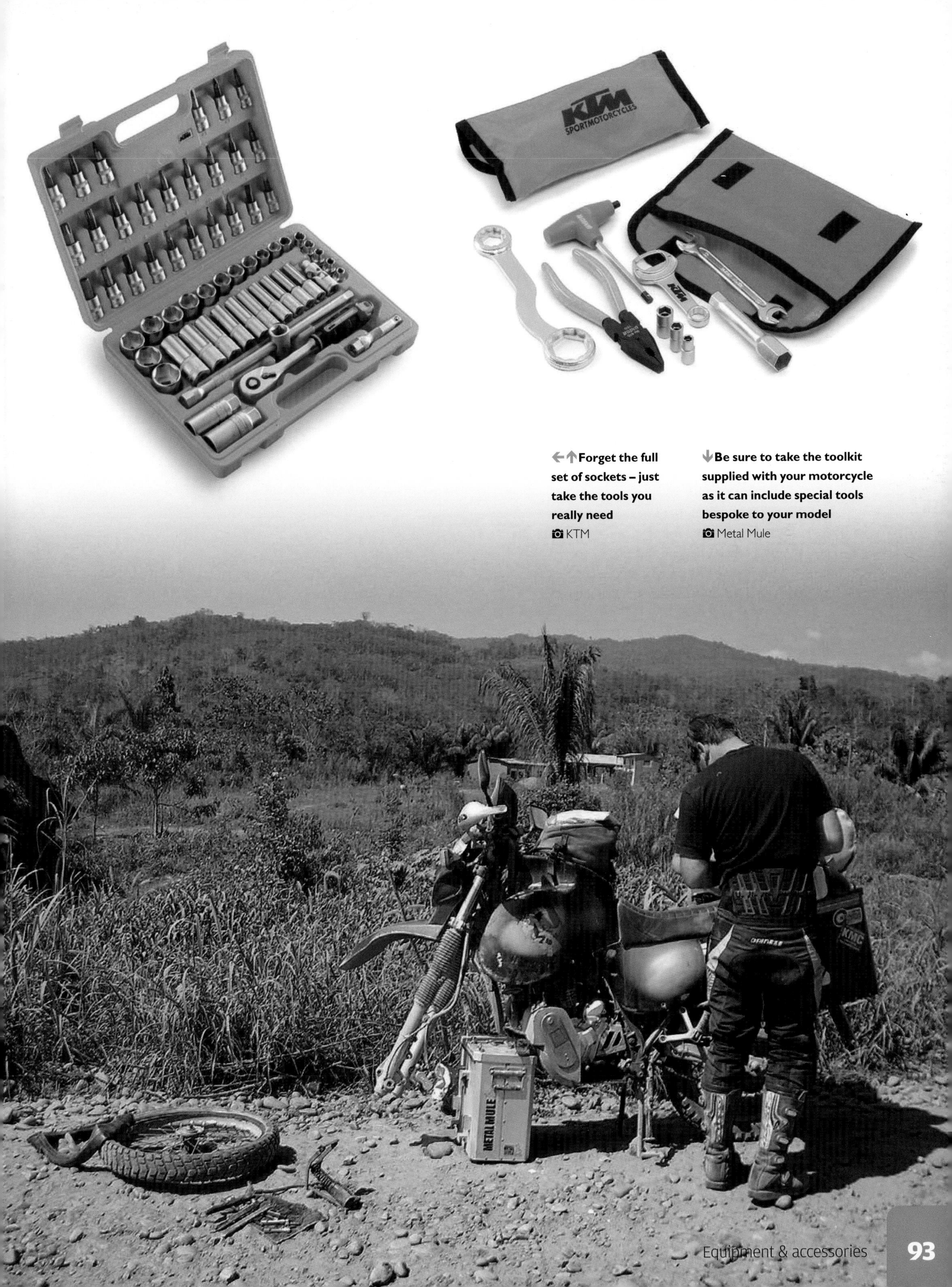

←↑Forget the full set of sockets – just take the tools you really need
📷 KTM

↓Be sure to take the toolkit supplied with your motorcycle as it can include special tools bespoke to your model
📷 Metal Mule

BMW R 1200 GS Adventure
Prepared by Touratech

If you wanted a large bike with 'go-anywhere' abilities, if money was no object, if you had the physical strength needed to manoeuvre and lift the bike, and if you were convinced that a small single-cylinder trail bike with soft luggage just wasn't your thing, then this is probably the bike for you. Prepared by aftermarket specialists Touratech, this BMW R 1200 GS Adventure includes everything you could want. The 60-odd individual 'extras' added are around the same value as the bike itself, which means considerably less money to spend on the road once you get out there. That said, for many riders this represents the ultimate in adventure motorcycling, so feast your eyes, at least for a moment.

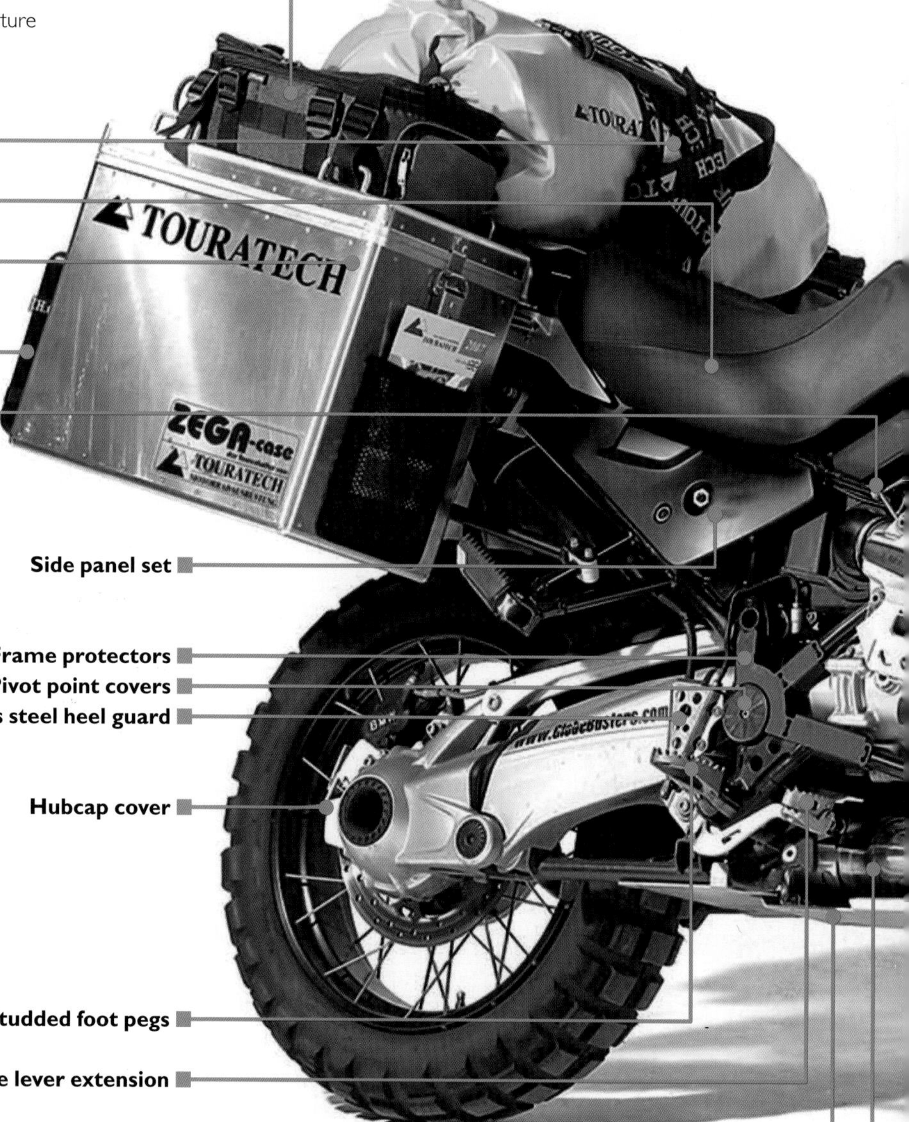

Front brake fluid reservoir guard

Articulated conversion fixing kit for Multiplo hand protector

Multiplo hand protectors

Large spoiler, silver, for Multiplo hand protector

Pannier bag

Day Trip Tankbag

Roll bag

Low Kahedo Line seat

Aluminium pannier kit, 35/41 litres, with black racks

Holder and 2-litre canister

Petrol line protection

Side panel set

Frame protectors

Pivot point covers

Stainless steel heel guard

Hubcap cover

Studded foot pegs

Brake lever extension

Aluminium sump guard extension

Exhaust connection tube without catalytic converter

Not visible

- Cockpit cover
- Adjustable gear lever
- Upgraded horn
- Hawker Odyssey upgraded battery
- Cigarette lighter socket
- Ceramic clutch
- Clutch housing bolts
- Clutch cover
- Clutch press plate
- Unifilter high-performance air filter
- Remus Hexacone rear silencer (carbon fibre)
- Front clutch fluid reservoir guard
- Throttle potentiometer cover
- Splash guard
- Adjustable cover strap for panniers
- ZEGA Bag 35 litres
- ZEGA Bag 41 litres
- Luggage rack support/ extension

TOURATECH
TOURATECH
www.GlobeBusters.com
TOURATECH
BMW
Spoiler for windscreen
Garmin GPSMAP 278
Handlebar bracket Garmin GPSMAP 276C, lockable
GPS bracket adaptor
276/278 power cable for R 1200 GS
Hard-part windscreen support
Antiglare shield
Hard-part windscreen
Xenon auxiliary headlight
Low-beam xenon light (with ballast unit)
Headlight protector
Oil cooler protection
Additional fog headlight left
Additional fog headlight right
Hard Part LA steering stop
Front Rallye mudguard
Crash bar bags
Cylinder guards
Kickstand support extension
Aluminium sump guard

Chapter 4

Luggage systems

📷 Adam Lewis

Successfully carrying your gear during an adventure trip requires some careful decisions early on in the planning stages, and making the right choice is key as you're going to be living out of your panniers for the duration of the trip. Almost irrespective of the type of trip you have planned, you'll essentially need a combination of luggage options:

Secure storage – this is an important issue when touring on a motorcycle, and having peace of mind to leave your luggage mounted to the bike is vital.

Convenient storage – for essential items that you need quick, regular access to, like money, maps, or your camera.

Cool storage – this can be handy for items like medication, batteries, and camera film.

Protective storage – motorcycles vibrate even on excellent roads; add a poor surface like gravel, add dust, add rain, and you have a very hard environment for your camera, video camera, and GPS. Too much dust and/or vibration and you may just find your equipment failing in the middle of a once-in-a-lifetime trip. Special protective equipment bags and boxes are available that offer protection from moisture, vibration, and dust.

Bulk storage – to carry items that simply don't fit in your other luggage, like clothing, sleeping mat, and spares. Whatever you choose, make sure it's waterproof.

↑ **Metal Mule's pannier system offers neat carrying handles**
Metal Mule

Hard versus soft luggage

The principal decision to make regarding your secure and protective storage is whether to opt for soft luggage or hard aluminium cases. The popularity of both solutions has grown significantly in recent years and a number of options are available from several suppliers. Many motorcycle manufacturers offer their own ranges of hard (plastic) luggage and these too can be a consideration, although they're unlikely to stand up that well to the rigours of an off-road adventure and are best suited to touring.

The second point to consider is the size of the load you plan to carry. A typical aluminium pannier can carry 30–40 litres, and soft bags 15–25 litres, but just because your bike has a load-carrying capacity of 'X', don't take that as a licence to load it up to the hilt. The choice of luggage type is also important if you're planning on riding with a pillion passenger, so always assess the weight you're placing on the bike and judge how this will affect its handling, particularly over rough terrain. Maintaining the weight as centrally and as low as possible will allow you a far better degree of control, balance, and manoeuvrability.

The hard or soft luggage debate is a favourite amongst overlanders, and there is no clear winner – it all boils down to personal preference and requirements. The table on page 100 outlines some of the pros and cons of each and offers some further considerations to weigh up before making a decision.

Deciding on your luggage system is really a personal choice that will be determined by your budget and the load you plan to carry. Research all the suppliers and products carefully to ensure you make the best possible choice.

→ **Centre of gravity is a real issue here with that heavy pack strapped to the back of the bike**
Metal Mule

Hard luggage options

Manufacturers-own
Yamaha

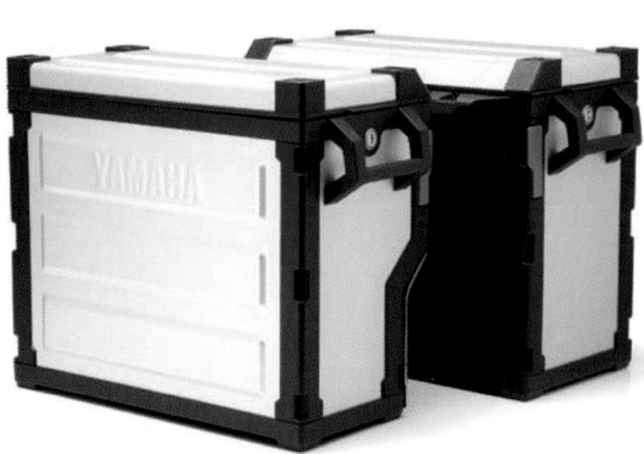

Aluminium
Touratech

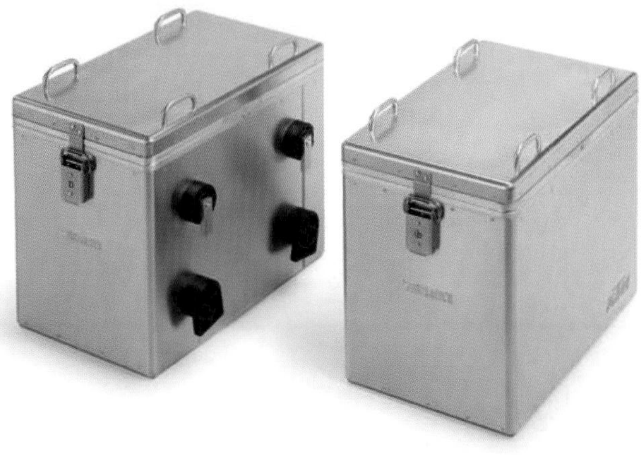

Plastic
Hepco & Becker

Soft luggage options

Frame-mount soft bags
Touratech

Throw-over
Andy Strapz

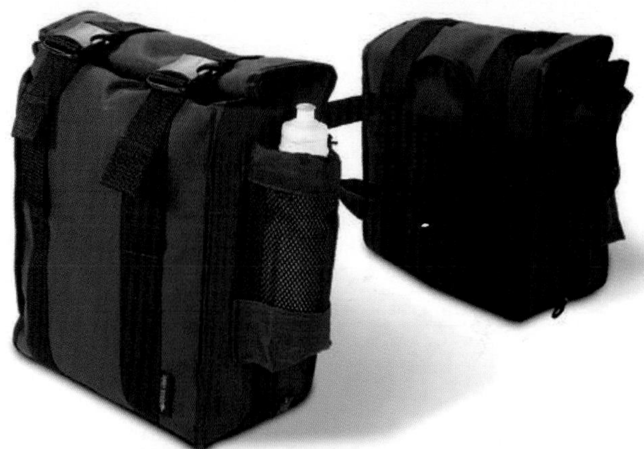

Tail packs
Touratech

Pros – hard luggage	Cons – hard luggage
Solid	Overpriced
Waterproof and dustproof	Heavy
More secure because they can lock properly	Arguably more dangerous in an accident
Easier to pack	Increases the width of the bike, which can be an issue in traffic congestion or on narrow tracks. Some places will allow you to bring the bike inside overnight, so it's useful if the maximum width of the bike will fit through a door
Gives you the option of securing additional luggage to the top of the pannier if needed	Encourages you to take more gear
Can be used for other purposes, such as a camping seat	Some locking systems can be over-complicated and very fiddly
Can act as a buffer in certain accident situations	Traditionally sit quite far back and high up, which doesn't help the bike's handling
Offers easy access to the contents	
Optional inner bags that fit exactly into the shape and size of the hard cases allow packing of items in liners, which then act as soft suitcases. Means the panniers can stay on the bike, which saves time and hassle	
They tend to come with a proper lock-set, which can normally be programmed to work with your ignition key	

Pros – soft luggage	Cons – soft luggage
Keeps the bike lighter and easier to handle	Not very safe and can be tempting to thieves
Encourages you to travel light	A soft bag is likely to rip, and once torn there's not a lot you can do with it, but you still need to carry your gear. An aluminium pannier might have a hole in it but could be bent back into shape until a proper repair is made
Soft luggage is arguably easier to source while hard panniers can have a longer lead time, as many manufacturers 'make to order'	Sometimes difficult to carry bulky or odd-shaped items
Offer a reasonable payload (15–25kg)	Robustness and ability to withstand the elements is sometimes questionable, but products are getting better all the time
Some more specialised bags have compression straps, making their overall size a lot smaller when fully compressed	Can be susceptible to the heat generated by the exhaust unless carefully mounted on the motorcycle
Can be used in combination with a small lockable top box	
With the right kind of rack, the bags can be mounted quite far forward and lower than hard boxes, which will ultimately help in handling the bike	

Globebusters

CROSS BRACING
Cross bracing the rear of the rack will add strength in the event of a crash – something that is often missing on OEM-fit panniers
UPPER MOUNTING POINT
Check upper mounting points on your motorcycle frame can take the loads you're intending to carry
D
VS
TT41
LOWER MOUNTING POINT
Many racks utilise the pillion footrest brackets for a lower mounting point
RADIUSED CORNERS The fewer welds the better, so look for corners formed by bends in the tubing rather than joints

Touratech

Racks and mounting systems

Once you've decided on the type of luggage, the next important consideration is the mounting kit – in other words some sort of rack system that allows the luggage to be attached to the subframe of the bike.

The rack you choose should be sufficiently robust and rigid to carry the anticipated load and also make mounting and dismounting the luggage a simple process. Some racks in fact offer the option of variable positions (different heights and angles) for the luggage, which can be useful if your load changes en route or for when you carry a passenger.

If you have an older bike, or you have specific requirements for your hard luggage, you may not find exactly what you want as an 'off the shelf' item. There are companies like Overland Solutions that offer bespoke manufacturing services for 'one-off' items, and this can be the answer to many problems, but there will be cost implications that you need to consider.

↑ A pre-assembled rack prior to mounting
📷 KTM

←← This BMW rack features a base plate on which the pannier can rest for additional support
📷 BMW Motorrad

← A bespoke rack and pannier set prepared by Overland Solutions
📷 Overland Solutions

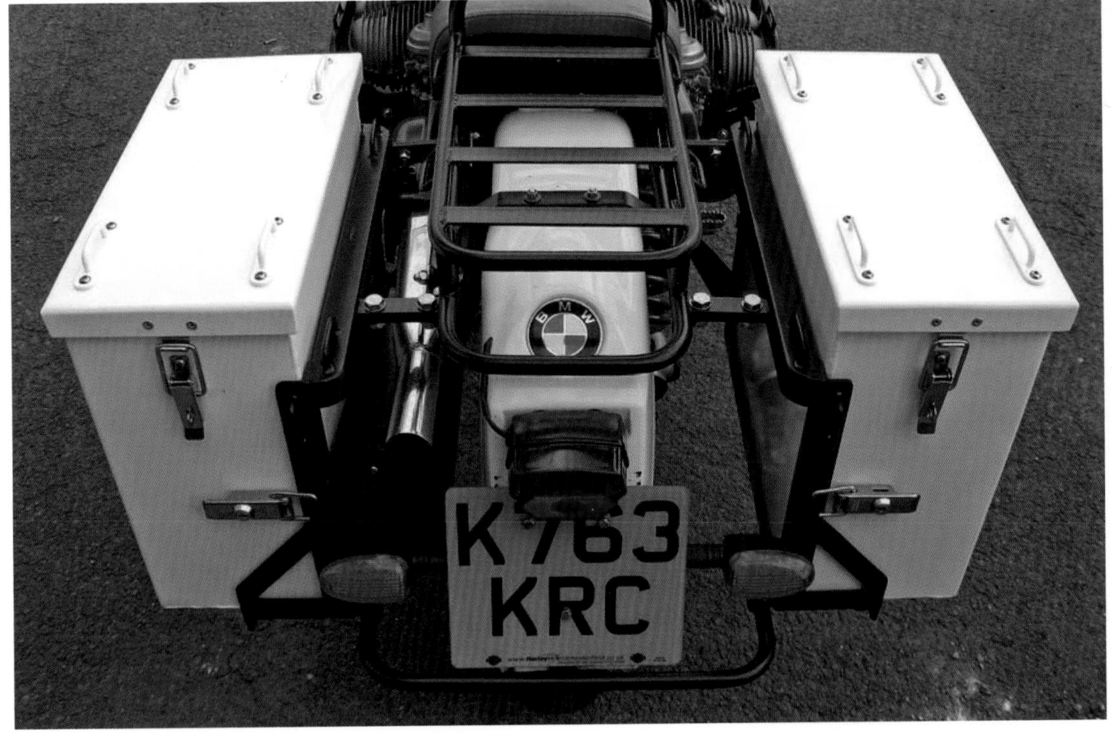

Building your own pannier frames allows you to select materials to suit your own requirements. Brackets can be tailored to fit around other modifications you may have planned

Making friends with a local fabricating company can help with the trickier bits of the build...

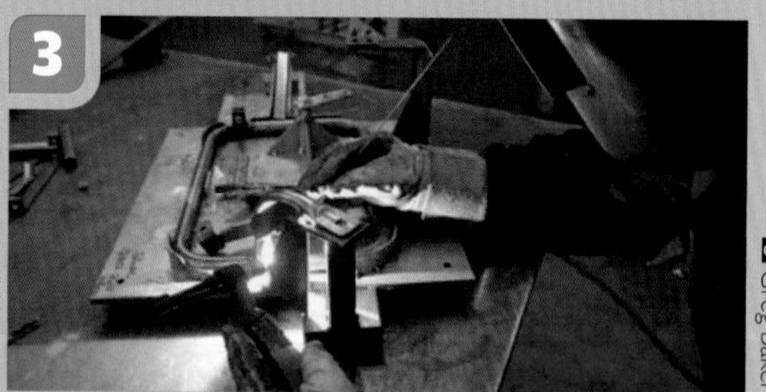

...and will ensure the rack will hold together under the strain – especially if you're not confident with welding

Greg Baker

DIY solutions

Unless you're confident of coming up with a design to carry your load, understand how different stresses will impact on the design and are sufficiently skilled in the art of welding, it's probably best not to attempt your own racking system and to opt instead for one of the many systems available through the main aftermarket suppliers.

If, however, you have the inclination and the necessary skills, it's feasible to fabricate a made-to-measure rack system for your bike and even your own panniers. Bear in mind, though, this can be a daunting task and is not for the faint-hearted, but a satisfactory end result is immensely rewarding and will usually give you exactly what you want from your equipment.

Depending on your level of skill and the tools available to you, various methods can be used to create your system. The main decisions when planning a rack are:

- Determining the weight you plan to carry.
- The material it will be made of – typically either steel tubing or square sections.
- How it will attach to the frame of your motorcycle – it should not be welded to the frame and instead will need at least four but preferably six mounting points (see page 102).
- How it will be braced – to take the required load and avoid flexing inwards under stress.
- How your set of panniers will ultimately be attached to the rack.
- You also need to be conscious of the size of the rack and ensure it does not prevent or limit access to your rear suspension unit or other key components.

One option, made from square sections of steel is a full or partial tray rack assembly on which the base of the pannier can rest. This alone is not enough to keep the panniers in place but it's a good starting point and can be supplemented by attachments connected to the frame. Bear in mind with this system that when the panniers are removed the rack will still be in place which may be an issue if space is a premium.

The alternative to the tray rack is a tubular frame onto which panniers are mounted. This requires some careful skill as the corners will need to be formed by bends rather than joints.

When it comes to home-made panniers, these can provide a strong and cheaper alternative to current aftermarket products but can be very time consuming if you are not proficient when it comes to working with aluminium. With a little imagination, a very effective and bespoke pannier system can be created from some 2mm anodised aluminium sheet, a strip or two of angle profile, a few rivets and low modulus sealant. Home fabricated aluminium cases can be made to the exact size and profile required, making them the ultimately flexible luggage system. Pay specific attention to waterproofing requirements and the fabrication needs for the pannier lids. Consumables needed include sealants for the inside and the outside of the panniers, superglue and acetate to clean the surfaces prior to applying the sealants.

As with any unique project, you'll most likely be working without plans, laying-up sections as you progress, so be prepared for some reworking along the way. Panniers can be made in your garage at home provided you have a basic workshop and access to some basic tools and consumables.

Custom, home-made components will need thorough testing so be sure to get out on your motorcycle and make sure everything works as planned.

← This Metal Mule pannier case is certainly not a DIY effort – it's worth considering the mounting solutions manufacturers have found when it comes to designing your own frames
📷 Globebusters

Alternatives

Army surplus ammunition boxes can be easily adapted for use as panniers, and will provide enormous levels of protection and durability. There is a plethora of sizes available, and whilst steel can be a little on the heavy side, the composite GRP cases are much lighter and easier to mount.

The plastic composite used in the manufacture of Pelican cases gives them a well deserved reputation for toughness and durability. Available in a variety of sizes, their simple design and construction means they can be used effectively in a variety of situations and can be mounted to almost any type of pannier frame.

← Don't overlook pre-existing cases when it comes to finding a solution for your panniers – army surplus ammunition boxes offer just the kind of robust protection that overlanding demands
📷 Greg Baker

→ **Tank bags come in various shapes and sizes so make sure you get one that fits the profile of your bike's fuel tank**
KTM

Other storage options

Tank bags – this is a great form of convenient storage and sits above your petrol tank. It's ideal for holding essential items to which you may need quick and regular access, such as important documents, cash, maps, cameras, earplugs, and gloves. One of their most useful features is a clear plastic sleeve into which you can slip your map, thus having it visible at all times. Some bags can expand and contract in size depending on your needs. It's important to ensure a secure fit to your bike before you purchase, as tanks and tank bags all come in different shapes and sizes. Bags can be attached by using magnets (which are heavy) or straps. The latter is the preferred choice given the uneven terrain likely on an adventure ride, and are essential as most modern tanks are made of plastic.

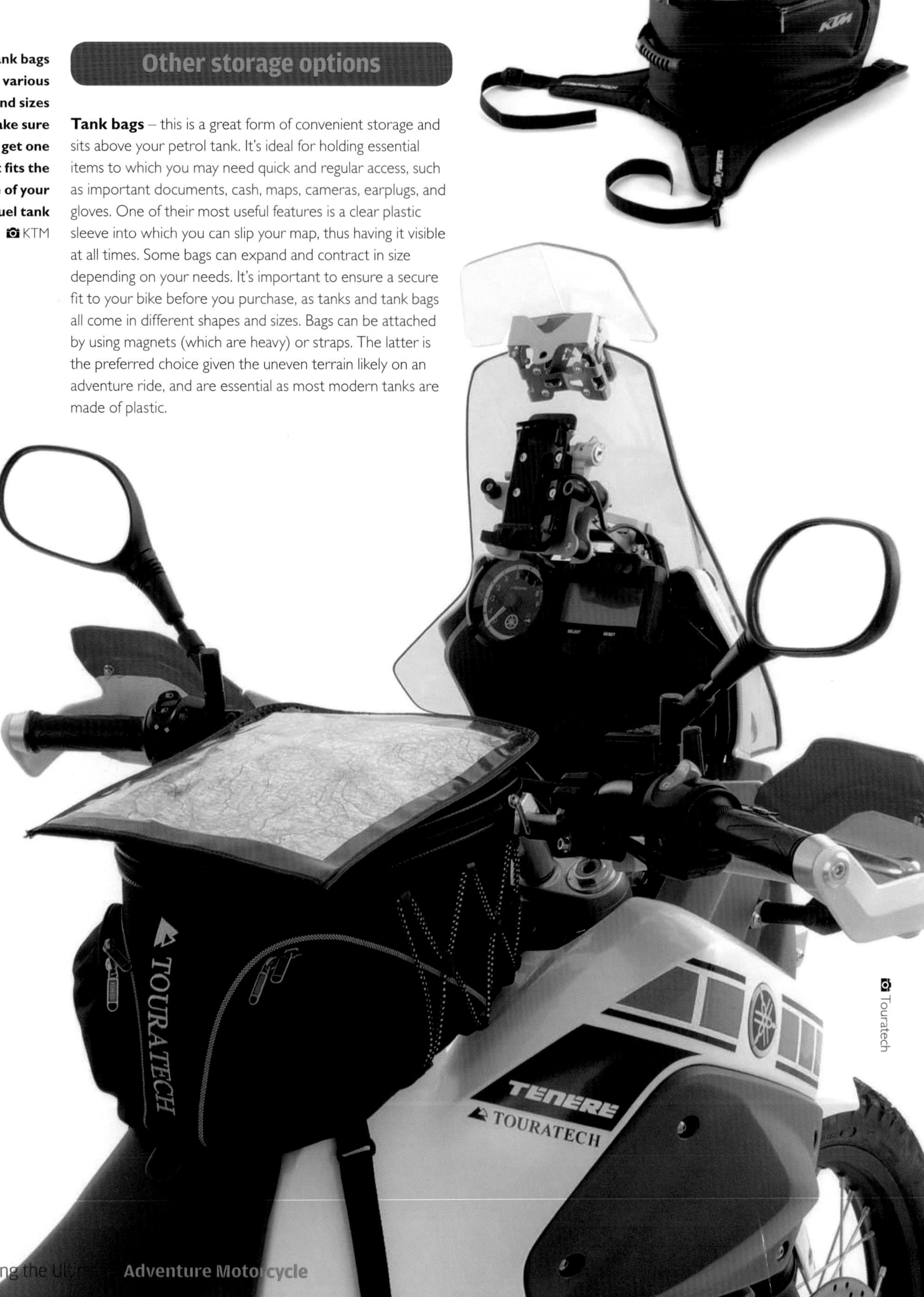

Touratech

Roll bags – for an extended trip, many riders also carry a 'roll bag', a robust, waterproof bag made from PVC and designed to offer flexible storage for bulky items. They come in a variety of sizes with carrying capacity ranging from 20 to 100 litres. To attach a roll bag to your motorcycle you need a flat surface of some kind behind the pillion seat. Alternatively, the bag can run across the top of the pillion seat and rest on your panniers, but this can hinder access to the panniers themselves.

Top boxes – some pannier sets include a top box. These fit on the carrier rail behind the seat, either as a permanent fixture or with a mechanism to make removing them fairly easy. They too can be locked and offer a reasonable level of security, but they shouldn't be overloaded as this can impact on the bike's centre of gravity and affect the handling, as the weight is placed high up and at one end of the machine. If your preference is for soft luggage but you want some added security, then a top box is a good idea.

Water storage – for long-distance desert travel you'll need to carry spare water, and the lower down you can stow it and the closer to the bike's centre of gravity, the less impact it will have on handling. Brackets to fasten bottles to your panniers are available and offer quick and easy access.

↑A roll bag offers waterproof storage and a good level of flexibility
Globebusters

↓Kriega's R3 waist-pack is 100% waterproof and made from ultra-tough materials ideal for the adventure environment
Kriega

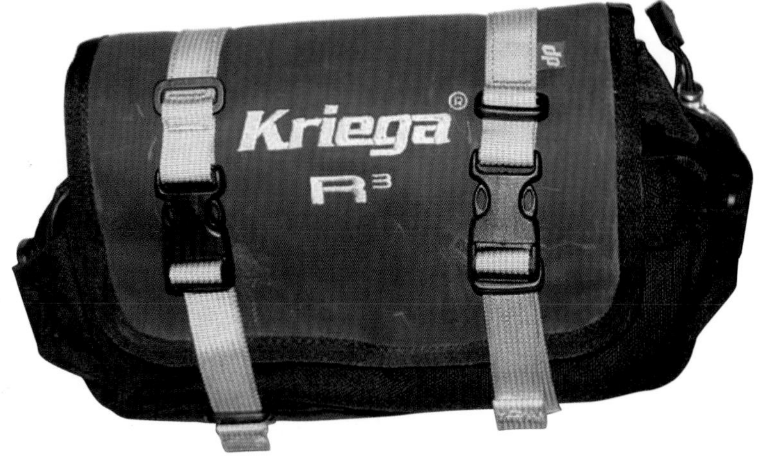

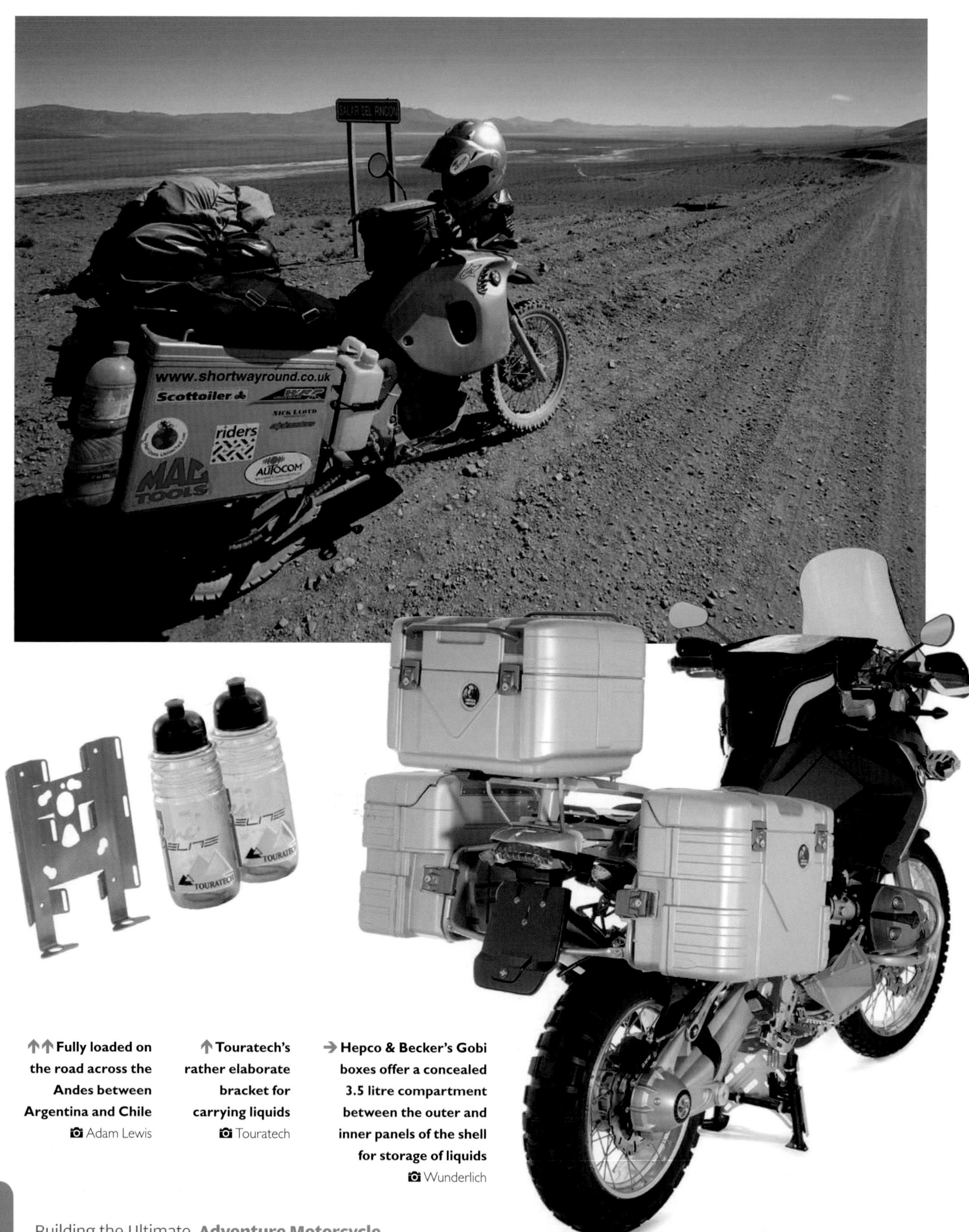

↑↑ Fully loaded on the road across the Andes between Argentina and Chile
Adam Lewis

↑ Touratech's rather elaborate bracket for carrying liquids
Touratech

→ Hepco & Becker's Gobi boxes offer a concealed 3.5 litre compartment between the outer and inner panels of the shell for storage of liquids
Wunderlich

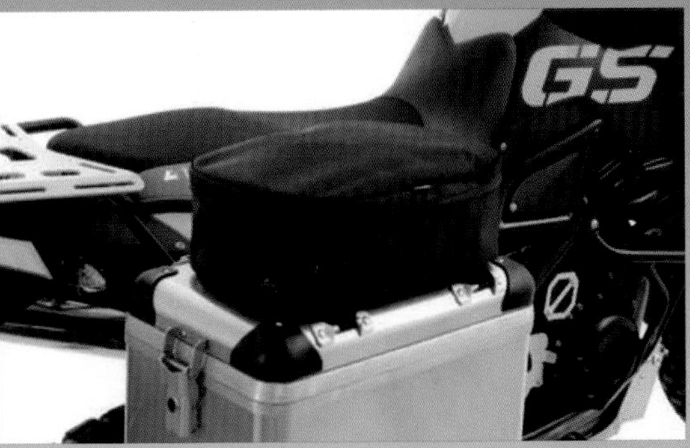

Tail bags offer easy access and are ideal for day trips
Pannier bags are not very secure for your possessions but do offer additional, expandable storage capacity
Touratech

Tail bags – these sit just above the rear light on a BMW and act as the ideal space for storing a spare set of gloves and/or levers – well out of the way but there if you need them.
Crash bar bags – Touratech produce a clever set of bags that can be attached neatly to the crash bars – not the best place for anything fragile if you happen to drop the bike, but certainly convenient and well located.
Pannier bags – if you're desperate for more capacity then a set of expandable bags on the top of your panniers is a good idea. These come with a non-slip bottom and straps to attach them to the top of the panniers. The downside is that they can make access to the panniers themselves rather difficult, but it's a very convenient place to store items you need to access regularly.

It's also really useful to consider a couple of different hiding places on the bike for essential things like emergency cash, a spare key, vital spares, and copies of important documents. Good locations include the space behind the headlight, beneath the seat, and inside the side covers.

When it finally comes to packing, apply the rule of mass centralisation – keep the load light and as close as possible to the bike's centre of gravity (CoG). Put heavier items in the panniers rather than in a top box or tank bag, as these are located too far away from the bike's CoG. The extra mass above the CoG has a direct impact on the bike's handling, making it slower to lean and turn at speed. Additional weight behind the rear axle will lighten the front end of the bike, further upsetting the machine's balance.

It will take several attempts to get your packing right, and as you spend more time on the road you'll get it down to a fine art and have easy access to all your most important gear. Remember to test the system before you leave so that there are no nasty surprises once you're out on the road.

Sorry officer, but my passport's at the bottom of my pannier and I'm having difficulty getting it out…
Wunderlich

Chapter 5
Personal equipment

BMW Motorrad

Having a well-prepared bike will not mean a great deal if you have various shortcomings in your personal equipment, which can make all the difference to an overland adventure.

Your kit will need to protect you from the elements and minimise the impact of an accident. Hopefully, by the time departure beckons you'll have had the opportunity to wear and test all of your essential gear – there's little point in throwing a new pair of boots on as you head off on the adventure of a lifetime only to find they're half a size too small. Your gear may need some adjustments, and subtle modifications can make all the difference on a long ride.

But it's not only about having the right riding gear. You'll be spending a fair bit of time off the bike too, whether that's asleep, eating a meal, or exploring the sights along the way. Your personal gear is just as important and there are some key choices to be made when it comes to tents, stoves, and sleeping bags.

→ **Touring helmet with peak and visor**
Lee Parsons

→→ **Motocross helmet and goggles**
Thorvaldur Orn Kristmundsson

Protection

Helmets

A good-quality helmet is essential and it's worth purchasing the best you can afford. The most popular helmets for adventure riding tend to be motocross in style – light and comfortable, worn either with a pair of goggles or with an in-built visor. An alternative to this is a helmet with a face that flips up and open. These can be very useful when stopping to ask for directions, as they reveal your face and allow you to be clearly heard – important when you're asking for directions. It's also less intimidating to the person you're talking to.

When trying on a helmet, make sure there are no uncomfortable pressure points (especially on your ears or forehead) and leave the helmet on for a couple of minutes to test if it really is a good fit. Try a range of different helmets before deciding and also make sure the one you choose has good ventilation, especially if travelling to hot climates. Also make sure you can't twist the helmet around too far or pull it off completely when it's strapped up.

Make sure you look after it properly, as it will take a fair few knocks when riding off-road. Keep it clean with a soft damp cloth and add a couple of drops of washing-up liquid in order to scrub off mangled insects and everyday grime.

The importance of a good helmet cannot be emphasised enough so be sure to make the right decision when buying.

→ **A 'flip-lip' is great for taking in the view**
Globebusters

↑ **Comfort on the bike is essential so be sure to choose your boots wisely**
Robert Wicks

← **These enduro boots feature a removable, stretchable neoprene inner, with the added benefit of an easy front-closing mechanism**
BMW Motorrad

Boots

Just as it's essential to have the right tyres on your bike, it's important to wear the right boots on your feet. A pair of comfortable boots makes all the difference, especially if you're doing a lot of walking and sightseeing en route, let alone looking for comfort and protection when riding.

Like an ordinary pair of shoes, good boots need to be broken in, so they may feel hard in the beginning. They should be durable and protective – don't for a moment think that a pair of hiking boots will do the job and help save on space. Your feet, ankles and lower legs need all the protection they can get, as they'll invariably get dragged under your panniers as you negotiate tough sections of terrain, and if you fall off they can easily get trapped underneath the bike. The boots should provide good levels of impact protection for the shins, instep, and ankles. A good set of boots may have metal sole inserts, heat shields, shin and calf shields, and padded heels to absorb shock.

Boots must also be comfortable, and you should wear long, relatively thick socks for additional foot protection when riding. The boots should be neither too tight nor loose. If they are too tight your feet may go numb, particularly if you're also cold. Check whether you can mount, ride, and operate all the controls freely. You should also be able to climb stairs, bend over, crouch, and pick up your keys from the floor when you're wearing them.

Many manufacturers now make a range of intermediate boots offering high levels of protection (much like a motocross boot with a quick release system) but with equally good levels of comfort such as you might find in a touring boot, and varying degrees of waterproofing. Ensure the fastening system works well and the clips are easy to lock and unlock. Try to purchase boots with aluminium buckles, which will last longer than plastic ones.

Comfort off the bike is also important (remember that you'll no doubt be walking around doing some sightseeing wearing your boots), so this sort of intermediate product is often the best possible compromise. For durability, try to choose boots that have removable soles – that way you can simply replace the soles when they begin to wear, as the boots themselves will last longer. Finally, beware of fancy features that may add to the price of the boot. If extra elements that make the boots look good aren't something you really care about, save your money and go for boots that are made for riding. The Dainese 'Virunga' and Alpinestars 'Vector' boots are good examples to consider.

↑**Unlined summer gloves are ideal for adventure riding. This pair from BMW features kangaroo leather palms and ventilation between the fingers**
BMW Motorrad

Gloves

Gloves are another important part of your clothing and serve to protect your hands against the elements, as well as in the event of an accident. It's important to make sure that your gloves keep your hands warm but not sweaty. Try on a few pairs before you buy, and select the right gloves for the right application. The gloves should fit snugly, but should not impede your ability to operate the controls, so your fingers must be allowed to move freely once in the gloves. Make sure that they offer ample protection and reinforcing to protect your hands, knuckles, and wrists.

A pair of good-quality motocross or enduro gloves work well in warm climates and you should choose a pair that's comfortable yet durable and with a good level of protection. A good pair should include neoprene protection over the knuckles, silicone fingertips for safety, a strong palm-covering with resistant overlays, and a long-lasting Velcro wrist strap.

If you plan to ride in extremely cold temperatures, such as Walter Colebatch on his Sibirsky Extreme expedition, then a set of heated mitts could be the way to go. He used Exo2's 'HeatMitts', which are designed to provide warmth and comfort for four to six hours on a single charge. Panels over the back of each hand keep the fingers warm while clever insulation ensures the heat generated by the panels stays in. The gloves also feature a breathable and waterproof membrane that provides comfort in all weather conditions.

If you're off on a long trip it might be worthwhile taking a spare set of gloves, particularly if you find a brand that works well for you.

Jackets and trousers

A proper riding suit comprising trousers and a jacket with suitable body armour is a worthwhile investment. With advances in fabric and armour technology, a textile suit is the best route to go for adventure riding. Leather used to be the preferred choice in the old days, but nowadays more modern materials (such as Kevlar and other reinforced materials) tend to offer similar or even better protection.

If possible, buy a suit that allows the jacket and trousers to zip together – this offers added warmth if needed, and also better protection by not exposing any skin in the event of a crash.

Another key consideration is making sure your suit is breathable – keeping the rain out while allowing sweat to escape. Look for a jacket and set of trousers with a removable inner liner, which can be used during both winter and summer. When it comes to buying, don't just try the suit on before you buy it, sit on a bike and make sure it's comfortable when riding. High-quality zips are essential, as are enough pockets, but make sure they seal properly. Ensure the armour is sufficient (knees, elbows, shoulders, and back) and that it all stays in place when you move around. Supplement the suit with a decent kidney belt for added comfort and protection of your lower back.

It's true that denim trousers can at least provide some protection, but they don't really protect against the elements, they take ages to dry, and when wet they become extremely cold. They're also likely to rip faster than leather or any other Kevlar or synthetic reinforced material. A proper set of riding trousers will also protect you from stones and other debris.

To further assist with 'climate control', use base-layer clothing made of 'wicking' fabrics, which allow perspiration to escape in the heat but retain body warmth in cooler temperatures.

Finally, as an added level of protection, you may want to consider a neck brace. This is a relatively new concept developed initially for the off-road race market, and comes in various guises. One version, introduced by KTM in collaboration with BMW, is made of carbon fibre and fibreglass-reinforced nylon. It's designed to help prevent extreme forward, rearward, and sideways head movements, as well as compression of the spinal column as a result of force on the helmet.

Slot for backpack drinking system tube
Reinforced in vulnerable areas
Stretchable, breathable mesh lining, with ventilation
Detachable sleeves
Waterproof outer pocket
Practical, easy-access pockets
BMW Motorrad
Stretch inserts for added comfort
Height adjustable knee protectors

↑ **Pack lightly to avoid carrying excess weight – as a rule of thumb, lay out everything you plan to take and then try to halve it before you even start packing**
Robert Wicks

Personal gear and equipment

Austin Vince proved on Terra Circa that it's possible to do any big trip without a tent or stove and with very little camping and performance kit. However, good equipment can make a huge difference. The improvements made in comfort and rest by wise investment will ultimately mean you have improved health, morale, and safety. The benefits of a good night's sleep, a good meal, and comfortable riding gear could really enhance your adventure.

There's an extensive range of kit available and one of the leaders in the field is Cotswold Outdoor, which has been supplying adventurers and expeditions to the far-flung corners of the globe for over 35 years. *Race to Dakar*'s Charley Boorman, GlobeBusters' Kevin and Julia Sanders, plus Simon Pavey, have all tested and used kit and taken advice from Cotswold. For more information go to www.cotswoldoutdoor.com.

Tents

This is your home, your refuge, and your personal space, so take time choosing the right model. Packed size, weight, pitched size, and the expected conditions all need to be taken into account. It's worth thinking about going up a size, as this will allow space for you, plus boots, helmet, and at least some of your gear. There are various types of tent available:

Dome – high at the centre and simple to pitch, usually with a small porch.
Tunnel – ground-hugging, stable, quick to pitch, and often with a large porch area.
Geodesic – bombproof construction and very stable, ideal for extreme conditions or at altitude.
Basha/Tarp/Bivi – super-lightweight and small, limited comfort and protection.

Tents either pitch inner or outer first, and many allow the inner to be left attached for quick pitching. If you're expecting it to be wet go for one that pitches flysheet first. If planning for hot climates, ensure the tent has a mesh inner that can ideally be pitched on its own.

Another consideration is doors and porches: storing and removing wet/muddy bike gear is much more comfortable in a dry porch than inside an inner tent. A well-ventilated porch with a wide opening provides shelter and safety whilst cooking in foul weather.

Understand the conditions you intend to use the tent in. You don't need a high-altitude tent if staying low in the summer, but you'll want to ensure that it's stable enough to stand up to a Saharan wind or a tropical downpour. Alloy poles and lightweight fabrics will mean a significant reduction in pack size and weight. Alloy poles are also more durable than fibreglass versions.

If travelling with friends consider having a small tent each. Then you may still be friends at the end of the trip!

Suggested products: Hilleberg Nallo 2GT, Vaude Taurus 1, Vango Banshee.

↑**Consider weight and size carefully when choosing a tent**
Cotswold Outdoor

↓**Adam Lewis sets up camp at Lago Liscanti in the Atacama Desert**
Adam Lewis

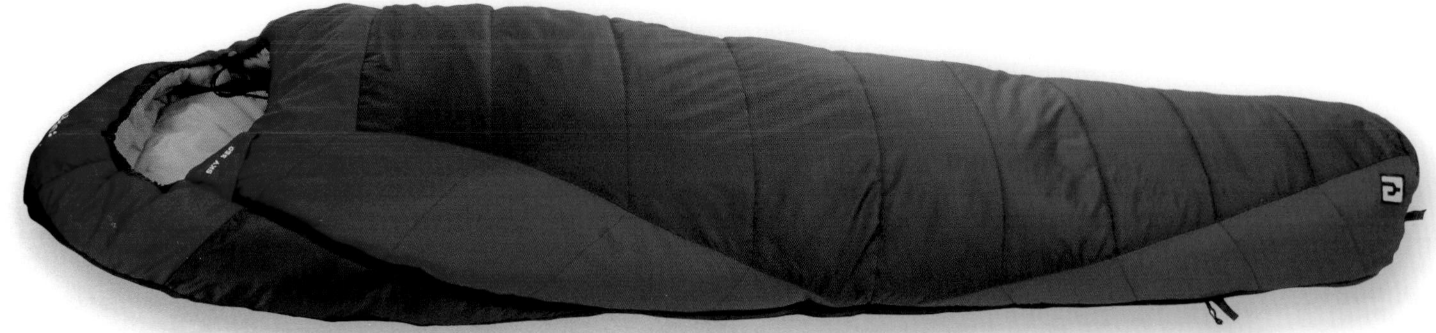

Sleeping bags

Invest as much as you can in a good sleeping bag and mat. Waking up cold, with stiff joints or feeling like your body has moulded to the shape of every rock beneath you, is no fun when you have 300 miles or 500km ahead of you.

When choosing a sleeping bag, consider the expected temperatures, available space, and weight. Synthetic bags (synthetic filling) are a good all-round option as they're easy to care for and will retain some insulation even if wet. They're the only option for those with allergies and also tend to be cheaper than down versions.

Down bags (filled with natural fibres such as goose or duck down) have the advantage of small pack size and less weight, as well as that cosy factor. However, avoid getting them wet and consider a dry bag for storage whilst travelling.

Sleeping bags are rated to a European standard and each bag is given four ratings:

Upper limit – the highest temperature at which an average male user would have a comfortable night's sleep (a sleeping bag can be too warm!).
Comfort – the temperature at which an average female user would have a comfortable night's sleep (women tend to sleep colder than men).
Comfort lower limit – the lowest temperature at which an average male user would have a comfortable night's sleep.
Extreme – a survival rating. This should be treated with caution and not relied on for general use.

Everyone varies on how susceptible they are to the cold, but the comfort lower limit is a good starting point. On a final note, use a liner. It will increase the warmth of the bag, will improve durability, will keep it clean, and can be used in a hostel or hut if hygiene standards are in question.

Suggested products: Mountain Hardwear Lamina 20, Rab Atlas 750, Ayacucho Solar 300.

Mats

Go for the best mat you can afford. Closed cell foam mats are cheap, effective, and robust, but it's also worth checking out self-inflating mats. Whilst generally more expensive they offer far greater comfort and a smaller packed size. They come in a huge range of sizes and thickness so try a few out.

A good mat and bag combination is key to a good camping experience. A good night's sleep makes you safer and more able to deal with the trials of the day ahead. Arguably this should be a more considered investment than your tent.

Suggested products: Thermarest and Multimat.

↑Consider the outer (shell) material as well as the inner (fill) material when choosing a bag
📷 Cotswold Outdoor

→Roll different mats out on the floor of the store and lie on each of them before making a choice
📷 Cotswold Outdoor

→ It's vital for a stove to be strong, reliable, lightweight, quick burning and compact
Cotswold Outdoor

→ This stove uses a self-sealing gas cartridge and is one of the smallest and lightest on the market and will boil a litre of water in just over three minutes
Cotswold Outdoor

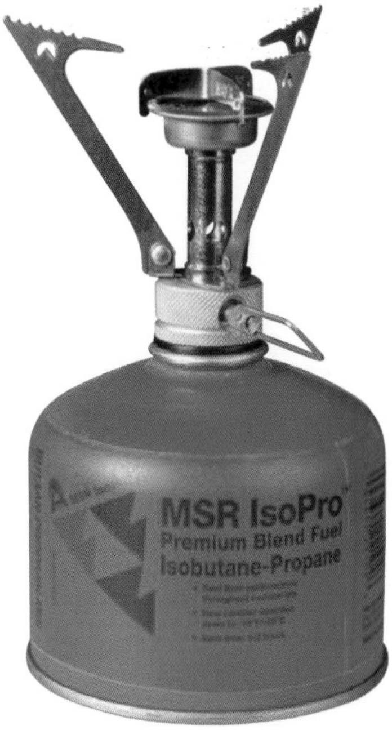

→ Panniers can double as a table in this clever arrangement from Touratech
Touratech

Stoves

A good stove can make a huge difference too. A hot meal at the end of the day or a quick cup of tea or coffee can be a real boost to morale. There are two main types:

Gas stoves – simple, cost effective, and convenient. Heat exchanger models and Piezo ignition have improved efficiency and ease of use. Outside of Europe fuel can be hard to find, and you have to consider how to dispose of empty cartridges.
Multifuel stoves – there are a lot of myths about these being complex to use. In truth, with a little practice they're as easy to use as a gas stove. They're easy to maintain, very efficient, and have the additional benefit that they can run on the same fuel as the bike (amongst other things), giving you a spare litre if needed.

Suggested products: Primus Omnifuel, MSR Whisperlite International, MSR Pocket Rocket, Jet Boil or Primus EtaPower.

Food

It's always great to use local ingredients and cook from scratch, but this isn't always possible, and pre-packed food certainly comes into its own as you venture off the beaten track.

Historically these meals have been an adventure in their own right. Fortunately this is no longer the case, with the latest boil in the bag or dehydrated meals actually tasting like real food! Flavours from curries to cooked breakfasts mean it's possible to get a good meal quickly by simply boiling a pan of water.

Energy bars, cereal bars, and gels are a great snack that can provide a quick energy boost to keep you focused. Keep well hydrated by using a hydration pack or regular drinks.

Suggested products: Wayfayrer, Travellunch, Go Bars, and the ever-useful Spork.

Touratech

Clothing

On an adventure trip it's important to have maximum flexibility in the clothing you take along. This can typically comprise base layers, mid layers, and insulation, which together will keep you comfortable and protected.

Base layers

Either synthetic fabrics or Merino wool. These work by 'wicking' moisture away from your skin, keeping you cool in summer and providing an insulating layer in the winter. A long day off-road can involve as much exercise as a run or climb. By drawing the sweat away from your skin the base layer will enable you to control your comfort and temperature far more effectively than a traditional cotton T-shirt. Base layers pack small, dry very quickly, and most contain an anti-bacterial element. This means you can wear them for longer and then wash and dry them overnight. Modern base layers don't need to be skin-tight so are no longer the reserve of adventure athletes – normal people can benefit from base layers too. Available in different thicknesses, you can combine them for an incredibly flexible solution to match any conditions.

Suggested products: Lifa, Icebreaker Merino Wool, Berghaus Tech Tee.

Travel clothing

Technical fabrics and the ability to treat them with mosquito repellent make lightweight travel clothing a real bonus to any expedition. They pack small and provided flexible options for different situations without taking up much space. Quick-drying and breathable, they work well as part of the layering system and are easy to care for on longer trips.

Suggested products: Craghoppers Nosquito shirt and Kiwi Trousers, Mountain Hardware Canyon shirts.

Mid layer

Traditionally a fleece, this provides an insulating layer under your armoured outer shell. For flexibility many lightweight fleeces are a better solution than one bulky piece. Also look at windproof fleeces, because they cut out a large percentage of the wind, reducing the wind-chill factor. A popular alternative to a fleece jacket is a thin insulated layer. These pack very small and have a high warmth-to-weight ratio. A well-chosen mid layer will double as the liner for an armoured shell as well as looking acceptable as a jacket on its own.

Suggested products: The North Face Windwall Jacket, Rab Generator Smock, Berghaus Ignite Jacket.

→ Base layers are fast drying and easy to wash – they can be rinsed out each night and will be ready to wear by the morning
BMW Motorrad

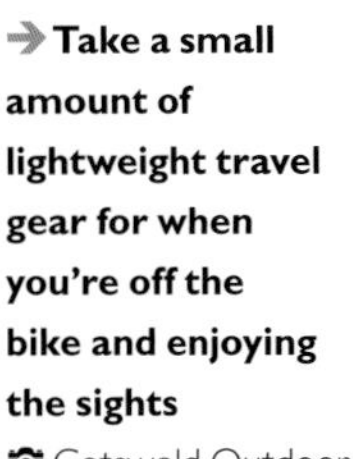

→ Take a small amount of lightweight travel gear for when you're off the bike and enjoying the sights
Cotswold Outdoor

→ You will find a water-resistant mid layer jacket very handy
Cotswold Outdoor

Survival equipment

In the event of an emergency, it's a good idea to either have a survival kit at the ready or be in a position to quickly gather the relevant items to take with you. Having a few key items can make the difference between life and death. Also, never forget that your mindset and your ability to remain calm and not panic are arguably your most important survival tools.

The importance of carrying an ample supply of water cannot be overemphasised. Humans will only last a few days without water, so it's worth taking as much with you as possible. The balance of the kit should be waterproof, compact, and lightweight, and should include:

- Water
- Water filter and purification tablets
- Food
- Emergency blanket
- Torch
- Sharp knife
- Compass
- Map
- Pen or pencil
- Lighter or matches
- Heavy-duty plastic bag
- Wire
- Basic first aid kit
- Personal medication

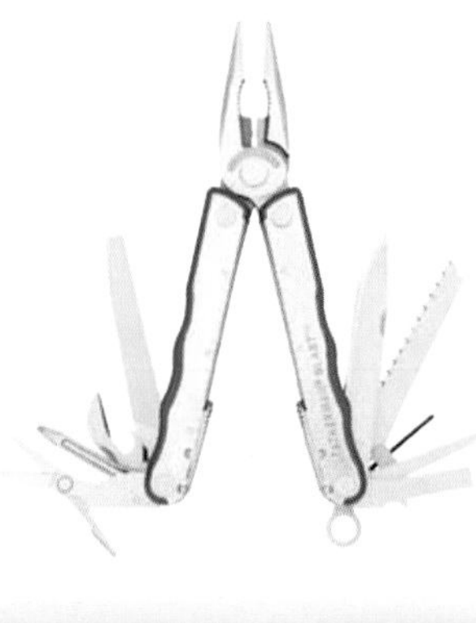

BMW Motorrad

PERSONAL GEAR AND EQUIPMENT TIPS FROM COTSWOLD OUTDOOR

- **Take your bike and panniers to the shop with you. Ask to try the kit on the bike to make sure it all fits.**
- **Take your helmet, clean boots, and gear with you and lie down in any tent with all the kit inside.**
- **Visit a Cotswold Tent Show, where you can see as many tents already pitched as possible and chat to the staff.**
- **Try to stick to meals that can be cooked in one pot – it saves space and washing up! Always take your rubbish away.**
- **Go for separate/different-colour dry bags inside a bigger duffle/pannier – keeps clothes, sleeping bags, and documents dry as well as improving organisation.**
- **Learn to pitch your tent and use your stove before you go away. If you've used the tent before check you still have the pegs and poles in the bag.**
- **Use small watertight bottles for fluids such as cooking oil and washing up liquid.**
- **Treat your kit with a waterproofing product such as Nik-wax.**
- **Try out a few different flavours/types of camp food before you go – choose the ones that work best for you and taste good. The start of the Silk Road is no place to discover you don't like the dehydrated chilli!**
- **When testing a sleeping mat, lie on it on the ground with a knotted rope underneath you to get a sense of the comfort level.**

Globebusters

Chapter 6

Case Study 1

Walter Colebatch

BMW G 650 X-Challenge

Walter Colebatch is a well-known adventure motorcyclist who has travelled the globe on two wheels for many years. His most recent challenge has been the Sibirsky Extreme Project – 31,000 miles (50,000km) across Central Asia, the Road of Bones, and the BAM Road, into the ultimate depths of Siberia. The idea was to push the boundaries of what is known and what is possible in terms of motorcycling in Siberia, and to set new benchmarks and ride new tracks that have yet to be explored by today's adventure motorcyclists.

Walter went to great lengths to plan and prepare a standard BMW G 650 X-Challenge for the depths of Siberia. This is the story of a remarkable machine.

Walter only got to collect the bike in late February 2009 and had less than six weeks to prepare it for the whole Sibirsky Extreme Project. He was scheduled to leave on 29 March 2009 and the bike was pretty much stock when he took delivery of it from Simon Pavey's Off-road Skills school. 'It had 375 miles (600km) on the clock and had just had its first service done. There were new Talon sprockets on the front and back and an F650 gear lever. It also came with one cracked mirror and a whole bunch of scratched plastic,' recalled Walter. There was much to be done to prepare it for the road that lay ahead.

↑ First launched in 2007 the G 650 X-Challenge is dominated by proportions of a typical enduro machine
BMW Motorrad

Origins

For this latest adventure, Walter knew he would need a very bespoke bike, and after much thought and careful planning he took delivery of a BMW G 650 X-Challenge, which began life as a BMW off-road school bike, based in what is now becoming BMW aftermarket HQ in the United Kingdom – Ystradgynlais in Wales. The BMW off-road school is there, Touratech is there, the BMW road riding school is there, GlobeBusters (BMW UK's adventure touring affiliate) is there, and expert bike-builder Bernie Wright is also based there.

Fuel tank

One of the most obvious needs for the bike was a larger tank, so one of Walter's first ports of call was the aptly named Hot Rod Welding in Holland, who specialise in the Xtank – a custom tank for the X-Challenge. 'I had toyed with the idea of a Touratech tank, then an Xtank, and even at one point considered both, giving over 30 litres of fuel both forward and aft,' said Walter.

Hot Rod Welding is run by Erik Bok, and his expert skills and ideas would come in handy for many of the tweaks that Walter wanted to implement on the bike, so before long, Erik's workshop became the base for Walter's bike preparation.

The Xtank is fabricated from 2mm sheet aluminium pressed shells, with four-point attachments and vibration dampers to form a strong triangular connection to the subframe. Walter had seen Erik manufacturing the Xtank

→ BMW placed the fuel cell under the seat on the X-Challenge and moved the fuel's mass down into the frame giving a lower centre of gravity and better balance
BMW Motorrad

→→ Hot Rod Welding in the Netherlands produced a custom tank giving a total of 30 litres
Sibirsky Extreme

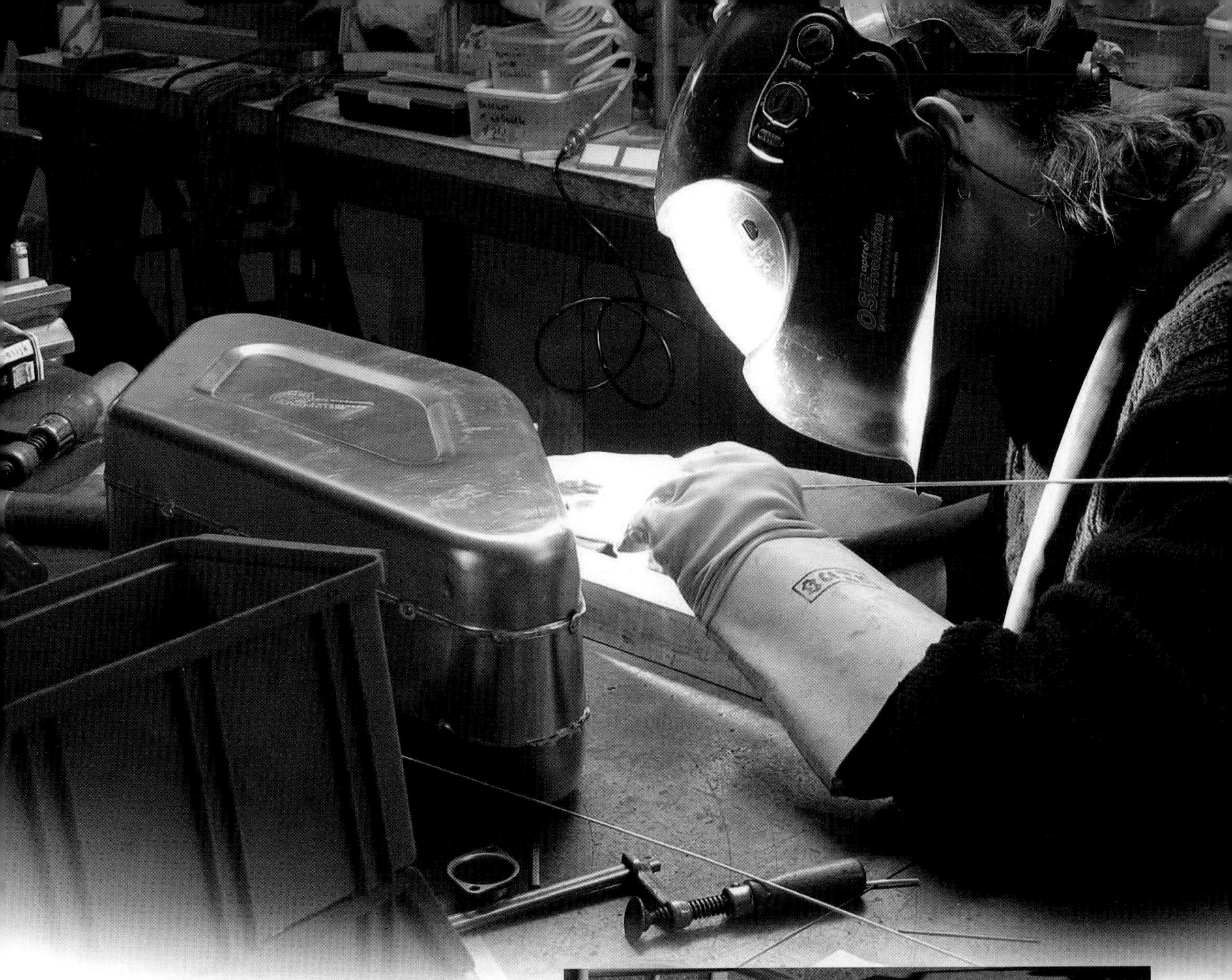

on an earlier visit to Holland, and asked if it would be possible to make a wider custom Xtank, with an extra couple of inches between the two pressed shells. 'When Erik said yes it could be done, it swung my mind in favour of the Xtank. If I could get a 10–13-litre Xtank, that would be enough, and it would be a neater, simpler solution.'

The initial plan was to add 50mm of width to the Xtank. Erik felt this would be the maximum he would feel comfortable with. The wider the tank, the more offset the mounting regime is, and this would lead to additional stresses – especially with the increased weight as well as the increased offset. 'At the last minute, as he was about to cut the 50mm strip, I got greedy. To hell with the risk, let's do 60mm,' said Walter. And so 60mm was added, giving the tank a volume of 12 litres (and the bike a total of 22 litres).

'Looking back, I probably should have stuck with the 50mm size. Erik was right – there are signs of torsional stress and the extra 0.8 litres I pushed for was probably not game-changing. That said, the tank worked very well,' said Walter.

The only problem in the whole fuel set-up resulted from an air leak where the electric connection for the main fuel tank penetrates the Xtank. Once that connection was sealed up with silicon, normal Xtank service was resumed.

A Remus aftermarket pipe helped to reduce weight
Sibirsky Extreme

Ortlieb bicycle panniers, a tank bag and roll bag formed the initial luggage system
Sibirsky Extreme

Exhaust

Walter had been trying to find a decent aftermarket exhaust for the bike. 'My first thoughts were not to worry about it, save some cash and stick with the stock exhaust,' he said, 'but I had a dream of having problems with the catalytic converter out in the middle of Mongolia or Siberia, and along with my drive to save weight and get more throttle response out of the bike I was determined to find a new exhaust option before departure.

'When I picked the bike up from the off-road school I managed to get my hands on a spare Remus exhaust and strapped it to the back of the X-Challenge – simple as that!'

Luggage system

The next 'essential' was luggage. 'I personally have never subscribed to the Germanic notion of steel or aluminium boxes – they're heavy, very heavy, and the frames required to support them are even heavier.'

A solid steel frame plus a pair of aluminium boxes will typically weigh about 20kg empty, and some custom-made three-piece sets weigh in at 25kg a set.

'Without wanting to get into the debate about hard versus soft luggage, I will say I've been riding to every continent over the past 15 years, and have never used hard luggage, never needed hard luggage, and don't see the need to start now. My opinion on them is that they're fine if you're sticking to highways and fast dirt roads, but are a major liability on anything more adventurous. They're also a lot more expensive!'

Walter had decided to try something a little different on this trip and picked up some Ortlieb bicycle panniers. They were super-light, waterproof, and easy to mount. 'When I got them in the mail I did have a few worries about the mounting system. They mount with 15mm closable plastic loops. In falls, I wondered how the plastic loops would hold up. Only one way to find out – suck it and see.'

Erik started from scratch with the rack. The pair had a few mounting points on the bike to work with, and knew they needed 15mm steel tube. One huge advantage of both soft bags and custom racks is the ability to move the bags forward. Standard fittings for hard luggage, even for bikes that are only ever going to be ridden solo like an X-Challenge, always have the luggage positioned as far back as possible. So not only is the hard luggage heavier, but it sits higher and much further back. This is bad for handling and puts additional stress on both the subframe and the suspension.

'We managed to rig it up so that the Ortlieb bags were carrying the weight in the same plane as me riding in a sitting position – *ie* very close to the shock. One thing we learned about the X-Challenge and luggage systems on the trip was not to believe for a minute that the aluminium subframe inserts where the mountings are located are man enough to do the job,' said Walter. Over the course of the first half of the trip as the threads all gave up they were increased from M6 to M8, and then M8 to M10. Each time it was just a matter of time before the next thread gave up. The only durable solution was to drill all the way through the frame and mount things through the square section frame using steel bolts, big washers, and Nyloc nuts on the other side. After modifying several of the mounting points in this manner, there were no subsequent failures.

Walter's early scepticism was right. The Ortlieb panniers did well, but ultimately the mounting system, which works for push bikes, was simply unsuitable for motorcycles. 'The mounting broke and I ended up reinforcing the mountings with steel and reinforcing the attachment to the rack with hose clamps/jubilee clips. The bags worked well, but could then not easily be removed from the bike – they were semi-permanently attached to it,' said Walter. 'Being a thinner material than the dedicated motorcycle panniers, they also suffered from abrasions, and a few holes began appearing after some falls.'

After nearly 22,000 miles (35,000km) he pensioned them off and replaced them with Ortlieb motorcycle panniers. 'These were good, well made, strong, and had a theoretically good mounting system, but the straps are too short and need to be extended. The only real downside was the size

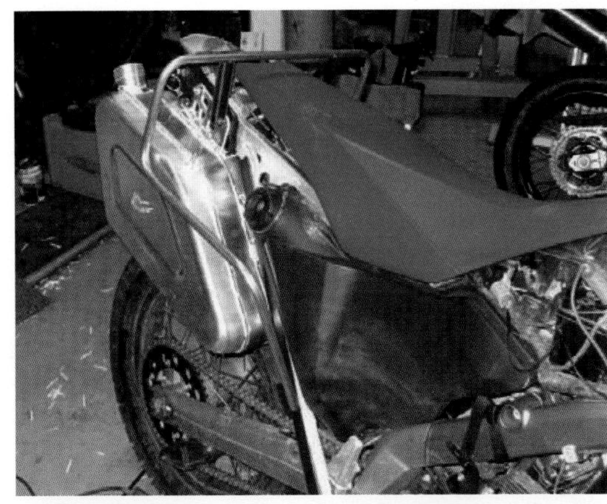

➔ The custom rack had to fit around the bespoke long range tank

Sibirsky Extreme

➔↓ The soft luggage was positioned well forward on the bike and lower than traditional hard luggage which helped lower the centre of gravity. A large tail plate would provide the base for a roll bag and other items

Sibirsky Extreme

– they're tiny. A bag that can barely take a sleeping bag and a couple of spare parts only is not big enough for this work.'

Walter's additional luggage consisted of a tank bag and a roll bag. 'The tank bag was good. There were some zipper problems as the trip wore on and I ended up replacing the zip at the same time I changed the cycling panniers. It was not completely waterproof, but enough that I was happy leaving my camera in there when riding through all-day rain.'

The roll bag from Ortlieb worked very well. 'The material they use is really tough. That bag has not one single hole in it after all the miles. There was battery acid splashing round there at one point which damaged a lot of the plastic at the back of the bike, but not the Ortlieb bag.'

Rally fairing

While Walter had been working on the luggage system in Holland, a phone call came in from Touratech UK – the front fairing and mounting system had arrived.

'The kit comes with Hella Premium DE lights as standard – a halogen low beam and 35 watt HID high beam, but as Touratech were backing me on this trip, I told them to save their money and not give me the Hella lights,' said Walter. 'I'm not a huge fan of them. The light spread is poor. They're nice and compact and weatherproof, but lighting modifications are my forte, and I was determined to do a lot better than the standard Des.'

There were two additional support brackets to double up the strength of the base of the tower (where it joins the neck of the frame). The instructions said: 'To be used in the event of extra hard riding'.

'I didn't think what I was planning to do qualified for that so left them off to save weight. I shouldn't have. The tower mount broke exactly where the additional support brackets would have braced it in the middle of one of the toughest roads in the world – the BAM Road in Siberia. I limped over 95 miles (150km) to the nearest village and had a couple of steel "bandages" fabricated to hold the whole front of my bike together!'

↑ It's not every day that a GB number plate makes it to Siberia!
Sibirsky Extreme

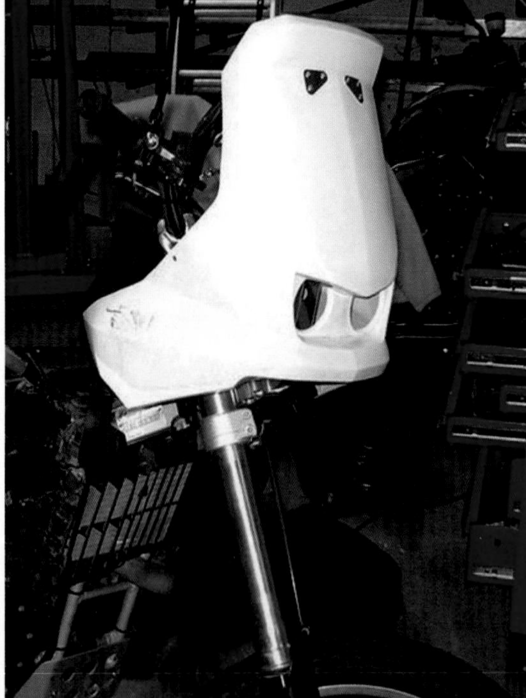

→ The fairing was supplied by Touratech
Sibirsky Extreme

Lights

'Some years ago I was riding two-up with my girlfriend in Bolivia. For whatever reason, one day we ended up having to ride the last 95 miles (150km) to Potosi in pitch darkness on a moonless night on a dirt track through steep mountains, 13,000ft (4,000m) up. All I had to see by was the poor standard headlight on the F 650 GS. It was the scariest three hours of riding in my life. It was largely guesswork, and if I got it wrong there was a massive drop waiting to break me, my girlfriend, and the motorcycle,' recalled Walter.

'I didn't plan on riding in the dark – no one really plans to ride in the dark when touring through Third World countries, but it happens. And if it happens when you have crappy lights, it's a real issue.'

Ever since Walter returned from that trip he has sought

the ultimate lighting solution and has worked on various headlight modifications and experiments.

'For this project I decided to take a pair of Audi A6 bi-xenon projectors – twin HID high beams but most importantly twin HID low beams. The lights would not run the standard Hella ballasts (which are bulky and heavy and a standard 35W) but HID50 slimline ballasts. They're about a third of the size, half the weight, and about 150% of the power of the stock ballasts. With twin 50W HID low beams, I would have the equivalent of about 350W of halogen light... on low beam! One big advantage of projector lights is the precise light cut-off on low beam. Despite pumping an enormous volume of lumens forward and on to the road, the razor-sharp beam cut-off ensures no stray light into oncoming traffic. Despite starting in the UK, 99% of the trip would be in LHD countries, and the headlights were LHD lights from the start.'

While Walter worked out how to seal them (the Audi projectors, like most car projectors, are open to dust and the weather at the bottom, since they normally sit in a closed plastic box), Erik built up a mounting plate for the two bi-xenon projectors.

The lights were then wired up with individual switches to enable:

- No lights to be on (useful when charging the battery or not wanting to drain the electrical system);
- Either light to be on; or
- Both lights to be on.

↑With a base weight of just over 140kg, the X-Challenge was one of the lightest possible bikes Walter could use as a durable adventure touring plarform
Sibirsky Extreme

←Considerable time was spent perfecting the lighting arrangement
Sibirsky Extreme

↑Walter set specific criteria for the seat and Dutch seat specialist Ray de Vries obliged Sibirsky Extreme

The front was rounded off with some LED running lamps, which served as parking lights/side lights, and would always be on when the ignition was on. 'Sometime after this was done, and with just one week to departure, some rationality crept into my head and I started imagining killing the electrical system with the heated clothing and then twin 50W HIDs as well. I switched back to standard 35W HID ballasts and bulbs to save 30W of power,' said Walter.

'My verdict – outstanding light both on low and high beam, particularly when both lights are on. My attempts at sealing the lights worked reasonably well given the fairly dusty conditions. Since then water and dust has been getting into the lamps, and they now need a very thorough clean-out and are working below peak efficiency with all the dust over the reflectors and lenses. On a final note, the electrical system on the standard bike is not the beefiest in the world, and the battery flattened a couple of times on the trip when running all my heated clothing. A modification I'll do in the new year is to put a 400W generator on the bike from an F 650 single, to replace the 280W stock unit. At that point, I'll revert to twin 50W HIDs.'

Seating

It was clear from the outset that the stock seat needed to be changed. 'I can ride 15 hours a day, seven days a week on a good seat, but one hour on the X-Challenge and my butt needed changing,' said Walter.

His Dutch connections again came into play. Ray de Vries is unique among motorcycle seat-makers. He actually rides bikes all over the world himself, and knows what it means to do long days on gravel roads, sitting down as much as standing up. He's done Bolivia and Mongolia and he knows what it's all about.

For this trip Walter needed a seat for all seasons and all purposes. It had to be wide and softer at the back, where he sat, and it had to maintain the narrow profile at the front so that it was unnoticeable when standing. Ray completely modified the stock X-Challenge seat shape and padding and re-upholstered it in black.

→Dutch-based Hyperpro provided the fully adjustable rear suspension unit Sibirsky Extreme

When it came to what material to use, Ray opted for three different types. 'I can't remember what and where,' recalled Walter, 'but think it was tough artificial leather under the tank bag, a slippery leather for the front where there would be contact with trousers when standing up, and a 'grippier' leather for the part of the seat where you actually sit when cruising – it's all thought of, designed for, and taken care of.'

So how did the seat perform after 31,000 miles? 'For me, perhaps the biggest unsung hero on the bike is the seat. I go for weeks on end without thinking about it and then suddenly realise the fact I haven't thought about it means it's perfect. What Ray has done to this seat is utter perfection. Anyone with an X-Challenge needs to have this seat – exactly like mine – because it's absolutely perfect for every kind of riding.'

Suspension

If there's one thing the Dutch do well, its suspension. 'It all started back in the days of Dutch company Koni being at the forefront of automotive racing suspension. Over the years, the wise guys at Koni began drifting off and starting their own companies, some of them motorcycle-related, like WP and Hyperpro. So while I was in Holland, it made sense to talk to a Dutch suspension guru, and that happened to be Bas at Hyperpro,' said Walter.

Bas didn't have to try too hard to convince Walter that the air shock just wouldn't work properly with a whole bunch of luggage on board, all day long. So a fully adjustable shock was built up around a purple progressive Hyperpro spring, adjustable pre-load fitted and progressive springs fitted to the forks. There wasn't much more Bas could do with the basic forks the X-Challenge comes with, but he did put in a thicker fork oil.

'The rear set-up was incredibly versatile. Set up correctly it allows the bike to handle like an unladen bike when loaded up, and that's a huge asset. I really like the combination of the top class damper with the progressive spring. It's very confidence inspiring on rough roads and at high speeds. I could never go back to stock suspension.

'And the front? Well, the front does the job. The progressive springs are a cheap way to gain some improvement and certainly enough for general adventure touring, but the quality of the rear set-up has now got me thinking (or drooling) about matching it with some sort of fork transplant for the front. It's probably not necessary to do anything to the front, but each change allows for faster, safer, more aggressive, more exciting riding,' concluded Walter.

↑ **When the scenery is this good you need to stand up and take it all in**
Sibirsky Extreme

Sibirsky Extreme

Cockpit

The final mission in Holland was to put together a workable cockpit solution – 'the office' for the next seven months on the road. The Touratech rally fairing comes with a mounting plate for a road book holder. 'That was something I didn't need, so it went into the scrap bin at Erik's. What I did need was a clipboard to hold maps and a good place to mount a GPS,' said Walter.

Erik made an aluminium clipboard and bolted the GPS ram mount to the back/top of it. Then the light controls (waterproof marine units sourced from an online boating supplier) were effectively countersunk into the map board.

The end result was a cockpit that was extremely functional and usable for travelling. 'I love paper maps, and I like to look at them when riding,' said Walter. 'If they're in a tank bag they're generally too low. You have to stop or at least slow considerably to look at them. The map board is up where a road book would be and does the same job... its navigation on the go.'

Having the GPS up on top of the fairing was a double-edged sword, though. 'You don't have to take your eyes off the road to see it, just change focus from far to near. No looking down. On the other hand, the Garmin Zumo is a heavy old unit. I will give them credit for durability, but they weigh a ton. Having that heavy lump of a GPS at maximum leverage with respect to how the whole front tower assembly mounts, results in a lot of vibration (or rather a magnification of vibration), and may have contributed to the "snapped neck" in the front subframe/tower assembly that I mentioned earlier. For future trips I'll have to rethink the GPS location – ergonomically its excellent, but for the bike's sake I might have to find some place better.'

Protection

With all the painted bits now back on the bike, Walter rode direct to Touratech UK, where his protection goodies were due. It was all there, less the bash plate. He proceeded to fit the hand guards and spoilers, radiator 'hard part', chain guide (rear), chain guide (front), and front mudguard (the rally fairing is not compatible with the original fender).

'I also picked up 20mm bar risers, but to fit them you really need to take the forks out or have a lot more dexterity than me, so I put them in my pocket and fitted them when I had the forks out for servicing while in the Ukraine,' recalled Walter. The large Touratech sump guard arrived a couple of days before he was due to leave.

His verdict?

Hand guards and spoilers – 'Very good and appropriately tough.'

Radiator 'hard part' – 'Not sure I needed it, in fact don't think it's been used at all as it's not scratched, but I guess it gives peace of mind knowing it's there.'

← An aftermarket chain guide for the front sprocket is essential on the X-Challenge
Touratech

Chain guides – 'Absolutely essential. The rotax engine is shaped so the generator cover is right in front of the front sprocket. I've twice seen 650cc rotax-engined bikes I've travelled with (including once on this trip) have major problems and risk breaking open the generator cover when chains come off. I had two chains break on me this trip, and the only thing protecting the engine housing was the front Touratech chain guide.'

Back chain guide – 'Similarly essential, as it stops the chain coming off the sprocket in rough riding when chain tension is fluctuating wildly. It certainly did the job, as no chain came off the sprocket in all the rough miles.'

↓ Back chain guide helps when the roads get rougher
Touratech

↑The Touratech bash plate is the best solution on the market
Touratech

↓An Acerbis front mudguard did the trick
Sibirsky Extreme

Front Acerbis mudguard – 'It did the job of keeping mud off extremely well – much better than the stock unit. But with this mudguard the bike can get hot and the fan works a lot, further stressing the electrical system. The rally bikes which also use this mudguard use a larger radiator. That's not really necessary for adventure touring, and besides, it's very expensive. I'm going to try a low front fender next year (from the KTM 990 Adventure) which will allow for better engine cooling and give me a good chance to compare the low versus high front fender.'

Bar risers – 'They were awkward to fit but did the job well enough and were relatively inexpensive. I still feel I could use more than the 20mm of rise. Rox make some well recommended risers that give 50mm of rise plus forward/back adjustment.'

Bash plate – 'I can't really say a bad word about it. I don't believe there's a better alternative on the market. The front bolts into threaded aluminium on the bike's frame. Like elsewhere on the bike, don't expect these M6 threads to last. Of the two M6 bolts that hold the plate on, one is now M8 and one is M10. The original M6 bolts have recessed Allen key heads, which are not the best. I think swapping them for normal headed bolts is a better idea.'

'In summary, there's a lot of Touratech stuff out there that could be classed as bling, but the reality is that much of their gear is designed for a purpose and works very well. The standards of machining are suitably impressive and while it's not cheap, the overall quality is very good.

'I wanted to keep weight low, so kept my Touratech bling at a minimum. For me there was no need for radiator stone guards, brake fluid reservoir guards, voltage regulator guards, brake disc guards and the like. I didn't get them and didn't need them. I was going to get a side-stand extension but forgot to order it and in the end never needed it. I also forgot to order the Neoprene fork socks. I regretted that and had to pick up a set (of KTM ones) in the Ukraine. The fork socks have worked though – no blown fork seals so certainly a recommended modification.'

Electrical

The final part of the preparation puzzle was the electrics, which were taken care of by extraordinary bike electrician Steve Hallam in his secret workshop in South London. 'Steve is one of those guys that you only ever hear about through word of mouth, yet his workshop has no fewer than 30 bikes in it, in various stages of electrical rebuild,' said Walter.

Custom bike magazine *Back Street Heroes* once described him as 'the most famous guy you've never heard of'.

Steve had prepared a couple of bikes for Walter over the years and has rigged up such outlandish ideas as a switchable twin ignition system for Dakar bikes – one magneto and one coil – just in case one system fails. 'Having considered my requirements, he proceeded to wire in five power sockets (three DIN and two cigarette lighter), both custom headlights – high and low beams, rewired the indicators, parking lights, GPS, heated vest and glove circuit, added a new fuse box, and in general tidied up my amateur electrical work,' said Walter.

The result was a completed bike.

Conclusion

'Every trip I go on gives me new ideas and tweaks to my existing notions of bike preparation,' said Walter. 'For me, the three essentials when it comes to bike prepping are:

- To make sure the bike can carry enough fuel to get you where you want to go
- To add sufficient protection to the bike to increase its durability and to ensure any reasonable fall can be absorbed; and
- To make sure it can carry the luggage you want to carry.

'In general, the rougher and tougher the planned route, the more the pendulum swings towards soft luggage. A general ride across Siberia on the Trans-Siberian Highway will be fine on a large bike with metal boxes, but the tougher and more ambitious the plan in terms of road/trail environment, the more the ideal bike and set-up switches to a lighter single-cylinder bike and soft luggage.

'I didn't really get everything I wanted from either type of side panniers I tried on this trip; neither the Ortlieb bicycle panniers nor the Ortlieb motorcycle panniers did the job I wanted of them, so I've decided to team up with a manufacturer to help design and produce the "perfect" motorcycle soft luggage.'

One concept Walter introduced on this trip was a 'map board' in the bike's cockpit. 'This was a huge success and something I'll be replicating in future,' he said.

'The larger adventure bikes like the BMW R 1200 GS come with seats that do allow you to ride around the world on them. People basing adventure bikes on smaller models, such as the F 800 GS or my X-Challenge for example, should have a serious think about getting a seat that will get you where you want to go without developing "monkey butt" by 5:00pm on day one – comfort is key to staying relaxed, and being relaxed is essential for good bike control and overall enjoyment.'

Any adventure bike build is going to be a compromise favouring the environment the bike is built to deal with. Some bikes are set up to deal with long days through sunny climes on endless asphalt. 'For the Sibirsky Extreme project, the modifications made to the bike were specific to the aims of the project: to cover significant mileage on forgotten dirt back roads and trails in Siberia, carrying 25–30kg of luggage, and giving me a fuel range of around 300 miles (500km); all on the lightest and most reliable motorcycling platform for the job.'

↑The map board and GPS combination is a neat idea but Walter was looking elsewhere before crossing this bridge
Sibirsky Extreme

Chapter 7

Case Study 2

Adam Lewis

Adam Lewis

BMW F 650 GS

In mid-March 2006 Adam Lewis and Danny Burroughs set off to ride around the world on a pair of BMW F 650s. Their route would take them across Europe and the Middle East, the infamous Karakoram Highway, India, and Nepal. From here they air-freighted the bikes to Bangkok for the Far East leg of the adventure. They then shipped to Christchurch in New Zealand, where, as can sometimes happen on long-distance overland adventures, the pair split up and went their separate ways, with Danny staying on in New Zealand while Adam continued on through Australia, East Timor, Indonesia, and Malaysia before shipping his bike from Singapore to Chile in South America. The first 18 months of the trip were featured in the Haynes book entitled *Adventure Motorcycling*.

Adam has since visited Chile, Argentina, Uruguay, Brazil, Paraguay, Bolivia, and Peru, but after three-and-a-half years and 83,000 miles (133,000km) on the road he's decided it's time to change his faithful BMW F 650 to a Suzuki DR 650. He's preparing the DR at a friend's house in Boston, so the 'second half' of the route will see him ride across the USA and up through Canada to Alaska before turning south to ride back to Bolivia, to pick up where he left off before his bike troubles.

Ahead of his departure, Adam carried out an extensive range of modifications to prepare his BMW F 650 for the arduous road that lay ahead.

Pre-departure modifications

Modification	Reason	Supplier	Comments
21in front wheel	Better handling off-road and more ground clearance	Talon rim and spokes built on original hub	Use in conjunction with modified rear shock
Stiffer fork springs	Better handling, particularly when loaded	Touratech	
Fork sliders	Protect fork stanchions from stone chips	Touratech	Can use gaiters
2003 Dakar screen	Improved wind protection	BMW	Needs home-made adaptor bracket if using on 2004 model, as screens are poor
Radiator guards	Stone protection	Touratech	
Handlebar risers (65mm)	Gain clearance between hand guards and clocks. More upright riding position when standing	Touratech	Requires longer front brake hose
Magura oversize handlebars	Strength. Magura are the only company that make heated grip compatible bars	Touratech	Can use any brand if not using heated grips
Hand guards/Brush guards	Protect levers in crashes	Acerbis	
Handlebar brace	Braceless handle bars	Homemade	
GPS mounting bracket	Vibration-proof lockable mounting	Touratech	
Large fuel tank (39 litres)	To balance loaded bike. Needed for extended runs in Patagonia and Australian Outback	Touratech	Supplied unpainted. Replace breather hoses with approved fuel pipe. Carry spare o-ring for Q/R fittings
Auxiliary wiring	Charging laptop, camera batteries, phone etc	Home-made	Use ignition-fed circuit to avoid blown fuses
Hawker battery	Long life, deep discharge, cold starting		Failed en route in Iran – faulty unit
Sump guard/bash plate	Protect engine cases	Overland Solutions	
Engine crash bars	Protect engine in a crash	BMW	Had to modify to use with Touratech 39-litre fuel tanks as both items use same mounting point in front of engine
Footrests	Larger size for better foothold	Racespec	Motocross size footrests. Require custom mountings
Side stand/footrest mountings	Improved design. Weight pushes through length of stand. Larger foot for soft ground. Mountings to suit non-standard footrests	Overland Solutions	
Centre stand	Needs lengthening to suit suspension modifications	Overland Solutions	Dakar models come without a centre stand
Rear suspension unit	Improved ride quality, especially when loaded	Öhlins, supplied by KAIS Suspension	Dakar shock shortened to mid-point between GS and Dakar length. Plain bearing fitted in cylinder head. Sprung and re-valved to suit load
Pannier frames and rack		Overland Solutions	Custom-made, including 'hidden' tool/spares boxes. Adjustable to allow for a pillion
Pannier boxes		Touratech, modified by Overland Solutions	Anodised, lockable clasps to suit frames. Stronger lockable lid clasps
Registration plate brace	Strengthen mudguard assembly	Touratech	

Adam Lewis

Pre-departure modifications

Modification	Reason	Supplier	Comments
Chainguard/speed sensor protector	Replace bulky enclosed OEM item	Touratech	
Exhaust system	Remove catalytic converter for using leaded fuel	Remus	
Scottoiler	Extended chain life	Scottoiler	Use large 'touring' kit. Carry a few spare 'injectors' and the screw-on nozzle for refilling; fitted to swingarm and bottom suspension linkage
Grease nipples	Longevity; ease of servicing		
Braided steel brake hoses	Extra length required for handlebar risers; improved braking performance	Venhill	
Headlight bulb	Improved performance bulbs		
Flexible indicators	Bend in a crash	Touratech	
Folding gear lever	Folds up in a crash	Touratech	Modified to operate correctly when wearing boots
Clutch lever – adjustable span	To suit small hands	Wunderlich	
Bike-to-bike jump start kit	Easy jump starting of bikes	Wunderlich	Access to battery requires removal of rack, seat, and cover. Add a fuse
Auxiliary power socket mounting	Requires moving when fitting 39-litre fuel tanks	Home-made	
Communications system	Bike-to-bike communications; music via MP3	Autocom	

→ **Adam's pannier rack was produced by Overland Solutions and included a neat tool box hidden out of view beneath the exhaust**
Overland Solutions

Post-departure modifications

Over the course of his journey, Adam's bike took a lot of punishment and required the implementation of a series of additional modifications to improve and strengthen it. These modifications are detailed in the table below.

Maintenance

An avid road, enduro, and supermoto racer, Adam not only meticulously recorded the modifications he's made but also a comprehensive list of his maintenance routine and the biggest issues he's experienced with the bike over the course of the ride.

Post-departure modifications

Modification	Reason	Supplier	Comments
Spherical bearing fitted to top of Öhlins shock	Multiple bush failures	Öhlins	See comments below on suspension
Increased lower subframe bolts from M8 to M10 and added Nyloc nuts	Multiple failures of M8 bolts		Plenty of material on frame lugs for modification
Cut away radiator fan housing to improve clearance to radiator	Housing had distorted due to heat and rubbed two holes in radiator		Had to send radiator away for welding
Removed solid oil return pipe (sump to oil tank) and replaced with flexible hose routed around the front of the water pump	Allows water pump replacement without the need to drain the engine oil. Lay bike on its side		Made new 'banjo' fitting by cutting both ends off original pipe and brazing together
Fitted washable air filter	Outback dust	Unifilter	Bike shops across Australia often oiled my filter free of charge
Fitted RaceTec 'Gold Valve' Emulators to forks	Improved handling off-road	RaceTech	Unbelievable difference. No more bouncing the front end out of ruts
Replaced aluminium seat bracket with steel version	Aluminium one broke		Home-made
GPS isolation switch	The Garmin 276c has a 'charge complete' light that stays illuminated even when the unit is switched off. This was draining the bike's battery		Home-made; use a switch with an LED

Suspension

Having used and worked with Öhlins suspension units extensively during their racing careers, they were the natural choice once Adam and Danny had decided to replace the OEM units. They chose a supplier that was known to them and explained the trip they were undertaking. The supplier contacted Öhlins directly to seek their advice, which resulted in a heavier spring being fitted and the unit re-valved. The hydraulic pre-load adjuster was also removed. Because Adam and Danny had fitted 21in front wheels to their bikes, a unit from the F 650 'Dakar' variant was used, shortened internally so that the length was exactly halfway between that of the standard GS unit and that of the Dakar. 'The front was one inch higher thanks to the 21in wheel and now the rear was one inch higher, but the problems started even before we set off,' recalled Adam.

He takes up the story: 'When I torqued up the lower bolt, the threaded insert in the U-bracket split, so I had a bronze one made at work and fitted a longer bolt with a Nyloc nut. Danny didn't have time to do this and a routine inspection in India revealed the original insert had split and fallen out, damaging the U-bracket, linkage, bushes, and bearings. When we removed Danny's unit we found the rubber bush in the top mounting had collapsed, allowing the cylinder head to foul the frame. When I checked my

Major suspension woes were part of everyday life on the road

Adam Lewis

R004
FNJ
Scottoiler
Bath Road Motorcycles 0117 9711447

shock, I too had vertical play and removed the unit to find the top bush had collapsed in just the same way.

'We concluded that the rubber bush was not compatible with the heavy spring and was being overworked by it. What was needed was a spherical bearing such as you'd find in one of the road-racing, motocross, or enduro units. We contacted our supplier, who seemed unaware that such a thing was available and instead sent us six replacement bushes.

'When the new bushes arrived I removed my unit to carry out the maintenance only to find the spring collar had broken. This appeared to have been caused by the impact of the unit cylinder head hitting the frame. I replaced the bush, had a steel spring collar made locally and wound off as much pre-load as I dared, as I was entering the "Raid de Himalaya", a Raid-style event held on public roads in the north of India. At the end of the first day I checked my unit for vertical play and found to my disbelief that the bush had collapsed after only 295 miles (473km). I had no choice but to withdraw from the Raid and fit my second bush. Danny and I searched every bearing shop we encountered in India and Thailand (without success) before another routine inspection of Danny's unit in Cambodia revealed yet another collapsed bush.

'As we unbolted the unit to replace the bush, one side of the U-bracket fell off! This was not repairable in Cambodia and Danny's father retrieved his original OEM unit from the garage and sent it via courier.

'While our bikes were aboard ship to New Zealand, Danny headed back to the UK and took the opportunity to talk to a senior Öhlins technician in Sweden. After explaining what had been happening, he agreed that we needed to fit a spherical bearing to the cylinder head.'

After a certain amount of haggling Öhlins acknowledged responsibility for the problem and arranged for the parts and all the work to be carried out free of charge. Adam concluded: 'I've ridden almost 45,000 miles (72,000km) since the shock was fitted with the spherical bearing and it has worked superbly. We stuck it out with Öhlins because the ride quality, for such a heavy bike, is exceptional. In Australia I had the unit serviced and apart from a standard service kit it needed an internal bush replacing (the coating had worn off) and the spherical bearing needed gluing into the cylinder head. I've lost no faith in Öhlins and will use their products again in the future.

'The top shock mounting bolt broke in Bolivia and consequently the U-bracket snapped (again). No parts were available at any of the South American distributors, but I managed to get it welded as a temporary repair and rode gently up to Lima, Peru, from where I shipped the bike back to Europe.'

← This is what three-and-a-half years on the road can do to your bike
Adam Lewis

Water pump

This was a weak point prior to departure, so Adam always carried a replacement impeller kit. The fault stems from a poor design in that the impeller end is supported by two seals, which, over time, wear a groove in the shaft causing water to leak. This is visible from the drain hole between the

← Adam stands alongside the fingers of a giant hand which reaches out of the sands of the Atacama Desert along the Pan American Highway in Chile
Adam Lewis

Adam fitted Race Tech 'Gold Valve' Emulators to the forks – these are essentially 'tuneable valves' that sit on top of the damping rods, held in place with the main springs. This makes them both simple to install and completely tuneable for all conditions and rider preferences
Adam Lewis

two seals that exits under the pump. It's not a difficult job but it is a time-consuming one. 'To help with the time and the need for finding a container for draining the engine oil, I replaced the steel oil return pipe (that runs from the sump, around the clutch cover behind the gear lever and up to the oil tank), with a flexible hose routed around the front of the water pump.'

Steering head bearings

'BMW have their own way of adjusting and securing the steering head bearings,' said Adam. 'I've now fitted four sets, which suggests their method isn't as effective as that of the Japanese. In Australia I had the opportunity to use the special tool listed by BMW and the first set I fitted using the tool did last longer – however, they still didn't last as long as I would expect them to, and the tool still requires the use of a torque wrench (the only hand-tool I don't carry). I fitted the next set using a non-calibrated torque wrench (all I could get hold of) and of course this set didn't last as long.'

Link arm bearings

'I've had to replace these on four occasions. They seem to be under a lot of stress (probably due to the heavy spring). They've dried up, flat-spotted, seized, and on one occasion stretched, elongating the holes, meaning I had to replace both arms as well as the bearings, bushes and seals.'

Batteries

Adam fitted a Hawker Odyssey battery prior to leaving

'Food first, then I'll fix it' – Adam makes camp
Adam Lewis

but it failed in Pakistan. 'All that was available was an $8 Pakistani-made one which lasted a week. In India I bought a cheap Indian battery which lasted until Thailand, where I bought a decent Japanese battery. When the bikes arrived in New Zealand my battery was dead (despite having been disconnected during the voyage). I finally managed to buy a genuine Yuasa battery (yippee!). However, thanks to my own stupidity, when I replaced the water pump in Queenstown I forgot to remove the battery and managed to partially dry out a few cells whilst the bike was leant over on its side.

'My bike regularly failed to start on cold mornings and on those occasions I would park it in the sun whilst I had breakfast, which usually did the trick. Although operating below par it did last until Chile, where I bought another Japanese battery. The location and type of battery is also an issue. With the fuel tank under the seat, the battery sits just above the cylinder head in the hottest part of the bike. Being a lead acid type, it tends to boil its brains out. Regular checks and topping up are necessary.'

Rear brake

'I don't know whether it's an F 650 thing, a single-cylinder thing, or a single front disc thing, but I find myself using the rear brake more on this bike than any other I've ever ridden. Unfortunately, though, the rear caliper is prone to binding and overheating and has boiled the fluid and glazed the pads on several occasions. This excess heat seems to have damaged the seals on the sliders, preventing them from staying clean. I've found that a repair kit called a "caliper pin cover set" from Motorworks contains exactly the same seals.'

↑Maintenance at regular intervals has been key to keeping the bike going
Adam Lewis

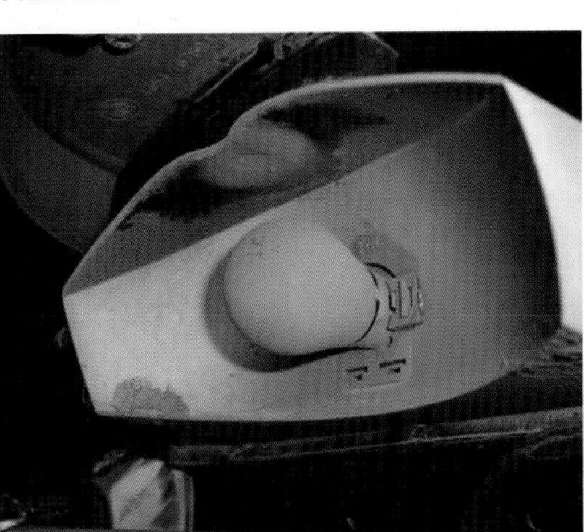

←Yes, dust does get everywhere
Adam Lewis

KNOX
Scottoiler.de
WRP
NICK LLOYD
riders
MAC TOOLS
AUTOCOM

↑**Early morning on the world's largest salt flat. Salar sits at 3,656m (11,995ft) above sea level in southwest Bolivia**
📷 Adam Lewis

Miscellaneous

'The Touratech flexible indicators bounce around a lot, causing the arms to split, and I've glued them several times. The bolt at the rear of the engine cradle broke so many times that I bought a length of M8 threaded bar and started making my own, but stopped counting after making six. Other than that, six fork seals, one clutch cable, one oxygen sensor, numerous head and tail light bulbs, a few fuses, and a fuel tank Q/R snapped whilst riding,' said Adam.

Conclusion

The BMW F 650 offers comfort, fuel economy, and roadside reliability. On the downside, it wears parts prematurely, it's not great at cold starting or starting at altitude, and experience shows that you need to carry a lot of tools if you're on a long trip.

The Suzuki DR 650

As has been said, Adam has decided to switch to a Suzuki DR 650 for the remainder of the journey. Replacing his BMW F 650 is an opportunity for him to take a slightly different approach and incorporate much of what he has learnt over the last four years on the road. 'Well, if you really want to travel off the beaten track then weight is the key,' he said. 'My F 650 took me to places I would never have believed possible prior to leaving home but at great expense to the chassis. A lighter bike and kit mean its gentler on its suspension so requires lighter springing, which in turn puts less strain on surrounding components – at least, that's my theory,' he added.

Air-cooling, adjustable tappets, and a three-bolt front sprocket on the DR 650 all bode well for overland travel. Being Japanese it uses a very small range of fixings, which in turn reduces the number of tools required and will add to the weight-saving.

'Unlike the F 650, it needs no special tool for the steering head bearings and a trial run proved I can break the bead of the rear tyre using just my feet and two tyre levers. That was something I couldn't do on the F 650 so

→**Preparation begins on the Suzuki DR 650**
📷 Adam Lewis

Nothing standard here – Adam's new dash set-up takes care of everything
Adam Lewis

I had to carry a heavy cramp to do the job. My toolkit for the BMW weighed a staggering 5.75kg and whilst I haven't yet been able to weigh it I think the DR toolkit will weigh in around 1–1.5kg.'

Fully laden but without food and water, the F 650 weighed 300kg and Adam is hoping the Suzuki will weigh in at around 220kg. 'I'm hoping that it won't just mean it's more reliable on the kind of terrain I've traversed so far, but that I'll be able to tackle routes that I would have considered off-limits on my F 650.' A smaller, lighter package will also reduce the cost of airfreight as Adam makes his way around the globe.

Another thing he wanted to ensure was that all tools and spares were carried on the bike, and not in his luggage. 'On many occasions I've had the opportunity to ride without luggage, but I've always been concerned about not having all I needed to repair a flat tyre or other issues.'

Of all the other overland motorcyclists Adam has met, the DR 650 has been the equally most popular bike, together with Kawasaki's KLR 650, followed by the BMW F 650 and Honda Africa Twin. 'Every DR 650 owner I've met has had the same thing to say about them – "They're bombproof!"'

SUZUKI DR 650 PREPARATION

The 2006 DR 650 was far from stock when Adam purchased it at the end of 2009 and came with the following modifications:

- **Progressive fork springs**
- **Trailtech 'Vapour' dash**
- **ProTaper 'evo' handlebars**
- **Barkbusters**
- **IMS 18-litre fuel tank**
- **39mm Kehin Flatslide carb**
- **Utah Sport bash plate**
- **Lock-wired neutral screws**
- **Large footrests**
- **Footrest lowering kit**
- **2in taller seat**
- **8.1kg rear spring**
- **GSX R 1000 silencer**
- **DRZ 250 tail light**

Before resuming his journey in South America, Adam plans to make a series of modifications to the bike. These are based on his countless experiences on the road over the past few years and a clear understanding of what it's going to take to give him the ultimate adventure bike:

- **Racetec Gold Valves fitted in forks**
- **Braided steel brake hose**
- **Screen**
- **Heated grips**
- **GPS mount (Garmin 276C)**
- **30-litre Safari tank and steel mount**
- **B&B bash plate**
- **Renazco 1in lower rally seat**
- **Scottoiler**
- **Rack with detachable hoop**
- **Pelicase mounted to a lockable Q/R**
- **Moto-Sport pannier frames**
- **Andy Strapz (soft) panniers**
- **Reworked (stock) rear suspension sprung to suit**
- **Some way to carry two 5-litre water containers**
- **Autocom (transferred from the BMW)**
- **Additional wiring for laptop and iPod charging (with isolators), GPS, heated vest**
- **Larger foot for side-stand**
- **Some way to carry two inner tubes**
- **Stove tap**

Keep up to date with Adam's adventure by visiting: www.shortwayround.co.uk.

Chapter 8

Competition rally raid

motorcycle

KTM

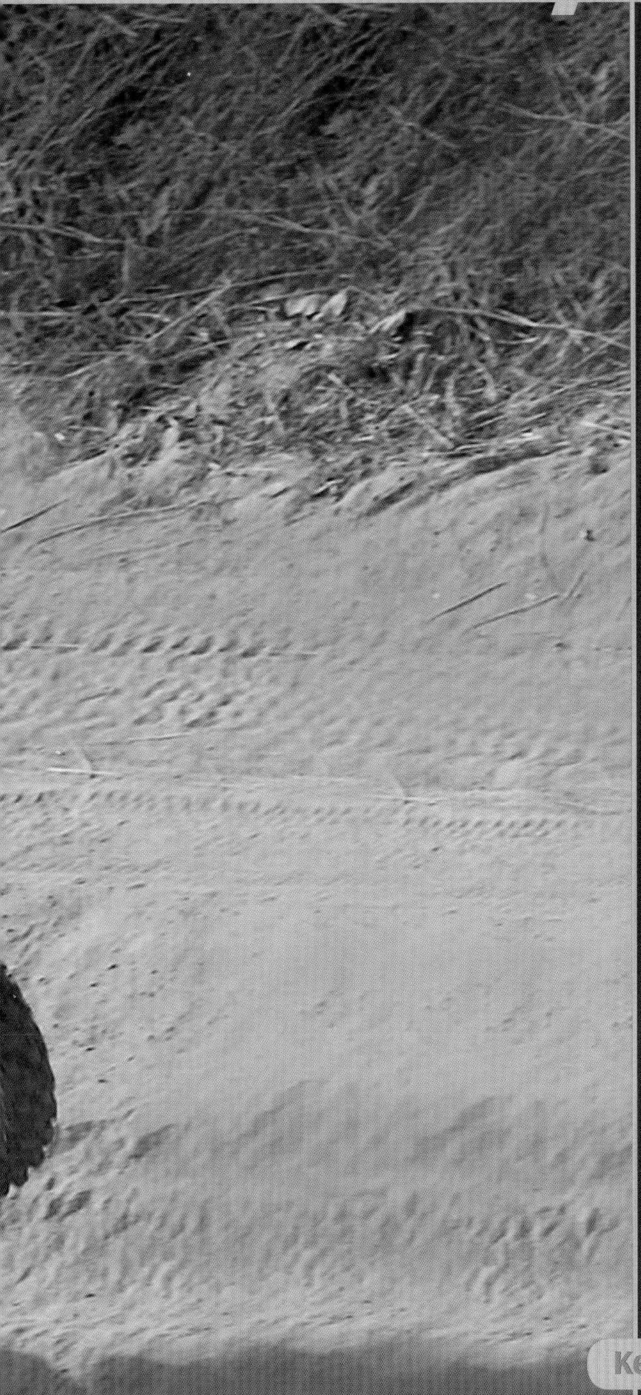

For many adventure riders, the epitome of adventure motorcycling is captured by the brave individuals who participate in rally raid events, best typified by the legendary Dakar. These are arguably motorsport's toughest events and quite literally push both man and machine to the very limit of their endurance.

Competition rally raid motorcycles share certain similarities with modern adventure bikes. Not only are they often the source of styling and design inspiration for what appears on the showroom floor, but the primary concerns of rider comfort and reliability are just as important. The other key similarity is the need for carrying capacity – not for camping gear, but for extra fuel, water, and spare parts.

KTM have been the leader in the rally bike sector for many years and a good example is their standard 690 machine – when comparing the rally bike to the standard model, the differences, particularly if you begin looking beneath the surface, are striking. Rally bikes are technical racing machines, designed to offer optimal performance, and put together to last through some of the most challenging environments for extended periods of time – the 2009 Dakar rally in South America ran for more than two weeks over a distance of more than 5,500 miles (9,000km). The other key point with a rally bike is that it's put together in such a way that when things do go wrong the rider is in the best possible position to repair or replace defective parts quickly and efficiently, as the clock is invariably ticking.

↑ **With a seat height alone of 980mm, just getting your leg over this beast is an achievement**
KTM

Key factors

In order to meet the extensive demands of the race environment, a rally bike enjoys a series of modifications, principally intended to:

- Strengthen the bike – in particular the subframe – to ensure it lasts the duration of the event (which in some cases can be as long as two to three weeks) and to overcome the threat posed by incessant vibrations.
- Offer the rider the maximum level of comfort over the duration of the rally.
- Provide the electronic components required for navigation, communication, and safety.
- Ensure the bike meets the technical regulations set by race organisers.

Writing in his book *Chasing Dakar*, Jonathan Edwards comments: 'The basic layout on a rally motorcycle is designed to put the rider in the most comfortable position possible. It is extremely important to have the handlebar position, foot peg location, seat height and controls adjusted so as to reduce rider fatigue while standing – one's ability to ride a motorcycle at high speed over unfamiliar terrain is directly linked to one's ability to control the motorcycle in a standing position.'

There isn't sufficient scope in this book to cover each point in too much depth so the following should be taken simply as an overview of the key modifications and accessories required for a rally bike.

Fuel capacity

Given the nature of off-road rally events, competing motorcycles must be able to go certain distances between fuel stops, as there's no assistance on the special stages. Regulations vary from event to event, but using the Dakar Rally as an example, bikes must have sufficient capacity to cover 155 miles (250km) plus an additional 10% as a safety margin.

The increased fuel capacity adds additional weight to the machine, which needs to be balanced out across the bike to ensure the handling isn't compromised. The importance of careful weight distribution is critical, whatever part is added to the bike, with the ultimate objective of maintaining a low centre of gravity without compromising on ground clearance. To achieve this, the fuel load (around 35–40 litres) is typically spread out across two front tanks (12–15 litres each) and two tanks on either side at the rear of the bike (5 litres each).

The fuel is used from the different tanks in a pre-determined order depending on the nature of the stage, so as to complement the handling of the bike. The tanks can also be drained simultaneously if the rider finds this to be of benefit.

Chassis

For many years the frame on a rally bike has typically been made of chromium molybdenum (chromoly) – described by one engineer as 'steel on steroids' – but more recently, with the introduction of smaller, 450cc capacity machines, aluminium frames have become more common and are further modified to deal with the harsh conditions of racing. The triple clamps are stronger and various tweaks are made to ensure increased stability and handling – essential elements in minimising rider fatigue.

Suspension

This is arguably one of the most important factors to consider when preparing a rally bike, given the weight and power characteristics involved, as well as the arduous and varying terrain that the rider will encounter. An adventure bike's suspension is relatively basic and can cope with some off-road riding but not with the stresses which racing places on a bike. Racing suspension needs to be set up in such a way so as to offer the rider optimal control across tricky terrain, but at the same time it needs to be progressive enough to take a large hit at speed and resist bottoming out.

↑**A look under the covers**
KTM

Engine

A rally bike engine requires increased oil capacity given the high speeds and hot climates typically found on rally events. Engines are fine-tuned to provide optimal performance within an agreed set of tolerances.

Lights

Most rally bikes have some form of enhanced lighting – normally in the form of a high-intensity discharge (HID) lighting kit – as being able to see at night is absolutely critical, and given the length of some of the stages it's always highly probable that some riders will be finishing stages in the dark. Most riders use LEDs, as normal bulbs are simply too vulnerable to the conditions. A second strip of LEDs on the rear light array acts as a warning light to alert other competitors at night if the rider and his bike are stranded.

↓**Engine protection needs to be substantial**
Overland Solutions

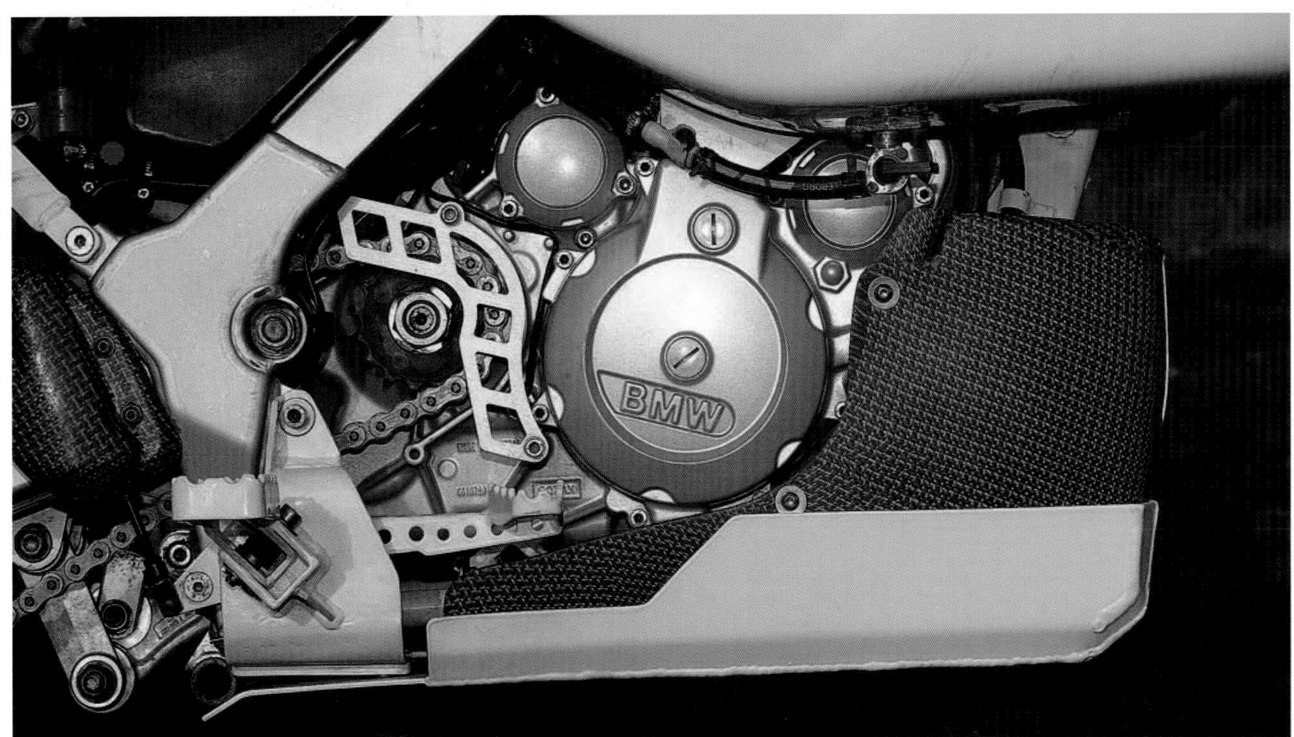

Foot pegs

To enhance rider comfort over long rally stages, large foot pegs are a must-have component. Competitors invariably stand up for the vast majority of the race stages and large foot pegs help considerably. Pegs are generally well oversized and extra 'grippy'.

Grips

Foam grips are highly recommended as they help reduce blisters and minimise vibration. Riders certainly find them more comfortable than the standard rubber grips found on adventure motorcycles.

Tyres

There is much debate about the different options available to riders when it comes to tyres. Today the discussion is about both the type of tyre and whether heavy-duty inner tubes or a mousse substance are the best solution for dealing with punctures.

Tyre choice is principally based on durability and traction and heavy-duty tyres are ideal given the long distances involved and their strong sidewalls, which are able to support the additional weight being carried. They're also more likely to survive a heavy impact from hitting a rock.

The puncture issue is a tricky one – tubes on their own are a massive risk, as the chance of puncture during a long stage is very high. The mousse is a solid foam insert that's fitted into the tyre where an inflated inner tube would normally be located. It's impossible to puncture this insert. Once the tyre with the mousse is mounted on to the wheel, it takes shape in the wheel in the same way that an inflated inner tube in the tyre would.

The mousse is fitted with a lubricating jelly (between the inner wall of the tyre and on the outside of the mousse) which helps keep it at as low a temperature as possible by reducing the friction between the mousse and the inside of the tyre.

When an impact is taken by the wheel, the tyre and mousse compress, as any normal piece of foam would under compression. When the wheel and tyre are free from this compression the tyre and mousse resume their original shape and allow the tyre to maintain functionality despite the puncture.

The downside of using a mousse is that it can have a tendency to break up in the hot conditions of a desert rally. The high speeds that rally bikes reach also contribute to this, and in the course of a long day in the desert the mousse begins to lose its self-healing properties, which in turn can affect the handling of the bike as it deteriorates inside the tyre.

Michelin have led the way for many years with their Desert tyre and Rally mousse combination and more recently Pirelli have started developing a tyre and mousse application in conjunction with the KTM factory rally team.

Spares

Rally riders need to be self-sufficient, as invariably the regulations prevent any outside assistance during the special stages of the race. As a result they need to have a stock of items on board should they break down or crash. Space is

➔ Handlebar switches control the road book
Overland Solutions

very limited and every additional component adds yet more weight, but it's not uncommon for a rider on a long-distance rally to carry spares for the water pump, a spare clutch, coil, spark plug, spare inner tube (only the front tube, as it can be used in either wheel), and a set of spare levers and cables. Everything needs to be crammed into spare spaces on the bike, and this is all in addition to the requirement to carry typically three litres of water on the bike in a tank built into the inside of the sump guard.

Navigation equipment

Navigation sets rallying apart from any other kind of racing. It's a fundamental skill that must be mastered over time if participants are to enjoy any level of success in the sport, and it may even play a crucial role in your survival if you get lost. The array of navigation equipment on a rally bike can at first seem quite daunting, bit it's important to learn about each individual component as well as how they interrelate with one another and thereby provide the maximum amount of information to navigate with confidence. That said, the real test comes in being able to take in the required information from the instruments without losing focus on the trail – simply put, it's multi-tasking at another level.

The suite of navigation equipment typically includes a road book, GPS, and odometer. Each of these needs to be mounted on the bike in such a way that it's protected from vibrations and easy to read while crossing rough terrain. Given the space constraints on a rally bike, the instruments are generally mounted in a cluster off the frame where the steering headset is located, in front of the top triple clamp (where the handlebars are mounted and the forks are clamped) and the front screen, known as the 'front mask'.

↑ KTM's service trucks carry essential spares, tyres and personnel between checkpoints on the rally
KTM

← Rally riding requires a fine balance between watching the road and constantly checking the road book
Overland Solutions

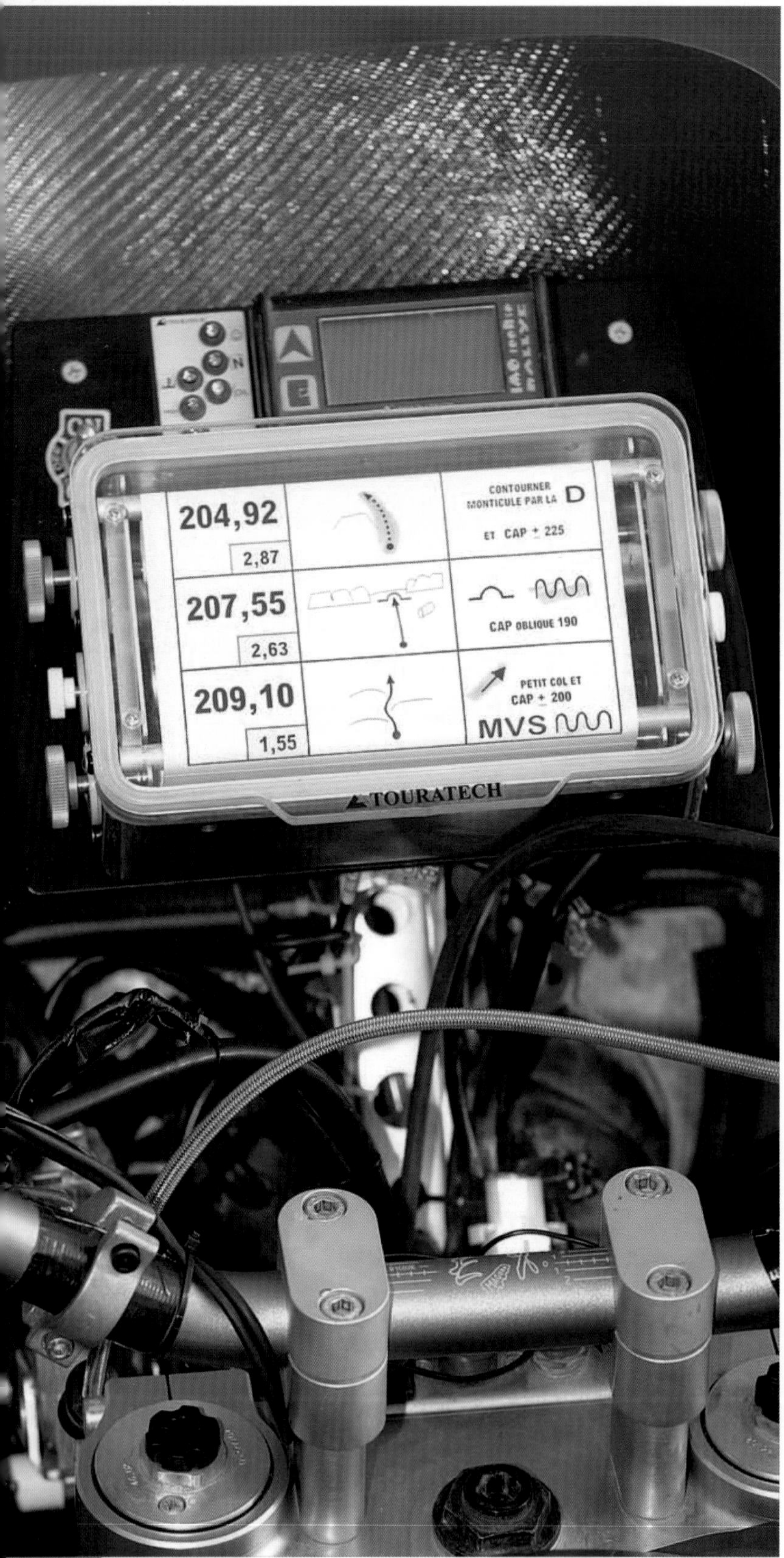

The road book

As we saw earlier, the road book is a set of detailed route notes in the form of a paper scroll which provides detail about the terrain and landmarks to be found along the trail at specific distance markers. It includes observations giving more information about each part of the route in the form of lexicon symbols and compass headings. In a major rally event, riders receive each day's rolled-up road book the night before that next day's start. Riders tend to spend a couple of hours reading the notes, and many tend to make coloured marks on their road book to highlight dangers and important landmarks. 'You don't have time to memorise much of the route, so you must learn to decipher the road book as you're racing,' says Charlie Rauseo of Rally Management Services, whose California-based operation promotes cross-country rally racing by providing rally training, products, services, and support for international rally racing (see www.rallymanagementservices.com for more information).

A good road book is typically a tough aluminium construction, with a strong motor that drives the rollers via rubber belts for forward/reverse operation. It should come with mounting hardware to fit to the motorcycle, and a strong two-way toggle switch. The belts can become clogged when sand and dirt enters the holder and this can have an adverse effect on the gears of the rollers, so avoid units with plastic gears which tend to strip themselves under wear. 'Road book problems are probably the most frequent mechanical failures during the Dakar,' says Rauseo, 'so use a quality item and learn how to fix it.'

← Riders use colours to highlight key points and dangers along the route
Overland Solutions

↓ Careful preparation of the road book is essential
KTM

↑Navigation skills are critical in top level rally events
📷 KTM

↑↑Road book courtesy of Nick Plumb, Touratech UK
📷 Nick Plumb

GPS and IriTrack System

Again using the Dakar Rally as the example, essential navigation equipment is compulsory for all competitors and is provided and controlled by the organisers, in particular the GPS. Use of any other system for navigation not explicitly mentioned in the regulations is generally forbidden and inevitably leads to disqualification from the race. It is each competitor's responsibility to correctly install the equipment before technical scrutineering takes place. Unlike the traditional GPS units common to adventure motorcyclists, a race GPS is a substantial and heavy piece of kit that works in conjunction with the Iritrack unit (see below).

'In the Dakar, the GPS has a very limited function,' says Charlie Rauseo. 'The rules change from year to year, but generally, the GPS will give you only your CAP heading (compass direction). There's usually no arrow pointing to a waypoint ahead. So you navigate using three sources of information: the ICO for mileage (distance), the GPS for your heading, and the road book for instructions on the route.

'In certain circumstances, the GPS will show an arrow directing you to the next waypoint, for example when you're within a one-mile (1.5km) radius of the waypoint. Outside of that radius, there's no arrow so it's imperative that you learn how to navigate using the road book, ICO, and compass heading without a GPS arrow.'

The GPS is integrated with the IriTrack System – a sophisticated communication system combining several data and voice technologies in a single unit that utilises satellite equipment to transfer information from the vehicle to the rally control centre. Inside the instrument is a GPS module, an inclinometer, a G-force meter, an Iridium satellite voice/data modem, and a microcomputer.

The system monitors the motorcycle's location and speed automatically and in real time, sending an alert to the control centre if the bike stops, takes a big hit, or experiences an inclination. The onboard computer records information every five seconds and sends this data every 120 seconds via the modem.

In the event of a serious incident the system allows a rider to trigger or request emergency help. If a brutal shock or a prolonged halt of the bike is detected, the system transmits an alarm message to the race control centre and indicates the competitor's GPS position. With the telephone function, the control centre can contact the rider through an automatic receiver pick-up and inbuilt microphone to establish dialogue and assess what assistance may be needed.

↑ This damaged fairing reveals the usually hidden IriTrack unit and assorted other navigational systems
📷 Meca' System

↓ The large lower bracket houses the ERTF GPS unit and is designed to absorb vibrations thanks to its integrated shock absorber system
📷 Meca' System

→ The typical rally bike cockpit is a complex environment to the untrained eye
📷 Robert Wicks

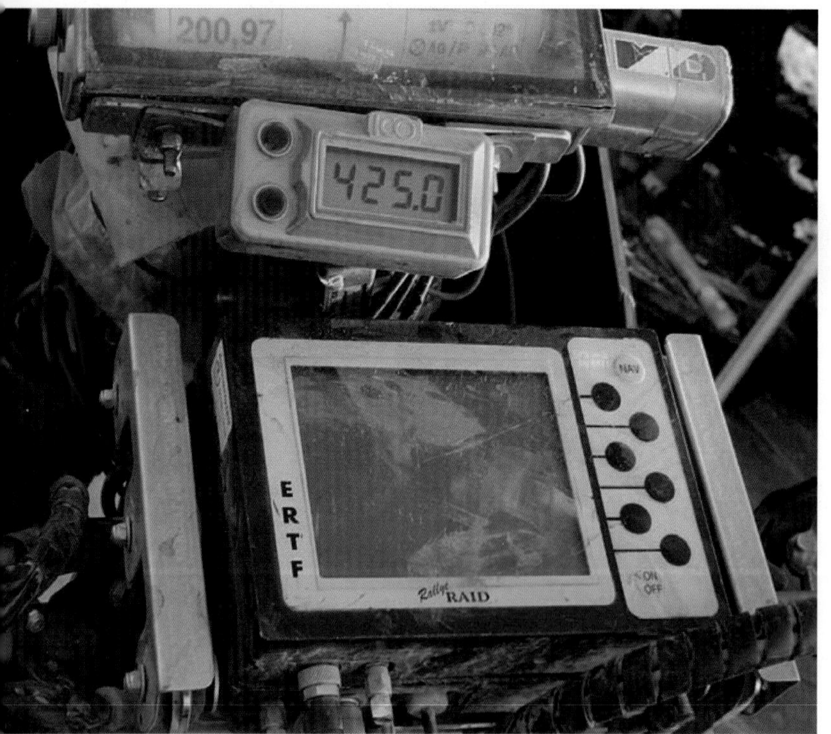

Repeater

An optional piece of navigational equipment is called a 'repeater' – a small unit that connects to the GPS via a cable. It features a screen that displays the compass heading and/or speed. This information is already available from the GPS, but the main reason for considering a repeater is that it makes navigation both safer and easier because it shows vital information up high, closer to the rider's line of sight when riding. This allows the rider to maintain more focus on the terrain ahead.

Odometer/trip meter (ICO)

An essential part of the rally navigation suite is an electronic odometer, the most popular of which are produced by ICO, so much so that this has become a generic name for such items. They're typically not supplied by the rally organisers but are still considered compulsory.

An ICO is a resettable digital odometer and speedometer linked directly to the rotation of the wheels via a pick-up sensor. It works independently and isn't linked to any other piece of equipment on the bike. It's such an essential piece of equipment that many bikes run a second ICO as a back-up, in case they make an error resetting mileage. Your life and correct navigation depend on having the right mileage, so it's good to have independent and redundant systems.

'Since the most common failure by far of the ICO is damage to the pick-up cable to the magnetic sensor on the front disc, it's possible to run only one ICO unit, but run two parallel pick-up cables with the second as a quick-change spare. The ICO cables and pick-up must be carefully routed out of harm's way,' says Rauseo.

Typical functions include:

- The ability to set your specific wheel size, which then allows for accuracy down to 15 feet per mile travelled.
- A handlebar thumb-switch for easy access to all functions.
- A display of the current speed.
- A clock which reads hours and minutes in 24:00 format.
- A peak speed indicator showing the top speed reached during an event.
- An aluminium plate for mounting the instrument to handlebar triple clamps.
- A sensor, which is mounted to the fork leg.
- A magnet with an aluminium plate for attachment to the front disc.

Typical dimensions are 100 x 50 x 30mm and weight is 120gm. It runs on two lithium batteries with around 200 hours of 'on' time.

Safety devices: Sentinel

Given the dangerous nature of adventure rally events and the varying speeds of competing vehicles (bikes, quads, cars, and trucks all participate simultaneously) safety is a

LED
FAN
LIGHTS
TOURATECH
STOP
TOURATECH
TOURATECH by ERTF
Dome
Snapon
TOURATECH
elf
france 2
w.com

'When a car or truck is near you, it may send a signal to your Sentinel which will sound the signal horn,' says Raueso. 'You're supposed to get out of the way. Remember that many cars do this a few hundred yards behind you, so you generally have plenty of time. Some cars don't sound the horn at all, which can be dangerous if they raise lots of dust passing you, and the fastest cars will catch most of the motorcycles.'

Sentinel is also fitted with a powerful alarm function with a range of up to 500m in open terrain which issues a warning if an accident has occurred or a vehicle has come to a halt but is out of sight. A sound and light sequence is triggered in all vehicles arriving on the scene, or approaching a vehicle that is stuck in the sand behind a dune.

↑Rally bikes need to be prepared for some of the harshest terrain
KTM

constant priority to both organisers and competitors.

The Sentinel system is put to good use in events like the Dakar Rally. Distributed by event organisers, it's effectively a safety horn, the function of which is to facilitate overtaking between cars, bikes, and trucks on the rally.

Sentinel is linked to the horn of the vehicle that wants to overtake. When the horn is sounded, Sentinel transmits the information digitally to the target vehicle up to 150m ahead in open terrain. The driver or rider of the target vehicle receives a sound warning (a 110dB buzzer) as well as a visual alert (a powerful 50-diode flashing light). He then replies to the vehicle following, whose race number has been digitally transmitted, by briefly sounding his own horn. The following vehicle then receives an 'OK to pass' signal (sound and light).

Development work

Once a rally event is over, the factory teams go through a post-mortem to see how their machine can be improved in terms of performance, reliability, and comfort. Invariably components are found which only just make the distance or are showing signs of the very severe loads they encountered. If the rally had lasted much longer these parts would have probably reached the limit of their reliable working life. There follows an extensive amount of development work to increase both the durability and the performance potential of the bike's components and systematically eliminate all potential sources of failure. You should undertake the same process after an expedition and seek ways to improve your own bike for the next adventure.

→The rally service park is a hive of activity after a day of racing
Meca' System

KTM
Typical rally bike specifications

KTM

Specifications

Engine type	Single cylinder, four-stroke
Displacement	654cc
Bore x stroke	102/80mm
Compression ratio	11.5:1
Maximum torque	69.5Nm/6,000rpm
Performance	70hp/7,500rpm
Starter	Electric
Transmission	Six gears
Carburettor	Keihin FCR 41
Control	4V/OHC
Lubrication	Pressure lubrication with two oil pumps
Primary ratio	36:79
Final drive	Chain; X-ring ⅝ x ¼in
Cooling	Liquid-cooled
Clutch	Wet multi-disc clutch, operated hydraulically
Ignition	Kokusan DC-GP 93-59
Frame	Chromium molybdenum, powder coated
Handlebar	Aluminium conified
Front suspension	WP-USD 52 MA
Rear suspension	WP-Monoshock
Suspension travel	Front 300mm / Rear 310mm
Front brakes	Disc brake 300mm
Rear brakes	Disc brake 220mm
Front/rear rims	1.6 x 21in/2.5 x 18in
Front/rear tyres	90/90-21in/140/90-18in
Transmission ratio	16:44
Battery	12V/8Ah
Wheelbase	1,510mm
Ground clearance	320mm (unloaded)
Seat height	980mm (unloaded)
Fuel capacity	36 litres
Weight	162kg

KTM

Typical rally kit parts

The key components that go into the make-up of a rally bike would typically include the following:

- Custom oil cooler
- Hand guards and deflectors
- Foam grips
- Rear dust lights and fuse box
- Switches for lights
- Oversized radiators (using originals)
- Steering damper
- Fuel caps
- Carb jets and needles
- Road book, switch, lights
- Rally computer
- Seat modification
- Horn and switch
- Cush drive rear wheel with disc
- Custom rally bar riser
- HID light kit
- 20-litre two-element front plastic tanks including supports and fibreglass trim
- Front petrol flexible hose kit with fuel pump
- Instrument support holder: stainless steel frame clamp, aluminium arc, roller support
- Frame clamp and damper tower support
- Fairing and lens support bar
- Road book and double ICO support plate
- Complete seat with suede cover
- Skid plate with removable water container and removable toolbox
- Low exhaust header
- Low silencer adaptor
- 5.5-litre aluminium right rear tank
- 4.5-litre aluminium left rear tank
- Rear petrol flexible hose kit with quick-release connectors
- External petrol tap
- Three-piece fibreglass unpainted fairing

←KTM rider Carlo de Gavardo clears a dune on the Dakar Rally
KTM

RALLY TRAINING

Anyone interested in getting into rally racing should consider a dedicated rally training course, provided you already have sufficient off-road riding experience. Be sure to choose a course which offers specific rally training rather than just off-road riding techniques, as they're related but different skills. The best schools offer both introductory courses, for those who want a taste of what it's like, and run advanced courses for competitors preparing for international rallies, where participants learn from experienced racers about navigating and keeping your head (and yourself) in the race.

Rally Management Services' Charlie Rauseo says: 'Cross-country rallies, unlike many other forms of off-road racing, involve a lot of mental training. You need to know how to manage your bike and body and learn to navigate using only a road book and compass heading.' His operation runs training events in various locations including Death Valley, California, covering everything from navigation training to desert, sand, and dune riding, as well as rally strategy and preparation training.

Appendix

Listings

Books

■ ***Adventure Motorcycling* by Robert Wicks** (Haynes, 2008)
An introductory guide to adventure motorcycling, this book covers every aspect of the trip, including basic practicalities, choosing the right bike, equipment, visas and carnets, riding techniques, maintenance, navigation, and how to deal with emergencies on the road.

■ ***Adventure Motorcycling Handbook* by Chris Scott** (Trailblazer Publications, 2005)
A great resource mixing hard-won practical advice with anecdotes and entertaining contributors' tales from around the globe, now in its fifth edition.

■ ***Adventure Riding Techniques* by Robert Wicks and Greg Baker** (Haynes, 2009)
The definitive guide to all the specialist skills needed for off-road adventure riding, written to give readers the confidence to undertake a long-distance adventure ride, whatever the conditions. This book takes a practical approach to adventure bike basics, riding techniques, crossing different types of terrain, riding positions, and survival. In typical Haynes style, using picture-led chapters and step-by-step instructions, this book covers all the key aspects of the techniques relevant to adventure riding.

■ ***American Borders* by Carla King** (Motorcycle Misadventures, 2008)
A thrilling armchair travel experience about a woman's solo 10,000-mile (16,000km) journey around the USA on a cranky Russian motorcycle.

■ ***Chasing Che* by Robert Symes** (Random House, 2000)
Covering an eight-month motorcycle tour of the back roads of South America, the author relates his adventures attempting to retrace the route taken by Che Guevara in 1952.

■ ***Chasing Dakar* by Jonathan Edwards and Scot Harden** (E&H Off-Road Productions, 2006)
An insightful guide with basic information for anyone interested in competing in the Dakar Rally.

■ ***Circling The Great Karoo* by Nicholas Yell** (Springbok Press, 2008)
Take a journey through some the most rugged terrain in South Africa with author Nicholas Yell on his old dirt bike, and enjoy his unique back-roads circumnavigation as well as interesting snippets of history, geology, and palaeontology.

■ ***Desert Travels* by Chris Scott** (Travellers' Bookshop, 1996)
Described as a light-hearted and readable account of various journeys by motorcycle in the Sahara and West Africa, as the author graduates from empty-tanked apprentice to expert dune-cruiser and desert connoisseur.

■ ***Dirt Bikes And Dreams* by Rod Brown** (Adventure Yarns, 2007)
A guide for the trail-bike adventure tourer which shows riders the easiest methods of setting both themselves and their bikes up for touring.

■ ***Distant Suns* by Sam Manicom** (Sam Manicom, 2008)
The third book by Sam Manicom as he continues his journey exploring Southern Africa and South America. The author is accompanied by his partner Brigit, and the book also covers the pros and cons of sharing travel with another person. For the die-hard enthusiast and non-rider, there is something for everyone in this wonderfully written story.

■ ***Dreaming of Jupiter* by Ted Simon** (Abacus, 2008)
Ted Simon's second round-the-world adventure (see *Jupiter's Travels*) comes to life in this wonderful book, a compelling account of the adventures en route, including breaking a leg in the middle of a vast plain in Ethiopia; a reunion with a camel rider he'd met 25 years before in Egypt; and crossing India and Thailand with Malu, 62, a former girlfriend. It's an evocative, poignant, funny and, as ever, very humble account of life on the road from one of adventure motorcycling's greats.

■ ***The Essential Guide To Dual Sport Motorcycling* by Carl Adams** (Whitehorse Press, 2008)
Aimed at motorcycling enthusiasts wanting to get the most out of riding on the road and off-road, with ideas on what to ride and how to enjoy the world's most versatile motorcycles – it's comprehensive, fun to read, and has good images.

■ ***Flat Roads And Twisties* by Ben Fourie** (International Motoring Productions, 2009)
A comprehensive adventure motorcycling resource for South African locals and overseas travellers alike – it includes chapters on general safety, routes, and areas to visit.

■ ***Going The Extra Mile* by Ron Ayres** (Whitehorse Press, 2002)
A handbook covering all aspects of overland travel by motorbike, with useful advice based on first-hand experiences from the author. The book is interspersed with black and white images and at the end has a resource directory of American companies and suppliers linked to the industry.

■ ***Good Vibrations* by Tom Cunliffe** (Summersdale, 2000)
Husband and wife team Tom and Roz ride Harley Davidsons across America. In Tom's own words: 'The ride of a lifetime was soon transformed into a pilgrimage in search of the American people who the Harleys dragged from under stones, off mountainsides, out of the swamps and the prairie dust. They looked after us, rode with us, worked with us, filled us with drink, took us to church on Sunday and to the cleaners at the poker table. A few threatened us. Most treated us like royalty'.

Robert Wicks

■ ***Planet Earth's Greatest Motorcycle Adventure Tours* by Colette Coleman**
(Motorbooks International, 2008)
Coleman's book offers a selection of routes from around the world, each with a brief description, advice on when to go, and introductory thoughts on the choice of motorcycle.

■ ***Into Africa* by Sam Manicom** (Trafford Publishing, 2005)
The first of a trilogy by the well-respected author and adventure motorcycle traveller, covering his journey from the British Channel Islands to Cape Town. As a gifted storyteller, Sam uses his ability to observe and capture everyday life and the people he meets along the way, enabling the reader to really experience his journey with him in a relaxed and narrative manner.

■ ***Investment Biker* by Jim Rogers** (John Wiley & Sons, 2000)
Investor Jim Rogers, who became a Wall Street legend when he co-founded the Quantum Fund, gives us his view of the world on a 22-month, 52-country motorcycle odyssey.

■ ***Jupiter's Travels* by Ted Simon**
(Penguin, 2007)
Possibly the most inspiring of authors and travellers, Ted Simon rode a motorcycle around the world in the 1970s. In four years he covered 78,000 miles (125,000km) through 45 countries, living with peasants and presidents, in prisons and palaces, through wars and revolutions. In 25 years this book has changed many people's lives and inspired even more to travel the world by motorcycle.

■ ***Kiwis Might Fly* by Polly Evans** (Bantam, 2004)
After learning to ride a 125cc motorbike, British-born Polly Evans flies out to New Zealand in search of 'the raw masculinity of the Kiwi man'. Upgrading later to a 650cc Suzuki Freewind, she finds the journey, the experience, and the men to be not at all what she expected.

■ ***Latin America In The Visor* by Angela Schmitz** (New Zealand Visitor Publications, 2007)
In this first of two volumes, the author takes the reader on a wonderful journey through South America – to the end of the world in Tierra del Fuego, to the Perito Moreno glacier in Argentina, to the Chilean Atacama Desert, to the waterfalls of Iguacu in Brazil, the silver mines in Bolivia, to Machu Picchu in Peru, and the tropical rainforests of Ecuador.

■ ***Lois On The Loose* by Lois Pryce** (Arrow Books, 2007)
With a promising career in broadcasting, but overtaken by an uncontrollable desire to get out there and see the world, the author packed in her career to ride her motorcycle solo from the northernmost tip of Alaska to the southernmost tip of South America. A great read for anyone considering a solo adventure.

■ ***Long Way Round* by Ewan McGregor and Charley Boorman** (Sphere, 2005)
Actor Ewan McGregor teams up with his friend Charley Boorman to travel from London to New York, through Europe, the Ukraine, Kazakhstan, Mongolia, and Russia, across the Pacific to Alaska, then down through Canada and America. Despite a support team in the background the pair face many of their own obstacles and encounters along their 20,000-mile (32,000km) journey. The pair went on to complete *The Long Way Down* – a trip from John O' Groats to Cape Town.

■ ***The Longest Ride* by Emilio Scotto**
(Motorbooks International, 2007)
Emilio Scotto recounts his world-record, decade-long motorcycle journey through virtually every country in the world, with more than 300 accompanying photographs. He set off from his native Argentina on a 1980 Honda Gold Wing called the 'Black Princess' on what is arguably one of the great adventure rides of all time.

■ ***Mi Moto Fidel* by Christopher Baker**
(National Geographic, 2008)
A bright red motorcycle proved the perfect vehicle to attract attention for a 'single male on a motorcycle loose on a libertine isle'. The bike drew stares, broke the ice, and made friends for Baker throughout his three-month, 7,000-mile (11,500km) Cuban ramble. Exposing the author to a cross-section of society and pursuits, the book has been described as an exotic escapade that fires on all cylinders.

■ ***Mondo Enduro* by Austin Vince** (Whitehorse Press, 2009)
In 1995 a group of British riders set off from London on Suzuki DR 350s for a journey that would take them across Europe and Asia to the Far Eastern edge of Siberia, then from Anchorage, Alaska, to Santiago, Chile, followed by South Africa, and finally back home to London. They called themselves *Mondo Enduro*, and this book is the trip log they kept throughout their journey. What sets this group apart from many other long-distance travellers is their unpretentiousness, their refreshingly low-tech approach, their gusto, and their marvellous upbeat attitude. The writing is fresh and immediate, and full of wonderfully understated British humour.

■ ***The Motorcycle Book* by Alan Seeley**
(Haynes, 2006)
This extensively illustrated all-colour book provides a comprehensive reference source for all motorcycle owners and enthusiasts, and is aimed in particular at those who are new to or returning to the biking scene.

■ ***The Motorcycle Diaries* by Ernesto 'Che' Guevara** (HarperCollins, 2004)
Documents 'El Che's' odyssey through Argentina, Chile, Peru, Colombia, and Venezuela on the back of a 500cc Norton motorcycle in the company of his friend Alberto Granado between 1951 and 1952, prior to his involvement in guerrilla warfare and becoming the Cuban Minister for Industry. Reaffirms the author's status as one of the 20th-century's most enduring icons.

■ ***Motorcycling Abroad* by Peter Henshaw**
(Haynes, 2006)
Written by past editor of *Motorcycle Voyager*, a magazine devoted to riding abroad, the book is targeted at the ever-increasing number of British travellers wishing to take their bike abroad, hire one while away, or even join a fully inclusive motorcycle tour. It covers everything from bike preparation and route planning to road safety, law, local regulations, extreme conditions, and emergencies. There's regional information about Europe, Scandinavia, America, Australasia, the Far East, and Africa.

■ ***Obsessions Die Hard* by Ed Culberson**
(Geotravel Research Center, 1990)
Chronicles the author's life-long dream of riding the length of the Pan-American Highway from Alaska to Argentina, including the infamous Darien Gap – an 80-mile (130km) stretch filled with jungles, rain forests, rivers, and swamps. A story of one man's struggle with his own obsession, this is an amazing tale of human endurance and perseverance in the face of staggering obstacles.

■ ***Old Man On A Bike* by Simon Gandolfi**
(The Friday Project, 2008)
At 73 years old, and following two heart attacks, Simon Gandolfi sets off from Veracruz on the Gulf of Mexico to embark on a five-and-a-half month journey culminating at 'the end of the world' – Ushuaia in Tierra del Fuego. This expertly written travelogue shares not only his journey of discovery in South America, but also to the USA and UK in the aftermath of the Iraq war, and the reality that is the corruption and resulting poverty for an overwhelming part of the South American continent.

■ ***One Man Caravan* by Robert Fulton**
(Whitehorse Press, 2003)
Originally published in 1937, the book recounts the legendary journey begun in 1932 by Robert Fulton on his Douglas twin motorcycle – an 18-month trip that included Turkey, Syria, Iraq, Afghanistan, India, Sumatra, Malaysia, Siam, Indonesia, China, and Japan. Adventurous by today's standards and tackled by a remarkable man, the book has now been reprinted to include Fulton's own photographs, maps, and charts.

■ ***Parallel World* by Nick Sanders** (Nick Sanders, 2009)
Parallel World charts Nick Sanders' seventh global circumnavigation and his fourth riding a Yamaha R1. Written on the road while riding an average of 12 hours a day across 41 countries and over 35,000 miles (56,300km) in less than five months, Sanders continues his record-breaking adventures.

■ ***Philosophical Ridings* by Craig Bourne**
(Oneworld Publications, 2007)
Philosopher and motorcyclist Craig Bourne answers numerous questions in this stimulating road-trip through philosophy.

■ ***Red Tape And White Knuckles* by Lois Pryce**
(Arrow, 2009)
In the style of a good old-fashioned adventure, seasoned adventurer Lois Pryce sets off to conquer

Africa. Without support, or even the usual 'taken for granted' gadgets such as a GPS or satellite phone, she tackles the Sahara, war-torn Angola, and the Congo Basin along the way. An inspirational read!

■ ***Riding High* by Ted Simon** (Jupitala, 1998)
Following on from his much praised *Jupiter's Travels*, Ted Simon recounts many untold episodes, both dramatic and hilarious, from his famous journey, as well as his efforts in later years to settle back into normal domestic life. The contrast makes it all too clear that great journeys become an expression of life itself and that, once begun, they continue as long as there's life left.

■ ***Riding The World* by Gregory Frazier** (BowTie Press, 2005)
A resource for novices and well-travelled riders alike, from the initial planning stages of routes, budgeting, choosing a bike, and modifications for travel, to research on sponsorship and motorcycle networking possibilities.

■ ***The Road Gets Better From Here* by Adrian Scott** (Virtualbookworm.com, 2008)
Having an affinity with Russia after travelling on Russian cruise ships as a child, and his fluency in Russian, the author travels 12,500 miles (20,000km) cross nine countries in three months to fulfil a lifelong dream. A novice with barely any experience and no back-up, the journey brings adventures beyond belief in Siberia, central Russia, Kazakhstan, western China, Turkmenistan, ancient Persia, and his destination of Istanbul.

■ ***The Road To Gobblers Knob* by Geoff Hill** (Blackstaff Press, 2007)
Geoff Hill takes his Triumph Tiger on a 16,500-mile (26,500km) journey along the Pan-American Highway from Chile to Alaska.

■ ***Rough Guide: First Time Around The World* by Doug Lansky** (Rough Guides, 2010)
Not specifically a motorcycling title, but an indispensable Rough Guide all the same. Covering the increasingly popular round-the-world travel option, this guide turns the planning process into a few easy steps that will make the most of your journey. Wherever you're starting from and whatever your budget, the guide covers key topics such as health, insurance, visas, advice on what to avoid, and the best places to visit.

■ ***The Rugged Road* by Theresa Wallach** (Panther, 2007)
One of the most amazing motorcycle journeys ever told, it details the guts, skill, bravery, and determination it took for two women to ride an early 1930s, 600cc Panther motorcycle with a custom-fitted sidecar and a trailer the entire length of Africa – in 1934!

■ ***Running With The Moon* by Jonny Bealby** (Arrow, 1996)
Two years after his fiancée unexpectedly died, Jonny Bealby takes up a journey to help find meaning in life – he sets off on a motorcycle trip around Africa in a story that is bittersweet, bold, and beautifully told.

■ ***Sahara Overland* by Chris Scott** (Trailblazer Publications, 2004)
Quite simply anything and everything you need to know about desert travel and the Sahara region. The author has an immense wealth of knowledge and experience in this field, which he brings together in a comprehensively illustrated guide coupled with numerous maps and local insight.

■ ***Scooters In The Sahara* by Dennis Robinson** (Dennis Robinson, 2006)
The story of an intrepid group of adventurers who rode from Carmarthen in Wales to Bansang in the Gambia on Honda C90 scooters. Not only were the team donating the scooters but also a fully-loaded van with medical supplies and equipment to the Bansang Hospital. Humbling for those who took part, and for the reader.

■ ***Sore Bums Rattling Around Asia* by Simon and Georgie McCarthy** (Simon McCarthy, 2005)
The first sign of a successful trip is that the co-authors weren't married when they did the trip but are now – especially when the trip was pillion until Nepal, when Georgie got her own bike! By the end of the journey the pair had travelled through 25 countries from England to Japan and back again.

■ ***Ten Years On Two Wheels* by Helge Pedersen** (Elfin Cove Press, 1998)
One of the best adventure motorcycling books available – if you can find a copy! This is a 200-plus page large glossy book with tons of photos and maps, recently updated to include Helge's latest journey through Siberia, Mongolia, and China. One man, one machine, and over 250,000 miles (402,000km) in the saddle – a fascinating read.

■ ***These Are The Days That Must Happen To You* by Dan Walsh** (Century, 2009)
Described as the pre-eminent biker-rebel of our generation, Dan Walsh sees the world in a different light during his hilarious and adrenaline-soaked bike trek around the world aboard a BMW F 650 GS Dakar.

■ ***Travel Time* by Herbert Schwartz** (Touratech, 2007)
A photographic journal covering five years and five tours of Tibet, Bolivia, Mexico City to Baja California, north to south through the Western USA, and through the Namibian desert up to the Angolan border, by founder and director of Touratech, Herbert Schwarz. The journeys – taken predominantly to test Touratech's products – have taken on a life of their own, and inspired this record of the different adventures.

■ ***Twisting Throttle* by Mike Hyde** (HarperCollins, 2009)
The witty tales of a mid-life crisis that took an ordinary Kiwi bloke alone around the USA and Australia on a motorbike, to fulfil what he calls 'Easy Rider-inspired dreams of his long-lost youth'. Both stories are told with self-deprecating wit and uncompromising humour.

■ ***Two Wheels Through Terror* by Glen Heggstad** (Whitehorse Press, 2004)
Departing from California in the wake of the September 11 tragedy in 2001, the author sets off to fulfil a lifelong ambition of circumnavigating South America. Travelling through Mexico to Colombia in a remote terrorist-run jungle, he is captured and forced to endure weeks of physical and psychological torture before finally escaping on another motorcycle. Gripping reading and a little different from the usual motorcycle adventure story.

■ ***Two Wheels To Adventure* by Danny Liska** (Bigfoot Publishing, 2004)
Liska was the first person to complete the 95,000 miles (153,000km) between the Arctic Circle and the tip of South America. The feat earned him the honour of being included in the *Guinness Book of Motorcycle Facts and Feats* as a 'champion rider' along the Pan-American Highway. A huge 755 pages of pure adventure, including a photo or illustration on every page, the book is now into its second edition.

■ ***Under Asian Skies* by Sam Manicom** (Sam Manicom, 2007)
The sequel to his first book *Into Africa*, this wonderful account details Sam's great adventure in the Australian Outback, Thailand, India, and Turkey, in his unique and effortless style.

■ ***Uneasy Rider: Travels Through A Mid-life Crisis* by Mike Carter** (Ebury Press, 2009)
Mike Carter sets off to travel 20,000 miles (32,000km) through Europe, reaching the four extremes of the continent – the Arctic Circle in the north, the Mediterranean coast in the south, the Portuguese Atlantic to the west, and the Iraqi border of Turkey in the east. An inspiring read.

■ ***Way To Go* by Geoff Hill** (Blackstaff Press, 2005)
Brings together two epic motorcycle journeys, from Belfast to Delhi on a Royal Enfield, and from Chicago to LA on a Harley Davidson. A thoughtful, hilarious, off-beat adventure story by award-winning travel journalist Geoff Hill.

■ ***World Understanding On Two Wheels* by Paul Pratt** (P.R. Pratt, 1980)
This is an excellent albeit rather dated introduction to overland travel, mixed with a travelogue of the journey taken by Paul Pratt over a course of 12 years in the 1960s and 1970s covering 115,000 miles (190,000km) across 48 countries.

■ ***Zen and Art of Motorcycle Maintenance* by Robert Pirsig** (HarperCollins, 2006)
This isn't as much about motorcycles as it is about philosophy. The backdrop is a 17-day motorcycle journey across the United States for author Robert Pirsig. The journey is punctuated by a series of philosophical discussions. The book sold over four million copies in 27 languages and has been described as 'the most widely read philosophy book, ever'. It was originally rejected by 121 publishers, more than any other bestselling book.

DVDs

- **The Achievable Dream**
- **Amazonas**
- **Long Way Down and Long Way Round**
- **Miles Ahead – endurance and adventure against the clock**
- **Mondo Enduro**
- **Moto Syberia**
- **The Ride – Alaska to Patagonia**
- **Riding Asia – London to Beijing**
- **Riding South America – Peru and Patagonia**
- **Siberian Extreme**
- **Terra Circa**

Websites

GENERAL INFORMATION AND FORUMS

www.adventuremotorcycle.org
Find up-to-date motorcycle touring companies, information on motorcycle tours and holidays, and the chance to log your own travel story.

www.adventure-motorcycling.com
Website of Chris Scott, who specialises in desert adventures and is the author of books including *Desert Travels*, *Sahara Overland*, and the *Adventure Motorcycle Handbook*.

www.advrider.com
A popular website forum for adventure riders. Includes adventure riding how-to's, ride reports, images, and technical information across more than 400,000 threads.

www.bigtrailbike.com
As the name says, this is for people with an interest in big trail bikes and the uses to which they can be put. The site shares technical knowledge on bikes, puts fragmented groups of riders in touch with each other, provides information on surfaced and unsurfaced roads, and features an international database of events, riding days, weekends, and touring holidays.

www.dualsportnews.com
Bi-monthly digital publication that covers models, gear and accessories, riding technique, technical tips, safety tips, and special events. Whether you're currently a motorcyclist, purchasing a first motorcycle, or simply enjoy reading well-written adventures, the site is worth a look.

www.flamesonmytank.co.za
Motorcycle information, safe-riding tips, on-road and off-road, trail riding, and touring in Africa. The 'Tour Reports' section offers a unique way to plan your adventure, including accommodation, equipment lists, information, and travel tips.

www.horizonsunlimited.com
The leading online resource for adventure motorcyclists. First created in 1997, with the addition of the HUBB (bulletin board) and e-zine in 1999 and 2000, the site has become a home and a focus for thousands of motorcycle travellers around the world. The site now comprises more than 6,000 pages of superb content and imagery. The HUBB has over 30,000 'threads' or topics and over 175,000 posts.

www.jamescargo.com
James Cargo has an experienced team of freight forwarders, a number of whom are bikers themselves, and they can arrange to get your bike pretty much anywhere in the world. With easy drop-off at Heathrow or Manchester, competitive quotes, and most importantly a great understanding of how precious your bike cargo is, you'll struggle to find better value for money or better service anywhere.

www.rac.co.uk
The Royal Automobile Club is the UK's longest-established motoring organisation with over 100 years' experience. The site offers great insight on carnets and international driving permits. Not all countries require a carnet or IDP, but it's well worth checking the requirements before you leave.

www.worldofbmw.co.uk
Official BMW website with information and links to BMW tours, off-road skills, equipment, bikes, and some excellent articles and interviews with adventurers.

BIKE PREPARATION, RIDING GEAR, AND EQUIPMENT

www.acerbis.it
Founded in 1973, Acerbis is a leading manufacturer of plastic accessories for motorcycles. It has branches around the world and sponsors many sports, especially motocross and enduro. It makes a good variety of long-range fuel tanks.

www.adventure-spec.com
Good source of information on long-range, unsupported adventure riding. The company specialises in a wide variety of equipment, tested to the maximum on adventure trips of their own and available through an online shop. Run by two keen adventure motorcyclists who had little luck in finding a reliable source for the obscure essentials required for independent off-road travel.

www.andystrapz.co.uk
Described as 'the world's best luggage straps', Andy Strapz are broad elasticised webbing luggage straps, with large patches of heavy-duty Velcro, that are designed to replace bungee cords. They're used differently, joining to themselves rather than using hooks, making them inherently safer. They were invented by Andy White, a senior emergency nurse, after a couple of near misses with bungee straps. In fact bungee straps are a major cause of permanent eye injury, and with Andy's lifelong passion for motorcycling he was determined to resolve their inherent dangers.

Overland Solutions

Appendix

Listings

■ **www.airhawk.com.au**
Manufacturers of an innovative air cushioning system that makes use of adjustable air inflation and multiple cells to provide a custom-fit to your personal contour for every ride.

■ **www.alpinestars.com**
Manufacturer of motorcycle riding apparel. The website includes news and product information.

■ **www.camelbak.com**
CamelBak is the originator of and world leader in hands-free hydration systems.

■ **www.cotswoldoutdoor.com**
Cotswold Outdoor started life in 1974 when the founders sold a range of basic camping accessories. Thirty years later the business is an award-winning retailer with numerous thriving stores and a highly successful mail order service, selling one of the most comprehensive ranges of outdoor clothing and equipment.

■ **www.dainese.com**
Leading supplier of quality riding gear, from helmets and gloves to trousers, jackets, protective gear, and boots.

■ **www.garmin.com**
Arguably the world's leading designer, manufacturer, and marketer of GPS navigation and communication equipment.

■ **www.happy-trail.com**
Specialists in manufacturing custom-engineered luggage systems and products for adventure motorcycling.

■ **www.hein-gericke.com**
With an extensive retail network across Germany, Great Britain, Italy, Belgium, and the Netherlands, as well as their excellent website, Hein Gericke offers a top range of motorcycling clothing and accessories for adventure biking.

■ **www.HID50.com**
Specialist supplier of high intensity discharge lighting.

■ **www.hotrodwelding.nl**
Small Netherlands-based company which specialises in working with stainless steel and alloys. They were the people who prepared the X-tank for Walter Colebatch's Sibirsky Extreme project.

■ **www.hyperpro.com**
Hyperpro is the leading producer of progressive suspension products for motor bikes. They produce steering dampers, complete shocks, front fork springs, and height adjustment kits for a vast number of bikes.

■ **www.kahedo.com**
German manufacturer of top-quality BMW-compatible seats and luggage.

■ **www.kriega.com**
Kriega packs are designed specifically for motorcyclists in terms of both features and performance, and their products carry a ten-year warranty. They offer everything from backpacks to hydro packs and waist packs. Their products are made of top-quality materials and are designed to last.

■ **www.mecasystem.fr**
French rally kit parts and accessories specialist.

■ **www.metalmule.com**
UK-based supplier of quality aluminium panniers, which have been extensively tested on overland adventures.

■ **www.ohlins.com**
Manufacturer of the world's leading performance suspension components.

■ **www.ortlieb.com**
Manufacturer of high-quality waterproof outdoor equipment, including bags and packs for everything from maps to photography equipment and personal gear.

■ **www.overland-solutions.com**
Overland Solutions specialise in preparing motorcycles to deal with extreme conditions or loads. The majority of their parts and fabrications are handmade to ensure top quality. These range from fabricating a basic side-stand to a fully prepared overland motorcycle for extreme riding conditions.

■ **www.pac-safe.com**
The company's philosophy is that 'when your gear's secure, you can do more', and they strive to provide innovative and high-quality travel security solutions, including secure bags, pouches, locks, and wallets.

■ **www.pelican.com**
Manufacturer of watertight protective cases, submersible flashlights, and quality torches. The company's cases are world-renowned and ideal for protecting photographic and video equipment, as well as a laptop if you're planning on taking one with you. The 'survival stories' on the website bear testament to the quality of the product.

■ **www.pivotpegz.net**
Manufacturer of innovative foot pegs with a unique and precisely tuned spring-loaded pivoting action that actively tracks with the motion of the rider's feet.

■ **www.rallybikecenter.com**
Rally Bike Center was started in May 2006 and is run by experienced Dakar mechanic and rally bike builder Ewout Grevengoed. The business prepares rally bikes, quads, enduro, motocross, supermoto, and adventure bikes at their premises in the Netherlands.

■ **www.rallymanagementservices.com**
San Francisco-based company specialising in preparation, running, and support of rally bikes and rally racing teams.

■ **www.rayz.nl**
Bike seats, by adventure riders, for adventure riders. If you want a bike seat made by someone who knows what it's like to cross Bolivia or Mongolia by bike, then this is the place to go.

■ **www.rsconcept.net**
French experts who specialise in rally bike preparation, bike rentals, and general advice on adventure motorcycling.

■ **www.rukka.com**
Rukka develops, manufactures, and markets technical and functional garments made from high-quality materials for leisure activities. They have an extensive range of motorcycle equipment, much of which is suitable for adventure motorcycling.

■ **www.stahlkoffer.com**
Midlands-based adventure pannier supplier for all BMW models, as well as the Suzuki V-Strom and Africa Twin models.

■ **www.touratech.com**
Leading supplier of an extensive range of off-road adventure equipment and accessories. A must-have item for most people in the adventure motorcycling fraternity is undoubtedly the Touratech Catalogue, with more than 1,000 pages crammed full with parts for your bike and your next adventure. German owner Herbert Schwartz is himself an avid adventurer and uses his expeditions to test new equipment before taking it to market.

■ **www.traveldri-plus.co.uk**
A large selection of waterproof bags, tents, luggage, and camping accessories for adventure motorcycling.

■ **www.wunderlich.de**
For more than 20 years Wunderlich have been developing high-quality motorcycle accessories and today specialise in parts for a range of BMW models. Their glossy catalogues are as extensive as they're mouth watering for the GS enthusiast.

TRAINING SCHOOLS

■ **www.adysmith.co.uk**
KTM off-road school run out of six different UK locations by one of the country's most experienced and respected off-road racers, Ady Smith.

■ **www.off-roadskills.com**
The place to go to develop and improve your off-road skills ahead of an adventure. Training takes place in the spectacular Walters Arena in Wales, offering 4,000 acres of terrain and trails to suit all riding abilities. The instructor team is headed up by seven-time Dakar Rally competitor Simon Pavey.

■ **www.rawhyde-off-road.com**
RawHyde's 'Adventure Camp' is the USA's most unique and critically acclaimed adventure riding school. It's an all-encompassing adventure experience that's much more than a simple 'rider training class'. You'll definitely learn a lot about riding in challenging conditions, and your confidence will grow immensely.

Sibirsky Extreme

ADVENTURERS AND TRIPS

www.benkapulko.com
Read about Slovenian Benka Pulko's five-and-a-half year global adventure which saw her log over 111,000 miles (177,000km), experience 75 countries on all seven continents, and earn her way into the *Guinness Book of World Records.*

www.berndtesch.de
Learn more about one of adventure motorcycling's more eccentric characters – Bernd Tesch. He's a travel-writer, publisher, journalist, and survival-trainer who produces and sells his own panniers and has more than 93,000 miles (150,000km) under his belt. He also runs an archive of more than 250 motorcycle travel books and a host of adventure travel meetings for enthusiasts.

www.josef-pichler.at
Learn about KTM specialist Josef Pichler's global adventures to all four corners of the globe, including the Amazon, Ethiopia, Kenya, Brazil, Chile, Argentina, Peru, Bolivia, Colombia, Ecuador, Egypt, Tibet, and the Sahara.

www.jupitalia.com
Official website of legendary adventurer Ted Simon. Author of *Jupiter's Travels, Riding High,* and *Dreaming of Jupiter,* Ted has inspired a generation of travellers and motorcyclists to get out and adventure on two wheels.

www.longwayround.com
Long Way Round is a documentary television series, DVD set, and book, documenting the 19,000-mile (31,000 km) journey of Ewan McGregor and Charley Boorman from London to New York on motorcycles. They travelled eastwards through Europe and Asia, flew to Alaska, and continued by road from there to New York.

www.longwaydown.com
Long Way Down is another a television series, book, and DVD, documenting Ewan McGregor and Charley Boorman's 2007 motorcycle journey south through 18 countries, from John O' Groats in Scotland to Cape Agulhas in South Africa via Europe and Africa.

www.nicksanders.com
Read about this extreme motorcyclist's expeditions and six trips around the world. Get information about movies, books, and other publications. Over the past seven years Nick Sanders has motorcycled around the world four times, on three occasions riding over 30,000 miles (48,000km).

www.racetodakar.com
Read about keen motorcycle enthusiast Charley Boorman's entry into the 2006 Lisbon–Dakar Rally. During the event he broke bones in both hands in a crash. He rode through the pain and on to the end of the stage before being forced to withdraw from the race.

www.sam-manicom.com
Sam set off to ride the length of Africa but his one-year trip turned into an eight-year epic across 55 countries and three books about his exploits. He's a keen advocate of motorcycle travel: 'The travel bug bites hard, but motorcycle travel bites deep and doing a long trip by bike is the stuff of dreams. I started to write because I wanted to share the fun.' His motorcycle is still his sole means of transport.

www.sibirskyextreme.com
The Sibirsky (Siberian) Extreme Project is a motorcycle adventure project led by Walter Colebatch with various other adventure motorcyclists, to attempt to ride into the ultimate depths of Siberia. The idea is to push the boundaries of what is known and what is possible in terms of motorcycling in Siberia and set new benchmarks and ride new roads and tracks that have yet to be explored by today's adventure motorcyclists.

TOURS AND ADVENTURES

www.bikershome.net
Outstanding accommodation and off-road adventure centre in Ouarzazate, Morocco, run by Peter Buitelaar and his family.

www.blazingtrailstours.com
Offering specialist Royal Enfield motorcycle tours in India. These guys know India like the backs of their hands and tours are designed to cater for riders of all abilities.

www.enduroindia.com
Enduro India has already established itself as the number one motorbike tour of India and is widely regarded as one of the must-have biking experiences anywhere on the planet. The trip involves 14 days of dawn to dusk riding through some of the world's most beautiful and inspiring scenery. Similar trips exist in the Himalayas and southern Africa.

www.globebusters.com
Pan-American Highway motorcycle expeditions run by round-the-world motorcyclists Kevin and Julia Sanders from their base in Wales. The couple run unique motorcycle tours the length of the Americas, through Northern Africa, and across some of the most rugged parts of Central Asia and on through China.

www.globeriders.com
GlobeRiders is a Seattle-based motorcycle adventure touring company founded by world-renowned adventurer Helge Pedersen. The company specialises in small-group, long-duration, scenic and cultural motorcycle journeys to areas of the world neither easily accessible nor commonly visited. They cater to experienced, self-sufficient riders who seek a more challenging and unique experience, and want to do it on their own machine.

www.graveltravel.co.uk
Since 1993 Gravel Travel has offered a variety of motorcycle tours exploring the back roads and remote tracks of Namibia and Southern Africa. These tours reach the remotest parts of the country and are personally guided to some of the most interesting and inaccessible parts of Africa.

www.ktmadventuretours.com
Official adventure tour service run by KTM in a variety of international locations including Italy, France, Romania, South Africa, Spain, Argentina, and India. Guides include the likes of renowned Dakar competitor Alfie Cox.

www.kaapstadmat.com
Cape Town-based adventure specialists offering adventure riding through what is arguably the most beautiful part of South Africa.

www.kuduexpeditions.com
Kudu Expeditions run top-notch expeditions ranging from round-the-world adventures to their renowned Paris to Dakar challenge. Kudu maintains the vision that no matter what your background or experience, you can achieve truly amazing things.

www.motoaventurepros.com
US-based team of highly experienced motorcycle enthusiasts dedicated to providing safe and affordable expeditions around the world.

www.motoaventures.com
Experienced Andorra-based tour outfit offering the highest standards and quality of guided motorbike tours in the dunes of Morocco and touring holidays in Southern Africa.

Appendix

Listings

■ **www.off-roadvietnam.com**
Adventure touring operation in Vietnam offering a wide range of tours and options including bike hire and other outdoor activities.

■ **www.perumotorcycling.com**
UK-based company specialising in motorcycle adventure holiday trips to Peru.

■ **www.trailblazers-spain.com**
Off-road adventure company offering activities in Spain and Morocco. Guides have excellent local knowledge and the company offers fully maintained machinery and riding gear.

■ **www.transamtrail.com**
A helpful resource for planning an off-road cross-country trip on the 'Trans-America Trail' – a west-bound ride that starts in north-eastern Tennessee and ends at the Pacific Ocean in south-western Oregon – some 4,800 miles (7,700km) of mostly off-road riding. The site has all you need to make your journey, including detailed road books and supporting maps.

BIKE MANUFACTURERS

■ **Aprilia**
www.aprilia.co.uk
www.aprilia.com

■ **Benelli**
www.benelli.co.uk
www.benelli.com

■ **BMW**
www.bmw-motorrad.co.uk
www.bmw-motorrad.com

■ **Buell**
www.buell.com

■ **Ducati**
www.ducatiuk.com
www.ducati.com

■ **Honda**
www.honda.co.uk
www.honda.com

■ **Kawasaki**
www.kawasaki.co.uk
www.kawasaki.com

■ **KTM**
www.ktm.co.uk
www.ktm.com

■ **Moto Guzzi**
www.motoguzzi.it
www.motoguzzi-us.com

■ **Moto Morini**
www.motomorinimotorcycles.co.uk
www.motomorini.com

■ **Suzuki**
www.suzuki.co.uk
www.suzuki.com

■ **Triumph**
www.triumph.co.uk
www.triumph.com

■ **Yamaha**
www.yamaha-motor.co.uk
www.yamaha.com

© BMW Motorrad

TRAVEL INFORMATION

■ **www.bradt-travelguides.com**
A leading specialised travel publishing company with more than 130 titles in its stable. Today Bradt has a reputation for being a pioneer in tackling 'unusual' destinations, and are a good source of information for adventure motorcyclists.

■ **www.embassyworld.com**
Provides a comprehensive list of contact resources for all of the world's diplomatic offices. Includes maps and a growing database of tools for the traveller.

■ **www.lonelyplanet.com**
Supplier of a great selection of travel guides. Especially useful for finding accommodation and advice in remote places, these guide books offer loads of valuable information which will help you to have a safer and more interesting adventure.

■ **www.maps.google.com**
A useful means of looking at distances and routes.

■ **http://maps.nationalgeographic.com/maps**
A comprehensive resource of international maps.

■ **www.masta-travel-health.com**
A useful resource for information on vaccinations and travel health.

■ **www.multimap.com**
World map with zoom function – useful for some basic planning.

■ **www.stanfords.co.uk**
Explore the world's largest map and travel bookshop with the widest range of maps, guides, and travel writing.

■ **www.sidestandup.com**
The world's only radio motorcycle road show with guest travellers, chat, interviews, and handy advice sessions every week.

■ **www.ttqv.com**
Touratech's mapping software site with downloads and loads of information on their innovative navigation and tracking equipment.

■ **www.weather.com**
A useful website for local and international weather.

■ **www.x-rates.com**
Useful currency conversion website.

■ **www.wanderlust.co.uk**
The UK's leading travel magazine for independent-minded and adventurous travellers looking for world-class information and advice about where to go, what to visit, and how to get there.

■ **www.whitehorsepress.com**
Comprehensive online portal selling motorcycle books, gear, luggage, maps, DVD, and related accessories.

OTHER WEBSITES

■ **www.atic.org**
If you're a fan of the Honda Africa Twin then this is the site for you – an independent group of Honda Africa Twin riders on the net, dating back to 1996 and now with more than 2,000 members united by the guiding philosophy of encouraging international co-operation and adventure with the common hobby of the Africa Twin.

■ **www.bmw-club.org.uk**
The BMW Club is the only officially recognised BMW motorcycle club in the British Isles and the Republic of Ireland. It has been in existence since 1951 and currently has a membership of around 6,500, not only from all over the British Isles but also Europe and the USA.

■ **www.bmridersclub.com**
Launched in 2006 by a small group of BMW enthusiasts in the UK who saw the need for a BMW club with down-to-earth attitudes and a common sense approach to club life.

■ **www.classic-motorbikes.net**
A useful online resource if you're interested in older bikes.

■ **www.dawntodusk.co.uk**
Information about the leading enduro in Wales which takes place in the dramatic and spectacular off-road venue of the 4,000-acre Walters Arena and comprises a 6-hour, 12-hour and 24-hour event.

■ **www.gsclubuk.org**
Founded back in 2001 as an Internet-based club for the BMW GS model range and their demanding owners, the club has created something of reputation for doing things well, whether it be its national events, local meets, exchange of technical information, or its fundraising for good causes.

■ **www.haynes.co.uk**
The world's leading publisher and retailer of illustrated workshop car manuals, motorcycle manuals, and motoring books. Publisher of *Adventure Motorcycling*, *Adventure Riding Techniques*, and *Building the Ultimate Adventure Bike*.

■ **www.knobblies.org**
Homepage of the Knobblies Trail Bike Club, with an extensive forum for all types of off-road enthusiasts.

■ **www.ridersarevoters.org**
Action group campaigning for improved conditions for bikes, encouraging riders to discuss issues with potential MPs ahead of the election and ultimately to vote. RAV work in conjunction with the British Motorcyclists Federation (BMF) and the Motorcycle Industry Association (MCI).

■ **www.trf.org.uk**
The Trail Riders Fellowship is the UK's largest trail bike riders' association and since the 1970s has worked to preserve access to, and helped to maintain standards of, public rights of way throughout England and Wales. There are 45 local TRF groups you can join and the routes available are a great source of off-road riding before you head off on an adventure. The website offers a wealth of useful information.

■ **www.ukgser.com**
UK-based motorcycling community, created by BMW GS enthusiasts for the benefit of like-minded individuals to enjoy BMW GS motorcycles. Has a wealth of GS-related material and interactive forums for a broad range of discussions. If you're new to the world of the mighty GS then this is your 'one-stop shop' for a wealth of information, help, and advice on all aspects of GS ownership.

■ **www.xt660.com**
The number one resource for owners of Yamaha's XT motorcycles. With forums covering everything from modifications to technical problems, if you're looking for help with your XT this is the place to find it.

To contact the author, please email adventuremotorcycling@gmail.com

Sibirsky Extreme

Index

Index

WITHDRAWN